Collecting the Dead

Collecting the Dead

Archaeology and the Reburial Issue

Cressida Fforde

Duckworth

First published in 2004 by
Gerald Duckworth & Co. Ltd.
90-93 Cowcross Street, London EC1M 6BF
Tel: 020 7490 7300
Fax: 020 7490 0080
inquiries@duckworth-publishers.co.uk
www.ducknet.co.uk

A catalogue record for this book is available
from the British Library

ISBN 0 7156 3284 1

Typeset by e-type, Liverpool

Contents

For my family

Plates

Acknowledgements

This book could not have been completed without the help of many people. Much of its contents is drawn from my post-graduate work and thus I am grateful to all those who provided assistance, agreed to be interviewed, and helped in a multitude of ways during the course of the PhD research.

In particular I would like to thank the Edinburgh University Library (Special Collections) for their assistance and for permission to publish from the Cunningham Papers, the University of Oxford for providing access to the Rolleston Papers, and the general assistance provided by staff at the Australian Institute of Aboriginal and Torres Strait Islander Studies, the Aboriginal and Torres Strait Islander Commission and the Foundation for Aboriginal and Islander Research Action. Thank you to Jack and Clare Golson, Jacquie Lambert, Tim Champion, Ken Colbung, Walter Palm Island, Nic Heijm, Paul Turnbull, and to all those who have extended their friendship, hospitality and assistance in the UK and Australia.

Considerable updating has occurred since the PhD and I would like to thank the Menzies Centre for Australian Studies and the Centre for Cross Cultural Research at the Australian National University for enabling me to undertake some of the necessary research. Particular thanks are due to Connie Roberts and Rhonda Agius for supporting the publication of the detailed story of what happened to the remains of their relative, Tommy Walker. Thank you also to Major Sumner for permission to publish his image on the cover of this book. Special thanks go to Jane Hubert, Fiona Handley, Gary Schwartz and Peter Ucko for their constructive criticism and reading draft versions of this manuscript, and to Lyndon Ormond Parker for his considerable help over many years. Thank you to Stuart Laidlaw for assisting with illustrations. Finally, I owe a debt of gratitude to my family, and to Vanessa Balloqui, Olivia Forge, Susan Morgan and many other friends for their encouragement and patience.

Introduction

In the United Kingdom, museums and other collecting institutions contain human remains. Some are kept in hospitals or pathology departments, others are housed in museums, archaeology, anthropology and anatomy departments. As exemplified by the scandal that surrounded the discovery that a doctor at Alder Hey Hospital in Liverpool had removed and kept organs from deceased babies without the consent of their parents, feelings can run high if it is perceived that body parts have been removed or used without the prior and informed consent of relatives.[1] Although this book is not concerned with pathology or medical collections as such, the human remains that it considers have also been controversial, and some have been the subject of heated debate and contested ownership for decades.

Unlike the collections in hospitals and medical institutions, those described in this book contain the remains of people from many different parts of the world and from many different cultures and ages, although remains obtained in Europe commonly form the majority. Collections were amassed from the later years of the eighteenth century until the first half of the twentieth century and were compiled to represent skeletally (but also sometimes with soft tissue) the different 'races' of the world, so that these could be measured, compared and analysed to understand human variation and origins. Such analysis was undertaken at a time when perceptions of human diversity were deeply rooted in notions of biological determinism and racial worth. These notions were themselves entangled within the contemporary colonial ideology and practice, supporting, and deriving from, a belief in European superiority.

While the cadavers that are today used for dissection in anatomy departments are 'left to science' by the deceased and their treatment is regulated by British law, the human remains that this book describes were not donated; indeed, many have been demanded back by their descendants or communities of origin in order that they can be given appropriate funerary rites. It is the contested remains in UK collections that form the subject of this book. Its focus is on indigenous Australians, not only because their human remains were frequently considered the most highly 'prized' in the nineteenth century, but also because Australian indigenous people have been at the forefront of repatriation campaigns in the UK. However, despite this book's concentration on Australia, the history of the removal of indigenous human remains for the purposes of scientific study is

1

mirrored around the world, and similar histories of how and why they were obtained can be found globally. Collectors in the UK maintained an international web of contacts through which human remains were gathered.

Although this book focuses on the collecting of human remains by UK institutions, this practice was not a purely British venture. Understanding human variation and origins was a primary scientific endeavour and most major European institutions were engaged in building their own collections. UK institutions generally stopped receiving remains from overseas in the first half of the twentieth century. However, indigenous remains continued to be collected after this time, but were usually kept in museums in their country of origin. The USA had significant collections of its own by the mid-nineteenth century. Collected remains are of varying age, ranging from those of people who died long before the arrival of Europeans, to those of individuals who died in the first half of the twentieth century.

One of the principal aims of this book is to provide an historical understanding of how and why human remains collections were amassed. With exceptions (e.g. Turnbull 1991, 1999) such information is generally lacking in the available literature yet is important for understanding the origin and substance of repatriation issues. The first half of the book examines the history of the collecting of human remains by UK institutions. The first two chapters explore the historical interest in human remains as sources of data for analysing human difference and origins, tracing both the development of relevant theories and the rise of human remains collections that occurred concurrently. Chapter 3 documents where remains were collected from, how they were acquired and how the broad collecting networks came into existence. Chapter 4 describes the contemporary responses of indigenous people, what motivated collectors and how they felt about the practice in which they were engaged. Chapter 5 examines how the collecting and analysis of human remains contributed to (and was the result of) general perceptions about Aboriginal and European identity, and studies its implications.

Throughout the book, various case studies are provided (for others see, for example, Fforde *et al.* 2002) which describe the pre- and post-mortem histories of known individuals whose remains were collected in the last two hundred years and have since been returned to Australia. These case studies provide important historical detail that is unavailable for the anonymous remains which make up the majority of collections.

The second half is devoted to an examination of what has become known as the 'reburial' or 'repatriation' issue, a term coined for the controversy that began to develop over thirty years ago when some indigenous groups began to campaign for the return of ancestral human remains from museums and collecting institutions, and their requests were refused. The issue was then, and continues to be in many places, highly contentious. For many indigenous groups, the knowledge that the human remains of their ancestors had been stolen and studied, and continued to be retained in institutions, was a cause of profound concern and outrage. For many archaeologists, physical anthropologists and museum professionals, the reburial issue raised not only fundamental ethical questions about the past, present and future practice of their discipline(s), but also the prospect of an imminent loss of potential research material.[2]

As a result of the sustained efforts of indigenous groups over the past thirty years, an increasing number of holding institutions now recognise that it is the appropriate authorities within originating communities who have the right to decide the future of their ancestors' human remains. The UK Working Group on Human Remains has recently provided evidence that refusal to return requested remains may be in contravention of the Human Rights Act (1998), although this has yet to be tested (see Chapter 9). However, despite this – and particularly in Europe – many museums continue to retain human remains against the wishes of claimant communities.

Today, calls for the return of remains are increasingly heard worldwide. Although voiced initially from Australia and North America, requests for indigenous remains in European museums have now come from most continents. In the USA, with the passage of the National Museum of the American Indian Act (1989) and the Native American Graves Protection and Repatriation Act (1990), Native American human remains (in collections under Federal 'control' – see McKeown 2002) are the property of tribes, and must be returned to them if requested. In Australia, Canada and New Zealand, museum policy and/or legislation to a large extent recognises that indigenous descendants hold pre-eminent rights to the remains of their ancestors. In Scandinavia there have been recent policy developments with regards to Saami remains held in Scandinavian institutions (see Schanche 2002, Sellevold 2002). In these countries, the importance of science is acknowledged with the recognition also that consultation must take place with appropriate indigenous authorities before any scientific analysis is undertaken. Chapters 6-9 document the development of the reburial issue in Australia and the UK, examining the landmark cases, the indigenous campaigns and the response of the academy.

The history of the collecting and repatriation of human remains demonstrates that such items are usually perceived differently by those who request the return of remains and those involved in their collection and study. Recognising the different ways that remains are perceived (why to some these remains are 'the dead' and to others they are 'data') is a central factor in understanding the reburial issue. Chapter 10 examines the different meanings attributed to human remains and concludes the book.

In gaining an understanding of the history of the reburial debate, readers should be aware that opposition to scientific use of the dead without consent is by no means an exclusively indigenous concern, either today or in the past (see Bahn 1984; Hubert 1989: 132-7). For example, in the UK, past centuries have witnessed a history of resistance to the use of bodies without consent by the medical profession. Richardson (1988) has documented the popular revulsion in seventeenth-, eighteenth- and early nineteenth-century Britain to the practice of dissection and grave-robbing. As Hubert (1989: 132-4, and see Bahn 1984: 132-3) has demonstrated, growing concern in twentieth-century Britain about the excavation of skeletons has in some cases led to reburial ceremonies. For example, the remains of a sailor from the Mary Rose were buried in Portsmouth Cathedral in 1984 partly in order to accommodate the feelings of those who believed the wreck to be a 'war grave' which should have been left undisturbed (Hubert 1989: 133; Southworth 1994: 23). In the UK, human remains have been excavated and studied on the understanding that they will be reburied in the future (Molleson 2003: 18). Prompted by concerns that the dead should be left to rest in peace, reports of the distress of descendants and others at the desecration of war graves or the improper clearing of cemeteries are commonly reported in the British Press (e.g. http://news.bbc.co.uk/2/hi/uk_news/england/2079562.stm; *Daily Mail* 28 August 2003). Neither is the need for the mortal remains of the dead to be returned to their country of origin solely an indigenous concern – many UK citizens dying abroad are brought home for burial. The UK Working Group on Human Remains (see Chapter 9) has recently reported that every year the British Home Office receives some one thousand three hundred requests for the exhumation and relocation of deceased persons (sometimes overseas), and this number is on the increase.

Revelations at Alder Hey Hospital and the discovery that parts of the bodies of those who died in the sinking of the Marchioness pleasure boat on the Thames in 1989 had been kept unbeknownst to their relatives have also recently received considerable press coverage and debate. Both incidents not only caused pain to grieving relatives but also generated wide public concern, in particular because they were characterised by the seemingly secretive way in which the body parts were removed and stored. This secrecy, along with the grief of relatives in these cases, finds parallels with the concerns of indigenous groups requesting the return of human remains to originating communities. However, the indigenous situation remains distinct and unique in the specific cultural beliefs which underpin requests, the continued frequent rejection of such claims, and the historical context in which collections were formed. Yet understanding of the intensity of concern raised by the whole 'repatriation issue' should not be difficult.

Throughout the book, the terms 'scientists' and 'Aborigines' are sometimes used as these have been commonly employed to refer to the main stakeholders in the reburial issue. However, the terms can be problematic and readers should be aware of their limitations. Of course, not all scientists study human remains and not all who manage human remains collections are scientists. Further, indigenous Australians do not always define themselves as Aboriginal, a term which only came into use post-contact (see Chapter 5), but instead by their local group or regional identities. In addition, to use these terms contributes to the assumption that these groups were always unified and polarised, which the history of the reburial debate set out in this book shows was not always true. It also suggests that the two groups are mutually exclusive, whereas there is an increasing number of indigenous archaeologists, museum, and heritage professionals. Because of its common usage, the book also employs the term 'reburial' even though returned remains may never have previously passed through funerary ceremony and may be accorded final disposition that does not involve burial.

The analysis of human difference from Hippocrates to Darwin

The physical variety of humankind has long been a subject of description and interpretation, contributing to definitions of human difference since at least the time of the ancient Greeks. This history is characterised by the persistence of, and tension between, two conceptual approaches to human diversity. The first, and most orthodox, advocated the essential unity of the human species and traditionally explained variety as the product of external factors. The second placed more emphasis on the differences within humankind, considering these to be both innate and immutable. Until the mid-twentieth century, each approach assumed a fundamental connection between biology and culture, an assumption that commonly led to the attachment of human 'worth' to physical characteristics; belief in the unity of humankind did not, as might have been expected, necessarily imply an egalitarian attitude towards other peoples.

The Greeks and the *'monstra'*

In the fourth century BC the Hippocratic Corpus employed environmental causation to explain the differences in physical and mental characteristics of various peoples in Europe and Asia (Lloyd 1978: 148-69; Stepan 1982: xi; Stocking 1988: 3). The Corpus provides what may be the earliest record of characteristic headform being used to define a group of people: the Macrocephali, so called because 'no other race has heads like theirs' (Lloyd 1978: 161). This shared feature was believed to have been caused by both nature and nurture – initially the result of artificial deformation, elongated headshape, it was thought, had eventually become an inherited characteristic. Although the Hippocratic Corpus assigned the finest temperament to the Greeks, allegedly because they were exposed to the best climate, in general the text takes a relativist approach to human diversity and there is little evidence of a belief in biological determinism or the ascription of inferiority to other peoples. Gould (1981: 19-20) has observed that in Plato's *Republic* (Book III 414d-415d), Socrates recognised the notion of innate social worth to be a lie.

The Hippocratic Corpus restricted its observations to the Mediterranean region, and did not describe the various 'monstrous' peoples then believed to inhabit areas much further east. Recorded by a succession of Greek writers, descriptions of the strange and remarkable inhabitants of the Indian subcontinent became widely available to the Latin world through the work of Pliny the Elder. Employing both physical and cultural criteria, some of the *monstra* in Pliny's *Natural History* were defined by their bodily features while others were distinguished by their unique behaviour. Although some of the beings are now known to be fantastic, such as the *Blemmyae* (who had their faces in their chests) and the *Cyclopes* (giants with a single eye found in the centre of their forehead) others, such as the Pygmies, did exist beyond the boundaries of the Classical world (Friedman 1981: 5-25; Stocking 1988: 3-4 and see Plate 1).

Pliny's compendium continued to be used as a record of human difference throughout the Middle Ages, its descriptions – or variations thereof – surfacing in the literature and art of that period (Friedman 1981: 9-19). The lack of any mention of the Plinian races in the Old Testament meant that medieval scholars were curious as to their origin and meaning. There was speculation, for example, as to whether the *monstra* were human, whether they were part of God's creation or victims of divine punishment, whether they were signs from God, and whether they were descended from Adam – perhaps the evil and deformed progeny of Cain (Friedman 1981: 87-130). As the geographical boundaries of the known world expanded, the presumed location of the monstrous peoples shifted accordingly, so that they maintained their position at the outermost ends of the earth. Always distanced from European civilisation in physical form and/or culture and geography, monstrous peoples were quintessentially alien.

The first European travellers to the Americas did not find the Plinian races they had expected (Stocking 1988: 4). However, the indigenous groups that they did encounter soon became the target of debates that had previously surrounded the origin of the *monstra*. Affirming orthodox belief in the unity of mankind, the Church debated and in 1550 eventually accepted the humanity of American Indians (Stocking 1988: 4). It was also in the mid-sixteenth century that physical differences between European populations began once again to be a subject of observation. Thus, included within anatomist Andreas Vesalius' *De Humani Corporis Fabrica Libri Septem* (1543) are descriptions and depictions of distinct skull shapes allegedly exhibited by the various inhabitants of different European nations. In a similar fashion to the Hippocratic Corpus, Vesalius and, later, others attributed these differences to tradition. For example, Blumenbach (1775: 114-15) noted that the wide heads and compressed occiputs observed in German crania were believed to have been produced by the practice of swaddling infants and placing them to sleep on their backs.

In the later seventeenth century, further encounters with different indigenous populations coupled with a new analytical approach to plant and animal diversity facilitated the scientific classification of humankind. Instead of following the biblical tradition and separating humans into three lineages fathered by Ham, Shem and Japheth, the earliest classifications usually contained four or five divisions (Stocking 1988: 4). Thus, in 1684 Francois Bernier proposed a system of classification that was the first to employ explicitly 'racial' divisions. He observed that while humans exhibited extensive individual variety there were still 'four or five species or races of men in particular whose difference is so remarkable that it may be properly made use of as the foundation for a new division of the earth' (Bernier 1684: 361, and see Stocking 1988: 4-5).

Although Bernier did not contemplate the origins of human diversity, this topic continued to be the subject of debate that could be divided between those who advocated unity and those who advocated plurality. An essay written in 1695 by 'L.P.' of Oxford illustrates the lack of consensus on the issue at the end of the seventeenth century, discussing the advantages and disadvantages of both approaches, for:

> the West Indies, and the vast regions lately discovered towards the south, abound with such variety of inhabitants and new animals, not known or even seen in Asia, Africa, or Europe, that the origin of them doth not appear to be clear, as some late writers pretend (L.P. 1695: 365).

Linneaus and typology

The next major step in the history of human classification was the work of monogenist Carl von Linneaus, which, for the first time, placed humans within the animal kingdom. Demonstrating the tenacity of the Plinian tradition, Linneaus' *Systemae Naturalae* (1735-60) classified 'wildmen' and 'monsters' within *Homo sapiens*. The rest of humankind was divided into four 'varieties' which used physical and cultural criteria as distinguishing characteristics. Thus, *Homo sapiens Americanus* was reddish, choleric, obstinate, contented and regulated by customs; *H. s. Europeanus* was white, fickle, sanguine, blue-eyed, gentle and governed by laws; *H. s. Asiaticus* was sallow, grave, dignified, veracious, and ruled by opinions; and *H. s. Afer* was black, phlegmatic, cunning, lazy, lustful, careless, and governed by caprice (Haller 1971: 4 and see Bendyshe 1865: 421-58).

Although Linneaus was the first to provide a taxonomy of the human species, his classification of humankind was not widely accepted. Even at this early stage, there was considerable disagreement about the number of human varieties and the criteria that should be used to define them. As the comparative anatomist Johann Friedrich Blumenbach (1775: 99) was to comment, 'very arbitrary indeed both in number and definition have been the varieties of mankind accepted by eminent men'. Thus, for example, Georges Louis Le Clerc, Comte de Buffon, divided humankind into six varieties and employed colour, disposition, figure and stature to distinguish between them (Buffon 1785: 57). Buffon was judgemental in his descriptions of various non-European peoples, his observations of

Australia's indigenous population illustrating early assumptions of a racial hierarchy as well as what may be a continuation of the Greek and medieval tradition of viewing peoples at the 'outermost ends' as inferior and bestial: 'the natives of the coast of New Holland [Australia] ... are perhaps the most miserable of the human species, and approach nearest to the brutes' (Buffon 1785: 94).

Whatever number of varieties they defined, Linneaus and Buffon only employed discernible external physical features for their respective classifications of humankind – an approach used in the 'systematic' method of taxonomy widely employed at that time. Indeed, zoology as a whole was largely dominated by the classification and description of organisms by their outward appearance. However, there was a small group of eighteenth-century zoologists who rejected this approach and instead advocated the prime importance of anatomy to an understanding of the animal organism (Visser 1985: 1, 23). This group pioneered the new morphological school of zoology, usually termed comparative anatomy, which emerged in the second half of the eighteenth century. Prominent amongst this circle were the Dutch anatomist and artist Petrus Camper, English surgeon-anatomist John Hunter and the German Professor of Medicine, Johann Friedrich Blumenbach (Visser 1985: 23-4; Stocking 1988: 5).

Camper: quantifying human difference

Camper's interest in comparative anatomy began in the 1740s, when as a student at Leiden University he had disassociated himself from the practice of classifying organisms purely by their external features, regarding anatomy as the key to understanding the natural history of the animal kingdom (Visser 1985: 24). Camper believed that artistic representations of Africans mistakenly depicted them as black Europeans, whereas he observed underlying differences in cranial structure. Having 'contemplated the inhabitants of various nations with greater attention' Camper (1794: 8):

> conceived that a striking difference was occasioned, not merely by the position of the inferior maxilla, but by the breadth of the face and the quadrangular form of the maxilla.

Although other scholars had previously reported that various groups of people exhibited distinctive head forms (Visser 1985: 107), Camper was the first to employ systematically a quantitative method to try to distinguish between them. In addition, he invented what may have been the first tool of craniometry – a device which held skulls in a specific position so as to facilitate their measurement (Camper 1794: 32-44). Using the facial angle (or Camper's Angle), an index that expressed the degree of facial slope relative to the cranium, Camper arranged human and animal skulls on an hierarchical scale:

1. The analysis of human difference from Hippocrates to Darwin

When in addition to the skull of a Negro, I had procured one of a Calmuck, and had placed that of an ape contiguous to them both, I observed that a line drawn along the forehead and the upper lip indicated this difference in national physiognomy; and also pointed out the degree of similarity between a Negro and the ape. By sketching some of these features upon a horizontal plane, I obtained the lines which mark the countenance, with their different angles. When I made these lines to incline forwards, I obtained the face of an antique, backwards, of a Negro; still more backwards, the line marks the ape, a dog, a snipe etc. This discovery formed the basis of my edifice (Camper 1794: 9).

As well as quantifying racial difference, a perceived similarity between apes and Africans, and the hierarchy inferred by this gradation of humans and animals, the facial angle carried with it an implicit measurement of intelligence. Camper was aware that Greek artistic tradition had always represented deities with a facial angle of 100 degrees – denoting wisdom – and that stupidity was widely associated with a decrease in facial slope (Haller 1971: 10-11). However, while this is implicit in his analysis (see Plate 2) Camper's works contain little of the outwardly negative descriptions of non-Europeans which other scholars, such as Buffon, commonly employed.

Although the facial angle initially met with severe criticism from Blumenbach (1795: 235-6) and later the naturalists William Lawrence (1844: 246) and James Cowles Prichard (1843: 46, 53; Stepan 1982: 34), both of whom questioned its reliability as a guide to racial difference, by the mid-nineteenth century it is believed to have been the 'most frequent means of explaining the gradation of the species' (Haller 1971: 11) and the 'standard parameter in the physical description of man' (Visser 1985: 107). Facial slope was simple to measure and the endurance of Camper's Angle is probably also related to the ease with which it 'attached' skull shape to racial worth (Stepan 1982: 34).

Despite describing a morphological similarity between apes and Africans, Camper (1794: 32) strongly opposed the view that 'the races of blacks originated from the commerces of the whites with ourangs and pongos; or that these monsters by gradual improvements became men'. Instead, he believed that all human races were of one species descended from a single pair 'formed by the immediate hand of God' (Camper 1794: 16). Rejecting the role of cultural practices, Camper (1794: 17, 22-31) contended that variety of headshape, and of other physical characteristics, was solely due to environmental factors.

Employing comparative anatomy to illustrate the principles of unity (today generally known as 'monogenism') Camper took the opportunity afforded by his public dissection of a 'Negro lad' in Amsterdam's anatomical theatre to demonstrate 'all those diversities in the cranium which nature has effectuated [sic]' (Camper 1794: 23). To facilitate his research into racial diversity he also assembled a collection of crania:

11

Exclusive of several skulls of my countrymen, and of the adjacent nations, I possess two English Negroes (the one was a young person, the other advanced in years) – the head of a female Hottentot, and of an inhabitant of Mogul, a Chinese, a youth of Madagascar, a Celebean, and finally the head of a Calmuck, that is of eight different nations (Camper 1794: 8).

In addition, Camper had acquired an African human foetus and the skins of Italians, Moors and a Dutch woman, and used these specimens to demonstrate the insignificance of variations in skin colour when compared to the overall similarity of the human species. Thus he observed that although the foetus exhibited African features 'the colour of the skin was not changed into black' (Camper 1794: 22), and that because the '*membrana reticularis*' of all the skins was 'to a greater or lesser degree of a dusky hue' (Camper 1794: 16) this was proof that no essential difference existed between them.

Early collections

Camper's collection of human crania was amongst the first to be amassed for the purpose of analysing racial difference. Collections of human remains were common by this time, but they invariably contained only European material. Indeed, by the late seventeenth century, the interests of medical gentlemen and the fashion for curiosity cabinets had combined to produce extensive private collections of European human remains (see Lunsingh Scheurleer 1985: 119). Collections of such material were also often associated with anatomy theatres either at universities, such as Altdorf, Copenhagen and Leiden, or in surgeons' guilds such as those at Rotterdam and Delft (see Schupbach 1985). Human remains of non-Europeans had figured in collections before the late eighteenth century, but had never before been procured for research into human diversity. Examples include the skin of a Moor housed at the Royal Society of England in 1681 (Grew 1681: 4), and an African foetus, various pieces of black skin and 'part of the hide of a Bashaw that was strangled in Turkey' (Day 1995: 71) which were collected by Sir Hans Sloane (1640-1753).

Camper's small collection of 'race' crania was surpassed in size and variety by that of his British contemporary, John Hunter. Hunter's collection of human remains from around the world demonstrates his interest in human diversity. In his famous portrait by Sir Joshua Reynolds, Hunter is depicted at his desk on which is propped a folio of drawings illustrating – in a graded series – the skull of a European, an Australian Aborigine, a chimpanzee, a monkey, a dog, and a crocodile (Turnbull 1999). This painting indicates that the relative status of the Australian 'race' was already decided by the time the quantitative study of humankind had begun.

By the time of his death in 1793, Hunter's collection of human and animal anatomical specimens included a number of European crania as well as at least two crania from the Caribbean, nine from various regions of Africa, two from New Zealand, six from Australia (including the skull of a Tasmanian) and one from Malaysia (Clift 1831). Eventually bought by the British Government in 1799, in 1806 the collection was moved to the premises of the Incorporation of Surgeons (later the Royal College of Surgeons of England) where a museum was built to accommodate it (Grey Turner 1945: 360). This museum formed the nucleus of the College collections, which, by the end of the nineteenth century, contained the largest anthropological collection of human remains in Britain.

Blumenbach's 'golgotha'

The collections of Camper and Hunter are historically significant not least because they represent the beginning of a science that aimed to quantify human difference by systematic analysis of skeletal remains. From this time onwards, human remains from around the world were scientific *desiderata* and not merely items of curiosity. However, although important precursors of the collections amassed during the next hundred and fifty years, those of Hunter and Camper contained just a few skulls from only a small number of different countries. The first collection assembled with the aim of representing *all* the different varieties of humankind with as many crania as possible was the 'golgotha' (Marx 1865: 8) at the University of Göttingen. Amassed by Johann Friedrich Blumenbach while Professor of Medicine from 1779 until his death in 1840, the collection contained eighty-two race skulls, including two from Australia donated by Sir Joseph Banks (Blumenbach 1795: 155; Wagner 1856).

Blumenbach's primary interest was the classification of humankind, a topic which he first tackled in his doctoral dissertation of 1775. From the start, Blumenbach disagreed with Linneaus' inclusion of humans within the same 'natural order' as the apes, believing that this distorted Man's spiritual and moral integrity (Haller 1971: 6). Instead Blumenbach classified humans in a separate category – *bimana* – to denote their unique 'external conformation, namely, the *freest use of two most perfect hands*' (Blumenbach 1795: 171). Initially, Blumenbach followed Linneaus' quadripartite division of humankind (Blumenbach 1775: 99-100), but by the third edition of *De Generis Humani Varietate Nativa* (1795) he had concluded that there were, instead, five varieties of humans. Nonetheless, Blumenbach agreed with Linneaus' taxonomic boundaries and upheld the unity of humankind, proposing that diversity had been produced by degeneration from a common primordial stock (Blumenbach 1795: 264-76).

Considering white to be the original skin colour since 'it is very easy for that to degenerate into brown, but very much more difficult for dark to become white', and noting that the 'beautiful' Georgian skull in his possession was the mean from which all others diverged, Blumenbach (1795: 269) argued that the Caucasians (named after the Caucasus

Mountains which now form the border between Georgia and the Russian Federation) had been the original peoples. The Americans and Malays were transitional forms between the Mongolians and Ethiopians respectively, the last two varieties being 'most remote and very different from each other' (Blumenbach 1795: 265). Although Blumenbach (1795: 275) assigned Australia's indigenous population (known then as New Hollanders) to the Malayan category, he noted that they 'graduate so insensibly towards the Ethiopian variety, that, if it was thought convenient, they might not unfairly be classed with them'.

Along with skin colour, features of the face and body, stature and constitution, skull shape was a principal criterion in Blumenbach's classification system. From examination of the skulls in his collection he believed that each human variety had a distinctive cranial shape (1795: 236-8). However, unlike Camper, he did not rely upon one measurement to distinguish between the skulls of different races:

> the more my daily experience and, as it were, my familiarity with my collection of skulls of different nations increases, so much the more impossible do I find it to reduce these racial varieties – when such differences occur in the proportion and direction of the parts of the truly many-formed skull, all having more or less to do with the racial character – to the measurements and angles of any single scale (Blumenbach 1795: 236).

Instead, Blumenbach assessed the skulls qualitatively, comparing their shape as viewed from one position only, the *norma verticalis*. From this perspective – above and behind the crania – he believed that all the racial characters manifested in a skull could be seen 'distinctly at one glance' (Blumenbach 1795: 237).

Like other monogenists, Blumenbach attributed racial variation to the influence of environmental factors. However, his analysis of racial difference in skull shape also considered the effects of national custom, the process that Camper had previously so categorically rejected (Blumenbach 1775: 115-21; 1795: 239-43). From observation of 'pathological phenomena and physiological experiments', Blumenbach (1795: 239) concluded that the bony structures were as 'liable to perpetual mutations [as] the soft parts of the body' and suggested that unique cultural practices which deformed the skull, whether through design or chance, were responsible for producing distinctive racial characteristics. Therefore, he considered it 'credible' that the custom of some Aboriginal groups of inserting a piece of wood through the nasal septum could explain, because of the continuous pressure that the peg would exert, the conspicuous smoothness of the front section of the upper jaw of an Aboriginal skull in his collection. However, although in his original dissertation Blumenbach (1775: 121) was willing to agree with the Hippocratic contention that, over time, features produced by artificial means could be inherited, by the third edition of *De Generis* (1795: 203-4, 243) he was not so sure:

1. The analysis of human difference from Hippocrates to Darwin

I have not at present adopted as my own either the affirmative or the negative of these opinions [whether physical characteristics acquired in life are passed to the next generation]; I would willingly give my suffrage with those on the negative side, if they could explain why peculiarities of the same sort of conformation, which are first made intentionally or accidentally, cannot in any way be handed down to the descendants, when we see that other marks of race which have come into existence from other causes which up to the present time are unknown, especially in the face, as noses, lips and eyebrows are universally propagated in families for few or many generations with less or greater constancy, just in the same way as *organic* disorders, as deficiencies of speech and pronunciation, and such like; unless perhaps they prefer saying that all these occur also by chance (Blumenbach 1795: 204).

The seeds of another major collection, at the University of Edinburgh, can also be traced back to the early nineteenth century. In 1798, Professor Alexander Monro Secundus donated his collection of anatomical specimens, and that of his father, to the Department of Anatomy at the University of Edinburgh. These donations formed the nucleus of an Anatomy Museum which, over the next hundred and fifty years, expanded to contain, amongst other items, natural history specimens, anatomical preparations and items to illustrate human and animal comparative anatomy. The collecting of overseas human remains by this museum began very early, although it was not undertaken to a large extent until the later nineteenth century. The Department of Anatomy may have contained the skull of an Aboriginal person as early as 1813 (Monro Tertius 1813: 378), although this could actually have been in the personal collection of its then Professor, Alexander Monro Tertius, who is known to have received an Aboriginal skeleton and three skulls from 'friends' by 1825 (Monro Tertius 1825: 224). Monro Tertius (1825: 203-4, 224, 227) also refers to 'four or five' Australian crania and two (or possibly three) Tasmanian skulls in the University's 'Museum of Natural History' and in the collections of the Edinburgh Phrenological Society (see below). It appears that Monro Tertius took a number of Aboriginal skeletal remains from the Anatomy Museum for his own collection: according to Turnbull (personal communication) ownership of these bones was still in dispute when Monro retired, and was only resolved when the collection was given to the Anatomy Museum after his death.

The great debate: monogenism vs polygenism

By the end of the eighteenth century, the unorthodox idea that human diversity was the product of multiple Creations was becoming increasingly prevalent. The theory of plurality, or 'polygenism', asserted that race differences were too great to have been produced by environmental factors and that, as separate species, the races must have been created already adapted to their specific habitats. As has been shown, this plural approach

15

was not new, but until the early nineteenth century it had never received serious widespread attention (Stocking 1968: 42-68). Contradicting the Scriptures, polygenism had never gathered sufficient support to challenge monogenism as the dominant theory of human origins, but by the second half of the eighteenth century it was sufficiently current to be refuted by both Camper (1794: 16,59) and Blumenbach (1775: 98). In 1778 Lord Kames (Henry Home) the Lord Commissioner of Justiciary in Scotland, strongly questioned Buffon's definition of species and the efficacy of environmental determinism, arguing that, 'certain it is, that all men are not fitted equally for every climate. Is there not then reason to conclude that as there are different climates, so there are different species of men fitted for these different climates?' (Kames 1778: 18). By 1799 Charles White, a Manchester physician, was convinced that the theory of unity could no longer be maintained.

White acquired an interest in anthropology during his later years, and was renowned at the time for his claimed 'discovery' that the 'Negro forearm' was longer, in relation to the upper arm, than that of the European (White 1799; Cunningham 1908: 22). Measurements of skeletal remains were used to support his assertion that there were 'numerous varieties of race, but wherever, and whatever feature, there is gradation from European to Ape in skelet[al] and other features' (White 1799: 56). For White (1799: 134), quantitative evidence provided proof that the European was most removed from 'brute creation' and, being superior in all ways, could be considered 'the most beautiful of the human race'. As Tucker (1994: 10-11) has demonstrated, data that did not conform to White's proposed gradation were manipulated into the 'correct' place. Although declaring that his purpose was not born out of malice towards the black race but purely to 'discover what are the established laws of nature' (White 1799: 136), White's preconceived notions of European superiority are abundantly clear:

> Where shall we find, unless in the European, that nobly arched head, containing such a quality of brain, and supported by a hollow conical pillar, entering its centre? Where the perpendicular face, the prominent nose and round projecting chin? Where that variety of features, and fullness of expression; those long flowing graceful ringlets; that majestic beard, those rosy cheeks and coral lips? Where that erect posture and noble gait? In what other quarter of the globe shall one find the blush that overspreads the soft features of the beautiful women of Europe, that emblem of modesty, of delicate feelings, and of sense? Where that nice expression of the amiable and softer passions in the countenance; and that general elegance of features and complexities? Where except on the bosom of the European woman, two such plump and snowy white hemispheres, tipt [sic] with vermilion? (White: 1799: 135).

Neither the doctrine of gradation nor White's assertion of European supremacy were innovative, and both were shared by polygenists and monogenists alike. Nonetheless there was an important distinction between the racialism set forth by the two paradigms: while the theory of unity contended that the 'lower' races had the potential to attain the physical and intellectual level of the European, for the polygenists the races were distinct species and their position on the hierarchical scale of humanity was thus innate and immutable.

Although the growth of polygenism was hampered by its seemingly anti-Biblical stance, in fact its advocates rarely denied the accuracy of the Scriptures. As one of polygenism's most ardent supporters contended, 'the plurality of species in the human race does no more violence to the Bible than the admitted facts of Astronomy and Geology' (Nott 1844: 5). Instead, polygenists attempted to incorporate their theory within an orthodox framework, often suggesting that while the Bible had only recorded one instance of creation – Adam and Eve – this did not prove that others had not taken place (e.g. Nott 1844: 6-7, 29). Kames (1778: 23), for example, posited that God had equipped the different races with unique features necessary for their survival in different climates following their dispersal after the destruction of the Tower of Babel. White (1799: 136) even argued that the Old Testament provided implicit evidence of additional Creations: if Adam and Eve had only begotten sons, where had Cain's wife come from? The opinion of the eminent American anatomist and craniologist, Samuel Morton (1839: 2-3) was perhaps more typical. He argued that scholars had 'hastily and unnecessarily' inferred that racial diversity had resulted from environmental factors only, asking:

> Is it not more consistent with the known government of the universe, that the same Omnipotence that created Man, would adapt him at once to the physical, as well as to the moral circumstances in which he was to dwell upon the earth? It is indeed difficult to imagine that an all-wise Providence, after having by the Deluge destroyed all mankind excepting the family of Noah, should leave these to combat, and with seemingly uncertain and inadequate means, the various external causes that tended to oppose the great object of their dispersion. We are left to the reasonable conclusion, that each Race was adapted from the beginning to its particular local destination. In other words, it is assumed, that the physical characters which distinguish the different races are independent of the external causes.

Polygenism's popularity advanced during the first half of the nineteenth century, in part because environmental causation increasingly appeared to lack empirical support (Stocking 1968: 42-68; Stepan 1982: 2, 35-40). It was becoming apparent that racial characteristics did not alter when exposed to a different environment (e.g. Lawrence 1819: 10-124; Stepan 1982: 37-8) and, consequently, some monogenists began to rely less heavily on environment as a causal factor. Thus, Georges Cuvier, France's leading comparative anatomist, considered there to be little evidence to support the role of environment in biological variation (Stepan 1982: 39), while in Britain, the eminent naturalists and monogenists James Cowles Prichard (1813) and William Lawrence (1823) both argued that racial variation had resulted from spontaneous and inheritable alterations in physical form that were preserved by isolation and interbreeding (see Stepan 1982: 35-40). Such alterations were thought to be the products of civilisation, for:

> The savage may be compared to [wild animals], which range the earth uncontrolled by man; civilised people to the domesticated breeds of the same species, whose diversities of form and colour are endless. Whether we consider the several nations, or the individuals of each, bodily differences are much more numerous in the highly civilised Caucasian variety, than either of the other divisions of mankind (Lawrence 1823: 100).

If proving (or circumventing) the efficacy of environmental causation was the main obstacle faced by monogenists, advocates of polygenism had to demonstrate that the human races were indeed separate species. Some looked for differences in human crania to provide supporting evidence. Thus for one of the later polygenists, Joseph Barnard Davis (1867: viii), the 'proofs' of man's diversity of origin:

> are derived from the essential peculiarities which are seen in the skulls of most races of people, and the distinguishing diversities of different races – for example, the crania of Europeans of African negroes, those of Australians, those of New Hebrideans etc. The sharpness of these distinctions may be said to be ethnognomic, and is most impressive when we compare the skulls of neighbouring races: – for instance, those of Guanches and Negroes of the West Coast; those of Boschemans and Kafirs; those of Negritos and Bisayans; those of Hindoos and the sub-Himalayan tribes on the one side, and the natives of the Indian archipelago on the other etc.

However, skull differences clearly did not provide irrefutable proof of polygenism, as monogenists had looked at similar data and had incorporated it within the theory of unity, as even Davis (1867: viii) admitted:

> The examination of the crania of infants and of children of these and other peoples puts the diversities alluded to in a striking light. Blumenbach, with his usual discrimination, made good use of this indelible impress of race-peculiarities in early life for the establishment of his quinary division of mankind, in the plate of his *Decas Tertia*, although its force as an evidence of something very like specific difference was wholly at variance with his system and was not attended to by him.

Most nineteenth-century biologists accepted Buffon's definition that species were groups of organisms that could only produce fertile offspring with their own kind. If the differences between the races were not in themselves conclusive evidence of polygenism, its advocates had to redefine the species concept and/or prove imperfect fertility between the races

(Stocking 1968: 48). Thus, the American polygenists Josiah Nott and George Gliddon (1854: 375) suggested that the term 'species' should define a 'type, or organic form, that is permanent; or which has remained unchanged under opposite climatic influences for ages' while their contemporary, Samuel Morton (1839: 82) proposed that if different 'organic types' could be traced as distinct entities far enough back in time to a 'primordial organic form', they should be treated as separate species, even if they were interfertile. Evidence for the permanence and longevity of the races was taken from Egyptian art which, it was argued, distinctly depicted the differences between blacks, whites, and Jews 'upwards of three thousand years ago as they are now' (Morton 1839: 2-3). Bishop Usher's calculation that the world had been created in 4004 BC therefore allowed only two thousand years for human diversity to have developed, a time period that the polygenists argued was vastly inadequate – especially as the races had shown no sign of subsequent change (Nott 1844: 8; Stanton 1960: 30).

As for human hybridity, most polygenists contended that physically similar races could produce fecund offspring, but those which were dissimilar, if they could interbreed at all, would only produce progeny that were to varying degrees either degenerate, sterile, or both (Nott 1844: 30-4; Nott and Gliddon 1854: 276-397; Walker 1866; Stocking 1968: 48-9; Stepan 1985: 104-12). Monogenists, meanwhile, continued to assert that races were inter-fertile and merely represented different varieties of the same species, often citing domestic animal breeds as analogous examples (Prichard 1813: 17-32, 39-40; Lawrence 1822: 473; Stepan 1982: 33-5).

The question of 'acclimation' (or acclimatisation) – whether races could adapt to foreign climates – also tested the central maxims of both monogenism and polygenism. Polygenists argued that because each race had been created to inhabit one particular environment, as immutable species they would be unable to survive in, or adapt to, any other. Thus Nott (1844: 19) cited the lack of successful European settlement in Africa and the detrimental effect of increasing latitude on the mortality rate of 'blacks' in America as evidence that 'the White man can not live in tropical Africa, nor the African in the frigid zone', further observing that 'a cold climate so freezes [African] brains as to make them insane or idiotical'. Monogenists, on the other hand, relying on the already tenuous efficacy of environmental causation, contended that initial problems would be overcome and races would eventually successfully adapt to their new surroundings (Stocking 1968: 54).

Polygenism and politics

By the 1830s, the polygenist assessment of acclimation and hybridity and its relegation of 'the black race' to a position of innate inferiority had found particular favour in America amongst those who opposed the growing

19

abolitionist movement (Haller 1971: 76-9). The polygenist contention that the black races would perish outside the tropical climate of the southern states, and that biological assimilation would be detrimental to both races, bolstered the belief that they were 'naturally' suited to slavery and would eventually die out if emancipated. South Carolina physician Josiah Nott, a slave owner who gave lectures on 'Niggerology' (Gould 1981: 69), was particularly vociferous in his use of polygenism as a scientific rationale for slavery (Stanton 1960: 66-72; Banton 1977: 57). With his colleague George Gliddon, previously the American Vice Consul in Cairo, he wrote the leading polygenist text *Types of Mankind* (1854). Declaring that 'I belong not to those who are disposed to degrade any type of humanity to the level of brute creation', Nott nonetheless considered that:

> a man must be blind not to be struck by similitudes between some of the lower races of mankind, viewed as connecting links in the animal kingdom; nor can it be rationally affirmed, that the Orang-outan and chimp are more widely separated from certain African and Oceanic Negroes than are the latter from the Teutonic or Pelagic types (Nott and Gliddon 1854: 457).

As well as employing such 'self-evident' visual data, Nott found scientific 'proof' of black inferiority in measurements that apparently demonstrated their smaller brain size. Thought to be constrained by their anatomy, the black races were thus deemed biologically unable to rise from servility, a position in which Nott, amongst others, argued they had achieved their most perfect state (Tucker 1994: 12-22).

Samuel Morton, cranial capacity, and early statistics

Nott made use of the first set of empirical data to be produced on the brain size of various races. This had been formulated by Samuel Morton who, by the late 1830s, had calculated average cranial capacities for the skulls in his collection at the Academy of Natural Sciences in Philadelphia. Morton, Professor of Anatomy at Pennsylvania Medical College, had become interested in collecting crania when unable to locate any skulls to show to his students during an introductory lecture on racial characteristics (Patterson 1854: xxxi). Aiming to determine 'ethnic resemblances and discrepancies by a comparison of crania' (Patterson 1854: xxviii), Morton set out to amass as many skulls as possible. Using an extensive network of friends and collaborators, in twenty years Morton accumulated over a thousand specimens – the largest anthropological collection of human remains at that time in the world (Morton 1839: v).

In classifying his collection, Morton (1839: 3-4) adopted Blumenbach's separation of humankind into five varieties although, in accordance with his belief that each was a separate species, he renamed these divisions 'races' and their sub-divisions 'families'. In a collection predominantly

North and South American in origin, but which contained representative samples of all five 'races', Morton took, on average, thirteen different measurements of each skull and subjected the results to statistical analysis. In particular, he used his data on cranial capacity to rank races on a scale that placed Caucasians at the top and the Mongolian, Malayan, American and Ethiopian races in descending order beneath (Morton 1839: 260). This hierarchy was widely adopted, the French physical anthropologist, Paul Topinard (1890: 229) stating over fifty years later that, 'the inferior races have a less [sic] capacity than the superior. Australians are the lowest on the scale in this respect'.

Cranial capacity was a measure of the internal volume of the skull obtained by a painstaking process that involved filling the cranium with white pepper seed, sand or lead shot, decanting the contents into a tin cylinder filled with water and measuring the displacement produced. Due to the generally held (and false) assumption that brain size was indicative of intelligence (Haller 1971: 18), cranial capacity, more explicitly than Camper's Angle, quantifiably linked skull form to mental ability. Morton's data was therefore extremely useful to those interested in scientifically 'proving' black inferiority, and while Morton himself rarely promulgated his results in the political arena, Josiah Nott was not the only pro-slavery scientist to do so. As Morton's obituary in the American South's leading medical journal stated:

we of the South should consider him as our benefactor, for aiding most materially in giving to the negro his true position as an inferior race. We believe the time is not far distant, when it will be universally admitted that neither can 'the leopard change his spots, nor the Ethiopian his skin' (Gibbes 1851 in Stanton 1960: 144).

Nonetheless, denial of the Scriptures was often perceived as too high a price to pay for scientific backing, and polygenism did not occupy the primary position in the ideology of slavery in mid-nineteenth century America (Gould 1981: 69). Most of those defending slavery employed the teachings of the Bible, which, interpreted in a certain way, provided ample 'evidence' to support their point of view (Gould 1981: 69-72).

By the 1830s the leading text in the field of craniology, Blumenbach's substantial treatise on the Göttingen Collection (*Decas prima (– sexta) collectionis suae craniorum diversarum gentium illustrata* 1790-1838) was becoming redundant; its deficiency in 'absolute and relative measurements' and its use of the 'defective three-quarter and other oblique views of many of the skulls' rendering it 'highly unsatisfactory to the practical cranioscopist' (Maury *et al.* 1857: 215). Furthermore, Blumenbach's results were increasingly considered unsound, being 'invalidated by the small number of specimens generally relied upon by him' (Patterson 1854: xxviii). Morton's approach, to take numerous detailed measurements from each skull in a collection that was considered large enough to compensate for individual variation, superseded that of Blumenbach and revolutionised the study of human diversity. Where there had only been aesthetic judgement and speculation, Morton, it was claimed, provided empirical data and 'objective' fact (Gould 1978: 503). However, as Gould (1978, 1981) has demonstrated in his detailed re-examination of Morton's data, the Philadelphian anatomist was far from objective in his method and analyses. Instead, Morton's results were a 'patchwork of assumption and finagling' (Gould 1978: 504) that consistently – through a variety of omissions and statistical errors – favoured his pre-conceptions about racial inequality. Yet Gould (1978: 509) could discern no evidence of conscious data manipulation, finding only an '*a priori* conviction of racial ranking so powerful that it directed [Morton's] tabulations along pre-established lines'. However, while it may have been implicit in his statistical analyses, Morton's subjectivity is clearly apparent in his descriptions of the defining moral characteristics of each race and family. Thus, Ethiopians were 'joyous, flexible, and indolent' and some tribes in this category constituted the 'lowest grade of humanity' (Morton 1839: 7), while the Circassians (members of the Caucasian race), surpassed all other peoples 'in exquisite beauty of form and gracefulness of manners' (Morton 1839: 8). For all Morton's computations, his racial distinctions were as much qualitatively based as they were quantitatively expressed.

Phrenology

Morton was one of the only craniologists publicly to consider using the principles of phrenology, the so-called 'science of the mind'. Although he did not wish to base his first analytical work, *Crania Americana*, on phrenology alone but instead to, 'present the facts unbiased by theory, and let the reader draw his own conclusions' (Morton 1839: i), Morton clearly regarded phrenology as having sufficient potential to include a list of pertinent measurements in this volume, as well as an essay on the subject by George Combe, one of phrenology's chief protagonists at the time.

Developed in the last years of the eighteenth century by Franz Gall and subsequently popularised by Johann Spurzheim and Combe, phrenology contended that the brain was the seat of the mind. Instead of being a homogenous unity the brain, according to Gall, was composed of different 'organs' that controlled different mental attributes (see Plate 3). For example, the organ of *Causality* found in 'the second frontal convolution underneath the frontal eminences' was thought to define 'the capacity to trace cause and effect'; and that of *Acquisitiveness* located 'in the front part of the first convolution of the temporal lobe' was believed to control the 'instinct of providing, covetousness, and the propensity to theft' (Hedderley 1970: 51, 54). Organ size reflected the degree of the associated function and, since the cranium was believed to mirror the shape of the brain, an examination of skull or head shape could be used to determine mental character (Cooter 1984: 3).

By isolating all mental phenomena in the brain and ascribing each a cerebral location, Gall was the first to use a purely biological approach to the study of mind and emotions. Perceived as undermining the Cartesian rationale for the existence of God, Gall's innovation was initially highly controversial (Cooter 1984: 5). Phrenology was also renowned for its reformist principles, teaching that the various 'faculties' could be improved with increased usage (e.g. Combe 1835: 89-99, 119-20). Appealing to a wide range of interests, phrenology had attained enough influence in the first half of the nineteenth century to effect reform in areas of education, penology and the treatment of the insane (Cooter 1984: 7).

Phrenological societies proliferated; by 1836 there were twenty-nine in Britain alone (Cooter 1984: 88-9) and for demonstration and research purposes, most phrenological societies acquired specimens of human and animal crania, busts, models and casts (Watson 1836: 113-66; Hollander 1920: 357). For example, extensive collections were maintained by the Edinburgh Phrenological Society and by James Deville, a commercial phrenologist practising in London (Erikson 1979: 36). As well as procuring the skulls of the famous and infamous, phrenologists were particularly eager to obtain indigenous crania in order to ascertain the typical mental character of each race (see the *Phrenological Journal* 1825 Vol. II: 1-19, 264-8, 533-43). Thus, in 1825 the *Phrenological Journal* (Vol. II: 268) published a request that its readers:

> going to distant countries ... avail themselves of the facilities which the science affords for the accurate and minute appreciation of character, and to collect skulls in elucidation of the origin, dispositions and talents of foreign nations.

Phrenology therefore provided an additional market for indigenous crania to that already established by the comparative anatomists. Phrenologists concurred with the widely held assumption that a positive correlation existed between brain size and intellect, and used cranial capacity as one method of determining racial character. Indeed, according to Combe (1835: 275-6) it was a fundamental principle of phrenology that large brains were always associated with 'individuals and nations distinguished for great aggregate force of mind, animal and moral and intellectual'.

When data did not fit in with pre-conceived notions of racial order, there were always alternative interpretations. Thus, for example, unable to equate the small cranial capacity of Morton's Peruvian skulls with the degree of civilisation this race was believed to have attained, Combe suggested that they had either been misidentified or artificially deformed, eventually concluding that the Peruvian skull depicted in *Crania Americana* was not typical of its kind (Stanton 1960: 38).

Like the early anthropologists, phrenologists also conceptualised racial difference in terms of rank:

> The New Holland skull rises a little above the Carib, but indicates a lamentable deficiency in the regions of the intellectual and sentimental organs. The organs of Constructiveness, Reflection and Ideality are particularly deficient while those of animal propensities are fully developed (Anon. 1825: 9).

Rejecting environmental causation as inadequate to account for the diversity in racial character, phrenology contended that the mental attributes specific to each race had been 'received from nature' and were, 'in exact accordance with the development of their brains' (Anon. 1825: 17). However, although this approach appeared similar to that employed by the polygenists, phrenology neither considered the races to be separate species nor believed their mental abilities to be fixed and immutable (Stanton 1960: 36). Instead, like monogenism, phrenology maintained that 'lower' races had the capacity to attain a higher position in the racial hierarchy. However, to the monogenists such improvement was really only a theoretical possibility – the environment effecting change so slowly that, for all intents and purposes, the status of each race was permanent (Haller 1971: 77). Phrenologists, on the other hand, believed that changes could occur over a relatively short period of time if members of the 'degenerate' races were encouraged to 'exercise' their 'weaker' mental faculties. Convinced that all races had the ability to ascend the racial scale, Combe (1841 Vol. I: 254) condemned slavery as a 'canker in the moral constitution of [America], that must produce evil continually until it is removed'. Combe (1841 Vol. II: 77) contended that black slaves had small brains which explained their submissive attitude towards slavery, while those of free blacks were notably larger, leading him to conclude that, 'the greater exercise of the mental faculties in freedom has caused the brain to increase in size; for it is a general rule in physiology that wholesome exercise favours the development of all organs' (Combe 1841 Vol. II: 112).

This reformist approach to racial hierarchy is apparent in Sir George Mackenzie's phrenological assessment of the skull of Carnambeigle, an indigenous leader from the Sydney area of New South Wales who was shot in 1816 by soldiers in a 'punitive' raid (see Chapter 3), and whose skull was sent to the Edinburgh Phrenological Society. Mackenzie, a Fellow of the Royal Societies of Edinburgh and London, became interested in the 'science of the mind' in 1816 and joined the Edinburgh Phrenological Society four years later. One of Scotland's most active supporters of phrenology, Mackenzie tried for many years, unsuccessfully, to gain its acceptance by the Royal Society (De Guistino 1975: 49-59; Cooter 1984: 55-7). While his examination of Carnambeigle's skull and the casts of two others from Australia led him to conclude that there was little hope that Aboriginal people would advance intellectually, Mackenzie saw potential for improvement, under proper direction, in their religious and moral 'faculties':

> Although, therefore, the progress of these people may be slow, and although their reasoning powers are not such as to lead us to think that their lower propensities can be under perfect control; still by working on love of appropriation, the sense of justice, and veneration; and by exciting the organ of attachment by acts of kindness, much may be done for these miserable beings in improving their religious and moral condition. Their lower propensities do not seem considerable when compared with foreheads that indicate more intelligence than they seem to possess, although they are large in proportion to their own. The first step towards improving such a people is to give them confidence, before any attempt is made to work upon their feelings. As their reasoning powers are weak and their self-esteem strong, much patience must be bestowed on them; and firmness being well developed, renders the necessity of patience and perseverance more apparent (Mackenzie 1820: 235-6).

Although phrenology shared a similar approach to racial difference with both the monogenists and the polygenists, used the same data set and analysed crania quantitatively, it was distinctly different in its conceptualisation of the association between biology and intellect. Comparative Anatomy assumed that skull size and shape reflected mental capacity and thus racial worth. Phrenologists, on the other hand, considered cranial morphology to be essentially plastic, responding in shape to alterations in the contours of the brain which had themselves been caused by changes in circumscribed mental attributes. Thus according to phrenology, the 'lower' races were constrained by their social and cultural environment and not by their anatomy.

Phrenology's popularity proved to be relatively short lived (Cooter 1984: 88-9); increasing marginalisation from the scientific world (which included exclusion from the British Association for the Advancement of Science in 1834) meant that membership of a phrenological society began to mitigate against entry into those with more scientific standing. Lack of credibility, religious opposition and divisive internal politics led to phrenology's decline in the 1830s and within a decade it had almost disappeared (Erikson 1979: 7; Cooter 1984: 89-94). However, while its principles and teachings were largely abandoned, phrenology's collections of crania remained, many becoming incorporated into those already assembled for anthropological study. Thus the Department of Anatomy at the University of Edinburgh received the collection of the Edinburgh Phrenological Society in 1886, which increased its holdings of indigenous Australian skulls by thirteen. Another major phrenology collection was that of James Deville in London, and in 1861 this was bought by private collector and craniologist Joseph Barnard Davis. Davis' collection was itself acquired by the Royal College of Surgeons of England in 1867. The College's museum was bombed in 1941 and much of what survived of its collection is now in the Natural History Museum, London.

Phrenology re-emerged in the later nineteenth century but by this time was entirely divorced from conventional science and orientated instead towards such popular alternatives as astrology and mesmerism. Nonetheless, whatever ideological differences this later 'pseudoscience' had with its earlier counterpart, its advocates continued to collect crania. Thus the Fowlers, a family largely responsible for phrenology's rebirth in Britain in the 1860s (Stern 1971), had a large collection of human skulls at the Fowler Institute in London. These items were probably acquired by commercial phrenologist Stackpool O'Dell when he bought the Fowler Institute building in the 1890s. The collection may then have passed into the hands of the British Phrenological Society, which still possessed skulls, kept with a storage company, in 1963 (BPS Council Minutes 2 September 1963, WI GC/17/1). The Society disbanded in 1966 and Symons (2003) describes transferring its books and museum collection (including skulls) to University College London a year later, noting that, 'the Society's artefacts are now in the Science Museum' (Symons 2003: 2).

By the mid-nineteenth century, fifty years of scientific research into human difference had generated the collection of a huge number of human remains from around the world (see Meigs 1858; Davis 1867: i-x). Attached to most scientific institutions and medical colleges, or in the hands of a smaller number of private collectors, anthropological collections existed throughout Europe and the USA, and were beginning to be amassed in the colonies (see Gould 1978: 503; Sheets-Pyenson 1988; Sutton 1986). In Britain, there were extensive collections in the anatomy departments of the Universities of Oxford, Cambridge and Edinburgh; in the Royal College of Surgeons of England; in the British Museum (Natural History); and in the Army Medical College at Fort Pitt, as well as in various private collections, the largest of which was that of Joseph Barnard Davis. Prominent collections elsewhere in Europe included that amassed by George Cuvier in the Musée de l'Homme in Paris; that in the Königlichen University in Berlin; that of Anders Retzius in the Caroline Institute in Stockholm; that in the Rijksmuseum, Amsterdam and that of Karl Von Baer in the Museum of Anthropology and Ethnography in St Petersburg (see Ucko 1992b).

Before 1859, research on skeletal remains had been undertaken in order to define and understand the structure of a human diversity which it is clear was already considered hierarchical. Comparative anatomy contributed to the monogenist/polygenist debate about the *origins* of humankind only in so far as it supplied evidence that could be used to support or contradict the contention that races were separate species. However, after 1859 a new purpose for quantifying human diversity emerged. With the publication of Charles Darwin's theory of evolution by means of natural selection, comparison between different races, between humans and apes, and between modern *Homo sapiens* and archaic forms of humankind, took on an entirely new significance.

2

Evolution, the great collections and the tenacity of 'race'

In 1859 Darwin first proposed that species evolve through a gradual process of natural selection. Darwin's theory was highly controversial for it not only denied the role of a Creator but also assumed a degree of shared ancestry between humans and the animal kingdom. Although Darwin did not specifically address the issue until 1871, the application of his theory to human origins and in particular racial diversity rapidly became a topic of debate in anthropological circles. For example, advocates of Darwinism, in particular Alfred Wallace and Thomas Huxley, contended that the theory of natural selection embraced elements of monogenism and polygenism and could reconcile the two schools by 'showing that both were right' (Wallace 1864: clxxxiv). According to Wallace's interpretation, in the remote past members of a homogenous race of proto-humans had slowly dispersed from their original habitat. As they encountered new environments their morphology had gradually altered 'in accordance with local conditions' (Wallace 1864: clxv) and they had evolved the 'striking characteristics and special modifications which still distinguish the chief races of mankind' (Wallace 1864: clxvi). When their mental faculties had advanced to a stage in which changes in behaviour rather than morphology enabled individuals to adapt to new environments, the 'mind' became the principal target of natural selection. 'Human' mental faculties then quickly evolved, in particular the capacity for speech, and from this moment the various physical forms of the different races had remained stationary. Wallace (1864: clxvi) concluded:

> If, therefore, we are of opinion that he was not really man till these higher faculties were developed, we may fairly assert that there were many originally distinct races of men; while, if we think that a being like us in form and structure, but with mental faculties scarcely above the brute, must still be considered to have been human, we are fully entitled to maintain the common origin of mankind.

Most polygenists were unconvinced. James Hunt, President of the Anthropological Society of London, an organisation which, unlike its rival the Ethnology Society, was predominantly polygenist in membership, was particularly derisive (Hunt 1866, 1867). However, his criticism lay not in the theory of natural selection *per se*, but in the presumption of its 'disciples', particularly Huxley, that modern races all belonged to the same species (Hunt 1866: 320; 1867: 118). Appreciation that Darwin's hypothesis provided a radically new theory of human evolution appears to have been largely subsumed by the necessity of fitting it within the circumscribed limits of either monogenism or polygenism. Thus Hunt (1866: 339) contended that no advance could be made in the 'application of Darwinian principles to anthropology' until the subject was freed 'from the unity hypothesis which has been identified with it'. In fact, as was already being demonstrated by German anatomist Carl Vogt, a polygenist and Darwinite, the theory of natural selection could easily be used within a strictly polygenist framework by arguing that the different races had evolved separately from different species of anthropoid apes (Hunt 1866: 339). Vogt's interpretation of Darwinism persisted, for example, in the work of the French physical anthropologist Paul Topinard (1890: 531-2).

While Darwin had used palaeontological evidence to support his theory of the evolution of animal and plant species, by the 1870s no transitional forms of fossil humans had been identified. Indeed, Wallace (1864: clxvi-clxvii) had used the similarity exhibited between available fossils and modern crania in support of his contention that human evolution from ape-like ancestors had taken place in 'a much more remote epoch than has yet been thought possible' (Wallace 1864: clxvi). For Wallace, the lack of transitional fossils was not proof that intermediary forms had never existed but merely reflected gaps in an as yet incomplete fossil record.

Instead of using palaeontology to provide evidence of a clear gradation from ape to human, Darwin looked to anthropology. Combining the concept of racial hierarchy with theories of social evolutionists such as Lubbock and Tylor (Stocking 1968: 113-32), Darwin concluded that each race represented a separate stage through which the human species had evolved:

> Differences ... between the highest men of the highest races and the lowest savages are connected by the finest gradations. Therefore it is possible that they might pass and be developed into each other (Darwin 1871: 66).

And:

> At some future period, not very distant as measured by centuries, the civilised races of man will almost certainly exterminate, and replace, the savage races throughout the world. At the same time the anthropomorphous apes ... will no doubt be exterminated. The break will then be rendered wider, for it will intervene between man in some more civilised state, as we may hope, than the Caucasian, and some ape as low as a baboon, instead of as at present between the Negro or Australian and the gorilla (Darwin 1871: 201).

According to Darwin, the 'primitive' races were no longer degenerate forms of Caucasians nor separately created inferior species, but humans who occupied the lower rungs of the evolutionary ladder. As such, they would be unable to compete with the more advanced races and, according to the principle of natural selection, would become extinct on contact with civilised nations (Darwin 1871: 282). Darwin (1871: 284-7) contended that this process had already occurred in Tasmania and was current in mainland Australia, New Zealand and other countries that had experienced European colonisation (and see Darwin 1859: 321-2, 329).

Darwin's new conceptualisation of the racial order had drawn heavily upon assumptions prevalent in both the monogenist and polygenist schools. Moreover, as the work of Wallace and Vogt demonstrated, even though the theory of natural selection made the dispute over the existence of single or multiple Creation episodes irrelevant, far from supplanting the unity/plurality debate, Darwinian theory had merely modified it. Monogenism and polygenism essentially represented contrasting attitudes towards human diversity, and both attitudes survived the Darwinian revolution. Thus the old subsidiary issues of hybridisation, miscegenation and acclimation persisted well after 1859 (e.g. Hunt 1870; Topinard 1890: 375; Stocking 1968: 47).

Although Darwinism has more in common with monogenism than the theory of plurality, it was the polygenist attitude which dominated physical anthropology (as this field was increasingly known by the end of the nineteenth century) for many decades after the publication of *The Origin of Species* (Stocking 1968: 42-68). Physical anthropologists continued to accumulate data about human *difference*, and did so on a scale far greater than ever before. Indeed, once freed from the Creation model, it was easy for the later polygenists to assimilate concepts of the 'survival of the fittest' into their own basic racist assumptions about the innate inferiority of the 'lower' races. As Joseph Barnard Davis (1867: 265) wrote of skull no. 1261 in his collection:

This skull is an excellent exemplification of Australian peculiarities, and most decidedly opposes the depreciators of craniological science. The superficial portions of the brain are very imperfectly developed in the race, and this gives rise to all their marked properties. Hence they have been rendered, by nature, utterly devoid of the power to receive that which is designated 'civilisation' by Europeans, i.e. an extraneous and heterogeneous cultivation, for which they have no taste or fitness, but which has to be thrust upon them by the high hand of presumed philanthropy, and under the influences of which their own proper endowments are constantly injured, and they themselves are inevitably destroyed.

In response to Darwinism, physical anthropology began to shift its focus away from taxonomy towards locating evidence of human evolution in the bodies of modern peoples. As Darwin (1871: 404) had looked upon Tierra del Fuegians and remarked 'such were our ancestors', so others scanned the 'lower' races for physical and cultural evidence that they were the modern representatives of past European populations that, like Pliny's monsters, had been 'expelled and driven to the uttermost parts of the earth' (Sollas 1911: 382). For example, W.J. Sollas, Professor of Palaeontology and Geology at the University of Oxford, asserted that the Tasmanians were survivors of an 'eolithic' (pre-palaeolithic) race (Sollas 1911: 70), that Australian Aborigines were the 'Mousterians of the Antipodes' (1911: 170), that the 'Bushmen' were survivors from the Aurignacian period (1911: 271-306), and that the Magdalanian people were represented by the 'Eskimo on the frozen margin of the North American continent and as well, perhaps, by the Red Indians' (1911: 383). Archaeology, it was claimed, provided corroborative 'evidence', and the material culture of modern 'primitive' races was compared with artefacts from the European palaeolithic (e.g. Dawson 1880; Tylor 1894).

A major avenue of research concentrated on examining the human remains of 'lower' races, in particular Australia's indigenous population and South African 'Bushmen' (see Skotnes 1996: 15-23; Morris 1996: 67-79), for 'primitive' characteristics – usually 'simian' features and/or those exhibited by fossil humans – in order to try to demonstrate a close evolutionary link to anthropoid ancestors. Thus, in order to determine the 'Place in Nature of the Tasmanian Aboriginal', Berry and Robertson (1911) of the Anatomy Department at Melbourne University compared measurements from fifty-two Tasmanian crania with those of fossil humans, primates, Negroes, Europeans, Veddahs and Kalmucks. Although admitting that the Tasmanians had morphologically progressed 'very much further' from '*Homo primogenius* and the anthropoid apes' than 'most writers would seem to believe', they nonetheless concluded that 'of recent man the Tasmanian stands nearest to *Homo fossilis*' (Berry and Robertson 1911: 67).

Dissection

The search for the physical evidence of Darwinian theory spread to the soft-tissue remains of indigenous peoples as, by the late nineteenth century, these became increasingly available to scientists in the West (e.g. Turner 1878, 1879, 1897; Berry 1911; and see Chapter 3). Although there had been some notable exceptions (e.g. Camper 1794; Soemmering 1784), prior to the late nineteenth century comparative anatomy had almost exclusively concentrated on skeletal material and, in particular, on the skull as, since Camper, the cranium had always been regarded as that part of the skeleton which best illustrated racial characteristics. As James Aitken Meigs (1858: 4), curator of Samuel Morton's collection, explained:

The human skull is so positively distinctive of race, that it claims at the hands of the student of Anthropology the most minute examination. The receptacle of the brain, of the organs of the senses and the masticulatory apparatus, it exhibits race-characters more striking and distinguishing than those presented by any other part of the bony system.

However, the collecting and study of crania to the exclusion of soft-tissue material had not gone unnoticed. In their account of the dissection of a 'Bushwoman', Flower and Murie (1867: 189) bemoaned the lack of available specimens and the consequent paucity of information about racial anatomy:

> with very few exceptions the arrangement of the muscles, vessels, viscera, and even the brain and nervous system constitute at present an unexplored field; and numerous well marked races of our species are passing away from the face of the earth without the slightest record being left on any one of these points. And yet in discussing questions, daily becoming of greater interest, relating to the unity or plurality of Mankind, and the amount of divergence of races, data such as these afford, whether their testimony be negative or positive, whether they tend to show absence or presence of variation from a given standard, cannot be neglected by the conscientious inquirer.

Despite Flower and Murie's complaints, the bodies of Khoisan ('Bushmen' and 'Hottentot') people did indeed exist in several museum collections. Thus the body of Saartje Baartman, the 'Hottentot Venus', who in life had been exhibited in Paris at the beginning of the nineteenth century, was dissected by Cuvier, and her skeleton, brain and reproductive organs placed in the Musée de l'Homme in Paris. In addition, by 1857, the Williamson Collection (then kept at the Museum of the Army Medical Department, Fort Pitt, Chatham (for a brief history of this collection see Fforde 1992c) contained the 'stuffed figure of a hottentot female' which had been 'prepared and presented to the museum by Andrew Smith, M.D., D.G.' (Williamson 1857: 68). Smith had also donated to this collection the body of Terrence Cannon, a young 'Bushman', which was then dissected by Staff Surgeon Williamson, who placed his skeleton in the Army Museum and sent several 'diseased organs' to the pathology department.

Australia

By the later nineteenth century, soft tissue human remains from Australia were beginning to arrive in Britain. The brains of indigenous Australians were analysed to try to find anatomical evidence for the assumed lack of intellectual development of Aboriginal people. For example, in 1888 H.D. Rolleston, Junior Demonstrator of Physiology at the University of Cambridge, examined an Australian brain to establish the differences 'between the brain of an educated moral man and that of a sensual animal-like savage' and to determine the correlation between 'the physical conformation of the cerebral hemispheres and the mental development of their owner' (1888: 32). Rolleston (1888: 33-4) concluded that the Aboriginal brain exhibited much greater 'simplicity' than that of the European in the areas of the brain traditionally associated with mental capabilities.

In 1908, Dr W.L.H. Duckworth, of Cambridge University's Department of Anatomy, examined four Aboriginal brains (one of which was that previously analysed by Rolleston) in research which aimed not to prove the 'low' evolutionary status of Aborigines, for this was then an accepted 'fact', but to find its anatomical manifestations. As Duckworth (1908: 69-70) explained:

> One of the chief points of interest concerning the brains of Australian aborigines is their consideration in the light of evidence derived from the other anatomical systems of these natives. That evidence points to their lowly status, because of the frequent characters very rare in the white races of mankind, but at the same time normal in the ape tribes. In fact, simian characters are frequent, though the Australian aboriginal has by no means a monopoly on these. But the brains of these natives have seldom been studied, owing to the difficulty of procuring material. The question at once arises then, does the conformation of the brain support the general conclusions (as to lowliness of status) suggested by the skeletal and other systems?

Although careful to point out that the Aboriginal brains in his possession could not be mistaken for 'anything but human specimens', and recognising the tendency for observers to see simian characteristics in all 'anomalous conditions of an anatomical nature', Duckworth thought that the four Aboriginal brains in his possession were recognisably different from those of Europeans and that, from the characters of 'lowly morphological value' which he believed they exhibited, they could be assigned to members of a 'lowly and probably darkly-coloured race'. However, while he believed that it might be possible with more specimens to distinguish between indigenous Africans and indigenous Australians he concluded that 'beyond this it does not seem to me probable that anatomical investigation will confer any power of racial diagnosis' (Duckworth 1908: 287).

Throughout the history of the collecting of human remains it was thought crucial to obtain the remains of people termed 'full-bloods' in order to ensure that they exhibited 'pure' racial traits, since it was believed that there was no point in measuring skulls to determine racial characteristics, if they had belonged to individuals of mixed descent. Along with their assigned status as one of the most 'primitive' of peoples, the high value attached to Tasmanian human remains was also based upon the belief that this was a finite resource as the Tasmanian 'race', because of its extermination by the colonists in the 'black war' on this island, had become 'extinct' in the 1880s with the death of Truganini, who consequently became known as the 'last Tasmanian'. The descendants of the original population were not considered Aboriginal, despite their self-identification as such. This type of racial determination was to have considerable consequences for Tasmanian Aboriginal people, dispossessed of land and identity, as their existence, and thus rights, continued to be denied by government into the 1980s (see Ryan 1981). As will be shown in subsequent chapters, the reburial issue has demonstrated that the validity of present day Tasmanian Aboriginal identity is still questioned by those interested in the scientific study of their remains.

The metric torrent

In the later nineteenth century, physical anthropology entered what one observer called the 'period of its efflorescence' (Stocking 1968: 47). The quantification of human difference became more extensive (one scientist taking five thousand measurements from each skull (Stocking 1968: 163)) and the number of remains in collections rapidly increased, largely in a continuing effort to distinguish between racial and individual variation (e.g. Davis 1867: xii-xiii). Thus, for example, the Anatomy Department at the University of Cambridge increased its holdings from 82 skulls, 12 skeletons and 36 bones in 1862 to 1402 skulls, 13 skeletons, 1800 bones and 280 specimens in spirit in 1891 (Macalister 1892: 936).

After the identification of the facial angle in the late eighteenth century, numerous indices for quantifying the skull and skeleton had been devised (Meigs 1858; Topinard 1890: 204-97; Hoyme 1953). Along with cranial capacity, probably the most extensively used general measurement of skull shape was the cephalic index. Introduced by Swedish anatomist Anders Retzius in 1844, this index was the ratio between the breadth of the skull and its length (Stepan 1982: 97). If a skull's cephalic index was less than 75 then it was termed long-headed or 'dolichocephalic'; if over 80 it was round-headed or 'brachycephalic'; if between 75 and 80, it was intermediary in form and termed 'mesocephalic'. Retzius' initial argument that primitive European brachycephals had been replaced by more highly advanced Aryan dolichocephals established the enduring principle that 'higher' races had longer heads. However, this principle became increasingly problematic as it was discovered that many 'primitive' peoples – such as Africans and the Australian Aborigines – had cephalic indices on a par with the Nordic and Teutonic races. Paul Broca, Professor of Clinical Surgery and the leading French physical anthropologist in the mid-nineteenth century, resolved the 'problem' by arguing that the skulls of the 'lower' races were elongated at the back (occipital dolichocephaly), in the area of the brain that was believed to control involuntary movement, emotions and sensations, whereas the skulls of 'higher' races were elongated at the front – the cerebral location of intellect and the higher mental functions (Gould 1981: 97-100). Again, anomalous data was manipulated to conform to pre-existing convictions concerning racial hierarchy. By 1906 the plethora of different measurements for skeletal material and the living body and the lack of standardisation in either led the XIII International Congress of Prehistoric Anthropology and Archaeology to appoint a Commission to establish an *International Agreement for the Unification (a) of Craniometric and Cephalometric Measurements, (b) of Anthropometric Measurements to be made on the living subject* (Duckworth 1913).

As more quantitative data became available, so the distinctions between the races became harder to define. Far from facilitating the definition of racial characteristics, the application of more metric techniques to larger samples of crania increasingly indicated that individual variation within each race was as great as the variation between them. Some craniologists disregarded this phenomenon. Davis (1867: xiii), for example, criticised Professor Theodor Waitz for asserting that 'small collections of race-skulls exhibit different forms of skulls strikingly, whilst rich collections fill up the apparent intervening gaps and show a continual transition from every one to every other', by arguing that this observation was only 'partially correct' and was more 'characteristic of a Professor of Philosophy than a Professor of Anatomy, essentially a science of observation'. According to Davis (1867: xiii):

> Although large collections, philosophically considered, must of necessity, by containing skulls which have some intermediate forms, tend to lessen distinctions, they, at the same time, serve to develope [sic] race characters more fully and to define the play of diversities round these race characters with more precision.

However, many other scientists soon began to recognise the difficulty in accurately defining races by physical characteristics. Thus, in his President's Address to the Anthropological Institute of Great Britain and Ireland in 1885, William Flower (1885: 378-9) explained that, while:

> the most ordinary observation is sufficient to demonstrate the fact that certain groups of men are strongly marked from others by definite characters common to all members of the group, and transmitted regularly to their descendants by the laws of inheritance .... Nevertheless, the difficulty of parcelling out all the individuals composing the human species into certain definite groups, and of saying of each man that he belongs to one or other of such groups is insuperable. No such classification has ever, or indeed can ever, be obtained. There is not one of the most characteristic, most extreme forms ... from which transitions cannot be traced by almost imperceptible gradations to any of the other equally characteristic, equally extreme forms, the relative numbers of which are continually increasing, as the long-existing isolation of nations and races breaks down under the ever-extending intercommunication characteristic of the period in which we live.

2. Evolution, the great collections and the tenacity of 'race'

Human 'types'

Faced with such evidence, the principal claims that racial characteristics were exhibited in the morphology of each individual became increasingly tenuous. Consequently, in the later nineteenth century the concept of 'race' received some modification as the idea of the racial 'type' gained ground (Stocking 1968: 56-9). According to the French physical anthropologist, Paul Topinard (1890: 446), 'by *human type* must be understood the average of characters which a human race supposed to be pure represents'. 'Type' therefore shifted the focus of racial characterisation from the individual to the group. Thus:

> It is more by the preponderance of certain characters in a large number of members of a group, than by the exclusive or even constant possession of these characters, in each of its members, that the group as a whole must be characterised (Flower 1885: 380).

In theory, only in isolated homogenous races would the features of the particular human type be discernible in each individual (Topinard 1890: 446). However, while homogenous races might have existed at one time, subsequent intermixture had made each type a 'physical ideal, to which the greater number of individuals in the group more or less approach, but which is better marked in some than in others' (Topinard 1890: 446-7). The task set by some physical anthropologists was therefore to recreate these primordial types from the confusing blend of modern races (e.g. Topinard 1890: 442-511; Stocking 1968: 58), an enterprise that required collections on a 'far larger scale than [had] hitherto been attempted' because, 'it is only by large numbers that the errors arising from individual peculiarities or accidental admixture can be obviated, and the prevailing characteristics of a race or group truly ascertained' (Flower 1881: 246). Although the target of analysis had been modified, the data set and the desire for more specimens remained the same.

By the 1900s, the 'metric torrent' propagated by physical anthropology in the previous half century had therefore unexpectedly weakened one of the fundamental underpinnings of the scientific conceptualisation of human difference (Stocking 1968: 163). It could no longer be accepted with confidence that 'race' was an empirical reality or that headform was an accurate indicator of human difference. The transition to analyses of human 'type' had circumvented these problems by relegating 'pure' races to the remote past with the hope that examination of modern peoples would provide evidence of their racial history and that, by doing so, the original 'types' could be ascertained. However, the efficacy of this method relied upon the age-old assumption that all racial characteristics were hereditary, a generalisation that was to be successfully challenged by the work of Franz Boas (1858-1942).

Franz Boas and the instability of human types

According to then contemporary theory, members of a race of people were physically alike because they shared a common ancestry. However, while eighteenth-century concepts of human difference had been preoccupied with lineage and genealogies, the comparative anatomists had been less interested in these aspects and as the study of physical characteristics had taken precedence, so consanguinity became 'almost a gratuitous assumption' (Stocking 1968: 165). Nevertheless, defining a race by the physical features shared by its members required these features to be stable and hereditary.

Franz Boas was an unorthodox physical anthropologist who approached the discipline not from medicine or anatomy but from a background of mathematics and an understanding of biology which was orientated more towards process than taxonomy (Stocking 1968: 166-94; 1974: 1-20). From an early stage Boas (1894a, 1894b, 1940) had been highly critical of the racial formalism which so invested the study of human diversity. With an approach that insisted upon strict empiricism, Boas systematically investigated many 'classic' anthropological issues, not to determine the classification of humankind but more to gain an understanding of the process of race formation. The results of his analyses contradicted many of the fundamental assumptions of physical anthropology. For example, his research into the 'half-breed' American Indian revealed that, contrary to the long held polygenist belief, individuals with Indian and European mixed descent appeared to be more fertile than 'pure' Indians and thus intermixture could be claimed to have had a beneficial effect (Boas 1894a: 193-4, 1940: 18-27, 138-48 and see Stocking 1968: 172-3).

Boas began to study the inheritance of headform in the early 1900s, and his most important research on this topic was conducted between 1908 and 1910 on behalf of the United States Immigration Commission. Initially aiming to investigate changes in headform in immigrant children born abroad and those born inside the USA, the initial results of Boas' research caused a shift in his focus of study. Expecting the headshape of immigrant children to reflect that of their parents, he found that his pilot study data unexpectedly revealed marked changes in cephalic index (Boas to Jenks, 3 September 1908, reproduced in Stocking 1974: 206-10; Boas 1903, 1911: 216-17, 1940: 28-85). Further research on a sample of almost eighteen thousand individuals confirmed these results, and Boas (1911: 218) concluded that although he could not explain what caused the changes in headform, 'the old idea of absolute stability of human types must ... evidently be given up, and with it the belief of the hereditary superiority of certain types over others'.

The tenacity of 'race'

By the 1920s, with the foundations of over a century's research into human difference having been shown to be increasingly suspect, there was a growing dissatisfaction with the quantitative analysis of the human remains of different peoples (see Stepan 1982: 162-9). It may have been such dissatisfaction, coupled with a proclamation by the Australian Government in 1913 that prohibited the export of all 'aboriginal [sic] anthropological specimens, including articles of ethnological interest, unless the exportation is by the accredited representative of an officially-recognised scientific institution and the permission of the Minister for Trade and Customs is obtained to such exportation' (*Commonwealth Gazette* 22 November 1913), which led to a rapid decrease in the number of indigenous Australian human remains sent to museums and institutions in the West. However, while some leading anthropologists were ready to admit that 'a race type exists mainly in our own minds' (Haddon 1924: 1), the study of 'race' continued, finding a particular niche in the socio-political sphere first within the eugenics movement and later in the racist ideology of Nazi Germany (Proctor 1988; Tucker 1994). Scientific rationale for the latter was provided predominantly by German physical anthropologists, who interpreted anthropometric and craniological data as support for the doctrine of Aryan supremacy and the 'innate' biological (and thus cultural) inferiority of various other peoples, in particular the Jews.

Outside Germany, the tenacity of 'race' and the concept of racial hierarchy is evidenced by the difficulty with which various anthropologists tried to mobilise their colleagues to condemn the scientific rationale behind Nazi racism. Barkan (1988, 1992: 279-340), for example, has documented in detail the considerable efforts of Franz Boas who, throughout the 1930s, endeavoured to organise British and American scientists to formulate a consensus of opinion on the race issue that would counter Nazi propaganda. However, his attempts were largely unsuccessful, for while influential physical anthropologists may not have explicitly supported Nazi racial doctrine, many continued to accept the basic existence of the concept and its role as a fundamental determinant of cultural and mental capacity (e.g. Keith 1931). Moreover, as demonstrated by Barkan (1988, 1992: 279-340), many of those who privately dismissed Nazi scientific racism were disinclined to air their views in public or to take an active role in combating its dissemination.

In Britain the lack of scientific consensus on the race issue was highlighted when, after two years of deliberation, the Race and Culture Committee established by the Royal Anthropological Institute in 1934 failed even to agree on a definition of 'race', let alone to fulfil its mandate to determine the degree to which race could be linked to culture (Barkan 1988: 194; 1992: 285-96). Nevertheless, British scientists were not completely silent on the issue. For example, in *We Europeans* Haddon and Huxley drew upon the recent work of geneticists and biometricians to demonstrate the fallacy of 'race' as a valid scientific term and suggested that its application to human groups 'should be dropped from the vocabulary of science' (Haddon and Huxley 1935: 107). Going one step further,

Firth (1938: 21) argued that, 'purity of race is a concept of political propaganda, not a scientific description of human groups today'.

Despite further attempts to organise scientists into a united front against Nazi racism (see Barkan 1992: 318-40), it was not until the growth of anti-Nazi sentiment during the Second World War, fuelled by revelations of the extremes to which German State policy had taken the doctrines of race theory, that a public scientific consensus on race was forthcoming (Stocking 1988: 11). This was achieved in 1950 by UNESCO, which issued the first of a series of statements on the concept of race. Opening with the statement that, 'scientists have reached a general agreement in recognising that mankind is one: that all men belong to the same species, *Homo sapiens*' (UNESCO 1952: 98, in Harraway 1988: 211), the UNESCO declaration ostensibly represented the return of the monogenist tradition to the primary position of scientific and moral authority (Stocking 1988: 11). Unlike its nineteenth-century manifestation, the monogenism reaffirmed by UNESCO was fundamentally egalitarian: the declaration stated that there was no scientific proof that human groups differed in their innate mental capabilities nor that miscegenation was biologically detrimental. This new theory of unity did not, therefore, conceptualise human diversity as a degenerating gradation from a European norm, but as a product of the 'operation of evolutionary factors of differentiation such as isolation, the drift and random fixation of the material particles which control heredity (the genes), changes in the structure of these particles, hybridisation, and natural selection' (UNESCO 1952: 98, in Harraway 1988: 211).

The idea of 'race' and the racial order which had been assumed, studied and reified by physical anthropology throughout its historical development appeared irrelevant to the new, more relativist, approach to human origins described by UNESCO. Not only had the measurement of human remains failed to answer the questions posed by physical anthropology, but even the questions themselves were, following UNESCO, considered irrelevant. The raw data which had been amassed – the remains of thousands of individuals procured throughout the world – were largely surplus to requirements. Nor could these remains be used by new developments in physical anthropology which emerged after the Second World War. There were few fossils for the palaeoanthropologists, and the studies which aimed to reconstruct the demography and pathology of past populations required not only well-provenanced remains in sufficient numbers to form a random representative sample of the population in question, but sufficiently advanced excavation techniques to ensure 'complete and accurate recovery of skeletal parts and information on their associations with one another and with other items' (Ubelaker 1989: 3). Few, if any, of the remains that had been gathered in the nineteenth and early twentieth centuries to classify and elucidate human diversity could match any of these criteria. It is therefore not surprising that, after World War Two and in some cases much earlier, collections received little attention, with their contents being placed in storage, or transferred to other institutions. With a few notable exceptions, hardly any indigenous human remains have been donated to British collections since World War Two, while in colonised countries the remains of their indigenous populations continued to be placed in museums, usually after discovery through archaeological excavation or chance disturbance. In Australia, collections continued to grow in many of the major State museums.

'Race' after UNESCO

Despite UNESCO's various statements on race, the concept itself was not abandoned. To the contrary, it was the subject of debate and description in mainstream anthropology journals (particularly *Current Anthropology*) and publications after 1950 (see Tucker 1994: 180-268). Coon's *The Origin of the Races* (1962), a polygenist script, demonstrated the continuing use of the concept of race and assumptions of racial worth, while the controversy it provoked showed that there were others who rejected such premises (e.g. Coon 1963; Dobzhansky 1963; Montagu 1963a, 1963b). Conforming to nineteenth-century stereotypes, Coon used the picture of an Aboriginal (Tiwi) woman in comparison with that of a Chinese 'sage' to demonstrate that cranial capacity was an index of intelligence. Montagu (1963a: 362), an outspoken opponent of such views, roundly criticised this comparison, asking with some exasperation:

> does it have to be re-proven every year that brain size within the normal range of variation characteristic of the human species at the *sapiens* level and characteristic of every human population has nothing whatever to do with intelligence?

Further illustrating how accepted the race concept continued to be, Livingstone (1962: 279) wrote in *Current Anthropology* that there were 'excellent arguments for abandoning the concept of race with reference to the living populations of *Homo sapiens. Although this may seem to be a rather unorthodox position among anthropologists ...*' (my emphasis). Echoing similar complaints made by scientists in the previous century, Dobzhansky's (1962) comment on Livingstone's article argued that races did exist, but that the problem lay in how to classify them. However, scholars were aware of racism and its dangers, although Dobzhansky, somewhat paradoxically, argued, 'to say that mankind has no races plays into the hands of race bigots, and this is least of all desirable when "scientific" racism attempts to rear its ugly head' (1962: 280). Racial analyses, and debate on the existence or non-existence of races, continued to appear in the pages of *Current Anthropology* for many years after this exchange (e.g. Brace 1964; Coon 1964; Count 1964; Montagu 1964a; Abbie 1967;

Coon and Hunt 1967; Kelso 1967; Mavalwala 1967; Robertson 1979; Robertson and Bradley 1979; Hall 1983; and see Shanklin 1994).

In 1982, Littlefield, Lieberman and Reynolds carried out an analysis of fifty-eight physical anthropology text books published in the USA between 1932 and 1979. They found that prior to 1970, the 'no-race' view was rarely expressed, but that after 1975 it had become the most frequent viewpoint, with 'only one quarter of the textbooks continuing to argue for the validity of the race concept' (Littlefield *et al.*1982: 646). Their analysis contended that this change could not be explained solely by the accumulation of new data or the 'self-correcting nature of empirical science' (1982: 646), because none of the arguments to invalidate the race concept were particularly new. Questioning why the race concept had persisted for so long, despite evidence and argument that it was inaccurate, Littlefield *et al.* proposed that the shift away from the race concept in the mid-1970s was due to the changing institutional and social context of anthropology as a discipline which had undergone a period of rapid expansion. This expansion, they argued, brought a large number of scholars and students into the discipline from a variety of backgrounds, altering its composition to one for which a 'no-race' viewpoint was more generally acceptable. The use of the term 'race' at this time appears to have been increasingly felt by some to be what would now be termed 'politically incorrect', reflecting not only the general rejection of the term, but also the fact that others wished to retain it and believed that its rejection was not based on scientific reasoning. As Brues (1967) wrote in her review of Coon and Hunt's *The Living Races of Man* (1965), 'It requires a degree of courage to write a book on Races of Man in this age of the New Prudery, when r-ce has replaced s-x as the great dirty word.'

More recently, Goodman and Armelagos (1996) examined the status of the race concept in physical anthropology in the 1990s. They observed that at the 1993 meeting of the American Association of Physical Anthropologists there was vigorous opposition to a resolution that sought to ratify an update of the second UNESCO statement on race. Attempting to understand this opposition, and after 'a reading of recent scientific literature, as well as wide ideological and social trends', their examination of the race concept in forensic anthropology and its use in medical research and human genomics led them to conclude that, 'racialism, [as] a theoretical stance, is alive and well' and that, furthermore, 'the re-emergence of race as a shorthand for human variation appears to be covariant with an escalation in biological reductionism and a search for simple explanations to complex problems' (1996: 175).

Looking back over the history of physical anthropology, claimed results of analyses consistently supported pre-conceived notions of a racial hierarchy. Scientific racism and quantitative analysis reified a pre-existing social concept regarding the ranked hierarchy of different peoples. Data that did not conform was either ignored or reinterpreted to 'fit' as required. Just as numerical data often attains the status of 'fact' and in doing so lends authority to scientific theory, so it is also exceptionally sensitive to unintentional manipulation. Gould proved this phenomenon when in his recalculation of Morton's data, he not only discovered the craniologist's own errors but later realised that on one occasion he had himself unwittingly 'chosen' a clearly incorrect number because it provided him with a 'good' result (Gould 1981: 66). Analysis of human remains set out to discover the physical manifestations of an identity already socially constructed by Europeans for Australia's indigenous population. Reflecting the 'lowly' position which had been ascribed to Australian Aborigines, first their skeletal and later their soft tissue material was perceived as 'simious', 'brutish' and/or primeval in form. This was taken to conform to the geographical location of Aborigines at the 'uttermost ends', the traditional home of all human beings considered uncivilised and bestial (see Gamble 1992; Bowler 1992).

That social concepts of race and racial hierarchy dominated physical anthropology is apparent in the tenacity of the race paradigm in science despite evidence within the academy that showed it to be false. Instead, the scientific establishment only began to turn away from this paradigm when, after World War Two, it increasingly became socially and politically untenable. However, the race concept continued to dominate physical anthropology textbooks until the 1970s, and remained a subject of heated debate in mainstream anthropological literature after that. Studies which bear the characteristic hallmarks of biological determinism, racial formalism, a concentration on human *differences,* and the implicit or explicit assumption of racial hierarchy (e.g. Coon 1962; Baker 1974) have appeared since World War Two and have been debated, commended and criticised (see above and Montagu 1964b, 1974). A more recent and extreme example (see Rushton 1994a, 1994b) received severe criticism (Chisholm 1994).

The study of human remains to locate 'evidence' of racial hierarchy lies in the past, but the results of a hundred and fifty years of grave-robbing remain, and the scientific value of such collections has recently been reasserted. Technical advances in the field of molecular biology mean that human remains collected in the nineteenth and early twentieth centuries are again being considered important for the study of human evolution and human diversity. For example, in the early 1990s it was claimed that the development of techniques which enabled DNA to be extracted from ancient bone, and possibly even from fossils, had the potential to answer many of the 'classic' questions posed by archaeology and anthropology, not least the relationship between modern humans and the Neanderthals (see Hagelberg *et al.* 1989; Brown and Brown 1992; Hagelberg 1990, 1992; Hermann and Hummel 1994). Hagelberg (1990) predicted that, 'opening up new avenues of research into the genetics and demography of our ancestors', the extraction of DNA from ancient bone would enable scientists to 'test hypotheses about human evolution, migrations and disease'. However, since the initial results achieved in the late 1980s and early 1990s, studies in ancient DNA did not advance as rapidly as expected, the main hurdle being the problem of contamination and the consequent difficulty in authenticating results (Brown and Brown 1992; Richards *et al.* 1995). In 1994, one researcher pondered whether, 'many archaeologists and archaeological scientists will be wondering if all the scientific excitement, media interest, and funding attracted by ancient DNA is a reflection of progress or merely self-deluding hyperactivity' (Hedges 1994: 861) and noted 'the enormous gap between the achievement of recovering one short ancient DNA sequence and the gleam in the eye of the palaeodemographer tracking migrations'.

In the mid-1990s there was progress in reducing the contamination of specimens (e.g. Richards *et al.* 1995) as well as some advances in the field of European palaeodemography through the analysis of modern DNA and its comparison with ancient DNA taken, for example, from the 5,000-year-old 'Ice Man' found in the Italian Alps in 1991 (Powledge and Rose 1996: 41-4). In 1997 it was reported that a sample of DNA has been successfully extracted from a Neanderthal skeleton (Krings *et al.* 1997), and since that time the process has been replicated (Relethford 2001). These studies concluded that Neanderthals had sufficiently different mitochondrial DNA to be considered a separate species to *Homo sapiens*, thus lending support to the recent 'Out of Africa' theory, which proposes that *Homo sapiens* emerged in Africa approximately 100,000 years ago and migrated globally, replacing other *Homo* species (including *H. neanderthalensis, H. heidelbergensis and H. erectus*) as it did so (Stringer and McKie 1996). This is in opposition to the other current major model of human evolution, the regional continuity hypothesis, which proposes that since an original migration out of Africa some 1.5 million years ago there has been a single evolving species, which has developed regional adaptations (Wolpoff and Caspari 1997). Discussions surrounding the conclusion drawn from the analysis of Neanderthal DNA and other fossil remains demonstrate how the two conceptual approaches to human origins – unity and plurality – are echoed in current scientific debate. While the number of ancient and fossil remains in today's collections is relatively small, the development of new research techniques (see, for example, Grupe and Peters 2003) indicates that human remains may always be considered a potential source of new scientific information.

3

Collecting the dead

As institutions in Europe acquired more and more human remains of people from around the world, so funerary sites in distant countries began to empty. The remains of Australia's indigenous population were sent to museums in Europe from the earliest days of colonial settlement. Museum catalogues (e.g. Williamson 1857; Davis 1867; Flower 1907; Hull 1960) show that by far the majority had been taken from any location in which Aboriginal people had placed their dead, but that some were taken before remains had passed through funerary rites.

Edinburgh University

The Anatomy Department at the University of Edinburgh housed a large anthropological collection of human remains and provides a good example of the wide variety of places from which Aboriginal human remains were taken, and how this process occurred (Edinburgh University's collection of Aboriginal human remains has now been repatriated to Australia, and much of its contents has been reburied (see Chapters 6 and 8)). By 1825, this institution contained the remains of a small number of indigenous Australians, but when Sir William Turner became Professor in 1867 the collection began to increase substantially, his term seeing the accession of the remains of over seventy-five Aboriginal people. After Turner, Daniel J. Cunningham (Professor of Anatomy 1903-9) and, to a lesser extent Arthur Robinson (Professor of Anatomy 1909-31) oversaw the growth of the collection which, by 1939, contained the skulls of over 1,660 individuals from at least fifty-five different countries. The largest component of the collection came from Australia and included the remains of at least six hundred Aboriginal people. Unlike other collections, that at Edinburgh University contained a very large proportion of post-cranial remains, nearly all of which were sent by this collection's principal donor, Dr William Ramsay Smith (see below). In Edinburgh, the post-cranial remains were kept in a workroom, while the crania were displayed in an annexe to the larger Anatomy Museum:

> At one end of the great hall is a cabinet, 18 feet high, and with 300 superficial feet of floor space, around which is a light gallery. This cabinet is occupied by a large collection of crania of the races of men, gathered in

various parts of the world, and, for the most part presented by former pupils, so that it forms a very representative collection (Turner 1919: 15-16).

Museum records vary in the amount of detail they provide about donated remains. Some identify the name of the individual, some supply a large amount of information about where and when and in what circumstances remains were obtained, others provide simply the name of the donor and the place of origin. Still others provide no information at all, only stating that a skull was from, for example, 'Australia'.

Many Aboriginal remains were taken from burial grounds, such as a skull described by Professor William Turner (ms, no date) of a man buried for five or six years, dug up 'from a black's burying ground where the trees facing the grave were marked and carved' and presented 'by my pupil Jas Howison'. Others were taken after they had fallen from tree burials, such as a skull 'brought by Mr Walter Dickson from the South Side of Lake Alexandrina in the province of S. Australia' (Turner ms, no date), or from funeral platforms, such as the skull taken, 'from a platform or funeral pile in thick tea-tree scrub adjoining the Coorong & mouth of the Murray: the body was rolled in coarse sacks'. Still others were picked up having probably eroded out of the ground, such as the skull 'found on the shores of Lake Bolac Western district Victoria' and donated by David Laidlaw in May 1892 and that 'picked up on Curtis Island' in 1879 and donated by Sir Arthur Mitchell (EADL Skull Catalogue). Other collections were sent remains taken from burial caves or disturbed through construction work, the latter being a more common source of remains in the twentieth century, and donated to museums in the colonies.

In a smaller number of cases, remains were obtained before they had passed through funerary rites – from, for example, hospital morgues, the scaffold, at least one University dissecting room, or from massacre sites. Because it is such individuals who often have the most information associated with them, some examples are presented in more detail below.

Hospitals

Some of those who procured human remains, and particularly those in the medical profession, had access to Aboriginal bodies lying in morgues, and to cadavers used for dissection. Remains from such sources were sometimes taken for scientific study and sent to institutions in Europe. Perhaps the most well-documented example is the mutilation of the body of William Lanne, the so-called 'last' male Tasmanian Aborigine, as it lay in the Hobart Hospital morgue (see Ryan 1981 and records of the official enquiry in the *Hobart Mercury*, February/March 1869).

3. Collecting the dead

William Lanne

Dr William Crowther (Honorary Medical Officer at the Hobart General Hospital) had been trying for some time to acquire the skeleton of a Tasmanian Aborigine for his friend, William Flower, Conservator of the Royal College of Surgeons of England. His previous request to the Colonial Secretary, Sir Richard Dry, for the body of another Tasmanian had been denied, and these remains were given instead to the Royal Society of Tasmania. Both Crowther and the Royal Society applied to Dry for Lanne's body, but after the Royal Society refused to waive its claim, stating that its right to Lanne's body was 'paramount to that of any other scientific institution in the world' (Agnew to the Colonial Secretary 5 March 1869, reproduced in the *Hobart Mercury* 19 March 1869), Dry conceded to the Society's requests but promised Crowther no hindrance 'should any further opportunity present itself of securing a skeleton for the Royal College of Surgeons from among the graves of the aborigines without violating the feelings of individuals or of the community' (*Hobart Mercury* 8 March 1869). Despite this agreement, Dry suspected trouble and ordered the General Hospital's House Surgeon, Dr George Stokell, to protect Lanne's body from mutilation.

According to the *Hobart Mercury* (8 March 1869), there was a general assumption throughout Hobart that Lanne's body would receive a proper burial and then, at some time in the future, his body would be exhumed for preservation at the Royal Society's museum. However, on the afternoon of 5 March 1869, Stockell met Crowther in the street and told him of Dry's orders. Crowther reiterated his claim to the body and said that Dry had promised it to him long ago. Stockell replied that the Royal Society had the best claim to the body, to which Crowther answered that Stockell was 'a fool to keep it in a paltry place like Tasmania, when it ought to be sent to a place like London' (*Hobart Mercury* 13 March 1869). They parted, agreeing to meet again later at 7 pm at Crowther's house. Stockell returned to the hospital and found Lanne's body unharmed.

At approximately 7 o'clock that evening, Dr Crowther and his son, Alfred William Crowther, were seen in the hospital morgue working on two corpses. Meanwhile, Stockell had arrived at Crowther's house as arranged but, finding that Crowther was not at home, soon feared the worst and made his way to the hospital. Informed by staff that Crowther had preceded him, Stockell discovered that Lanne's skull had been removed and replaced by that of a schoolteacher lying nearby. After making an unsuccessful search for Lanne's skull, he locked the morgue and returned home.

The following morning, Stockell told the Secretary of the Royal Society, J.W. Agnew, and one of its leading members, Morton Allport,[1] of what had happened. Fearing that Crowther would take the rest of Lanne's skeleton also, they ordered Stockell to secure Lanne's hands and feet for the Royal

Society, which he did. In later defence of his actions, Agnew stated that after the removal of the head 'can the removal of the feet and hands be regarded as the slightest consequence? If a barbarian shatters a valuable vase, is it blameworthy if some of the fragments are removed, in order that he may not have the satisfaction or profit of putting them together?' (*Hobart Mercury* 19 March 1869).

What remained of Lanne's body was buried on 6 March. Rumours had spread that his body had been mutilated and a number of Hobart gentlemen requested that his coffin be opened, 'in order to satisfy their minds that the ceremony of burial was not altogether a 'vain show' (*Hobart Mercury* 8 March 1869). But inspection of the coffin caused no alarm and the coffin was sealed before being carried to St David's church-yard by four of Lanne's friends, followed by over a hundred mourners. After the burial, Dry gave orders that a police watch be placed over it, but his orders were not carried out. Stockell and his men later disinterred Lanne's coffin and removed the body, placing the substituted skull in the coffin which they reburied, and leaving the grave in a 'perfectly decent and proper order' (*Hobart Mercury* 12 March 1869). Later, Crowther's party came to the cemetery and, discovering that they were too late, left the grave empty with part of the coffin visible, a skull lying on the grave surface and the surrounding ground 'saturated with blood' (*Hobart Mercury* 8 March 1869). The next day, news of the grave-robbing spread across the city and several hundred people, including the Colonial Secretary, gathered at the cemetery.

Following a Ministerial Enquiry, Dr Crowther was suspended as Honorary Medical Officer and, subsequently, his son was suspended as a pupil of the hospital. Meanwhile, Crowther had been trying to trace what was left of Lanne's body. According to an article (entitled *'Et Tu Brute'*) placed by Crowther in the *Hobart Mercury* (12 March 1869), he had discovered that Stockell had taken the body to an old disused room in the General Hospital where he had spent all of Sunday 7 March reducing it to a skeleton. A day later, unable to gain entry to the room in question, Crowther returned later with the police but the group was confronted by Stockell, who denied them access. Forcing their way through, Crowther did not discover Lanne's skeleton, but found instead what remained of the rest of his body, describing the room as a 'charnel house' (*Hobart Mercury* 12 March 1869).

A later enquiry into the treatment of Lanne's body sat for two days. Both Crowther and his son refused to attend, on the grounds that they had been prejudged at the previous Ministerial Enquiry, where their atten-dance had not been requested. The enquiry was terminated when requests for the scope of the commission to be enlarged were refused (*Hobart Mercury* 12 March 1869). In a final attempt to get Crowther on the witness stand, and in response to Crowther's printed accusation (in *Hobart Mercury* 12 March 1869) that Stockell had been responsible for taking

Lanne's skull, Stockell was officially prosecuted. However, in court Crowther refused to answer any relevant questions on the grounds that he might incriminate himself, and his son refused to appear. Stockell was acquitted (*Hobart Mercury* 16 March 1869). This ended all official enquiries into the mutilation of William Lanne's body, despite public outcry, not only because of the way that Lanne had been treated, but also because it was now clear that Aboriginal and non-Aboriginal bodies were indecently treated in the morgue, and were subjected to the publicly hated practice of dissection (*Hobart Mercury* 12 March 1869).[2]

But what then happened to Lanne's remains? Ryan (1981: 217) reports that Stockell had a tobacco pouch made from Lanne's skin, while other scientists took his nose, ears, and a piece of his arm, and that his hands and feet later appeared in the rooms of the Royal Society. Morton Allport wrote to Barnard Davis in 1873 describing various existing Tasmanian Aboriginal skeletons including that of Lanne, although failing to mention where it was located. He also reported that Lanne's skull was said to be in London in the possession of William Crowther's son. By at least the 1980s it was believed by both the Tasmanian Aboriginal community and Edinburgh University that Lanne's skull was in the collection of the University of Edinburgh's Anatomy Department. However, just before it became clear in 1991 that this skull was to be repatriated to Tasmania, the then Professor of Anatomy cast doubt upon its identity (Brocklebank and Kaufman 1992). Criticised as a strategy to retain the skull, these doubts were rejected by Tasmanian campaigners. Shortly afterwards, the Department's collection of Tasmanian human remains were returned to Tasmania (and see Chapter 8).

Lanne's story demonstrates the high value placed on Tasmanian human remains at this time, and the abhorrent lengths that two eminent Hobart doctors would go to acquire them. The doctors and their assistants mutilated Lanne's body (and a nearby cadaver) and desecrated his burial site, disobeyed direct orders from the Colonial Secretary, risked criminal charges and their careers, deceived members of the powerful Hobart establishment, and clearly acted against public opinion. The events in Hobart demonstrate the emergence in the later nineteenth century of collections in the colonies regarded by some as legitimate places to house valuable specimens, and by others who believed, like Crowther, that the colonies were 'not the place for such things'. Lanne's story also serves to demonstrate that the authorities were aware that obtaining the human remains of 'the aborigines' from the morgue might not be condoned by the general population. Nonetheless, Dry was willing to bow to scientists' demands as long as Lanne initially received a proper burial. While the wishes of scientists were considered paramount, there is no evidence that consent was acquired from either Lanne or his kin for the use of his body for scientific purposes. The outcry and enquiries that followed the discovery of Lanne's mutilation demonstrate the public hatred of dissection, with the realisation that it was not only Aboriginal remains that were treated in this way. Contemporary newspaper reports do not describe the response of Tasmanian Aborigines to the news of Lanne's mutilation but these can be inferred from the later distress and fear of one woman (Truganini – see Chapter 6) that her own body would be similarly treated. Finally, Lanne's story is also important because some one hundred years later, the request for the return of his skull was a key element in the start of the campaign by Aboriginal people for the repatriation of remains from UK institutions (see Chapter 8).

Adelaide

Although Lanne's case is famous, it is almost certainly far from unique. Australian indigenous human remains may have been taken from the hospital in Melbourne, as the British craniologist Joseph Barnard Davis received the skull of a man who had died in this institution (Davis 1867: 261), and a number of Aboriginal body parts were certainly sent by members of the Adelaide medical establishment, themselves eminent anthropologists (Jones 1987), to UK institutions in the late nineteenth and early twentieth centuries. The main individuals involved in this latter supply route appear to have been Edward C. Stirling, Director of the Adelaide Museum and Professor of Physiology at the University of Adelaide; Archibald Watson, Elder Professor of Anatomy at the same university, and William Ramsay Smith who, as well as being Chairman of the Central Board of Health, City Coroner, Inspector of Anatomy and a doctor at the Adelaide Hospital, was the supplier of the majority of Aboriginal remains sent to the Anatomy Department at his old university in Edinburgh.

Ramsay Smith (1859-1937) commenced medical studies at the University of Edinburgh in 1884, graduating with a B.Sc. (natural sciences) in 1888 and with an M.B., C.M. in 1892. In 1904 he graduated with a D.Sc. from the University of Adelaide and received his M.D. from Edinburgh in 1913. Aside from his medical career, Ramsay Smith was also a Fellow of the Royal Anthropological Institute of Great Britain and Ireland, and twice President of the Anthropology Section of the Australian Association of the Advancement of Science. He wrote extensively about Australia's indigenous population (1907a; 1907b; 1908; 1913; 1924).

Ramsay Smith's first donations to the Anatomy Museum (two animal specimens) were made in 1890 and 1891 while he was still a student at the University of Edinburgh (Day Book, EADL). His next donations, in 1899, were two human skulls from South Australia. In response to a request from Turner to supply additional Aboriginal remains, Ramsay Smith answered that he could send 'a fairly complete collection in the course of a short time', remarking that 'with less Hospital work and a more extensive field as Coroner and President of the Board of Health I hope to be able to enrich your collections and do something in new fields of investigation' (Ramsay Smith to Turner 17 January 1901, EADL). Ramsay Smith was true to his word and subsequently became the most prolific supplier of indigenous Australian human remains to the UK; he was also responsible for supplying a smaller amount of remains from other parts of the world. As he foresaw, he was able to use his professional positions to assist in locating and removing human remains.

Tommy Walker

Stirling, Watson and Ramsay Smith obtained remains from the Adelaide Hospital morgue as well as the University of Adelaide's dissecting rooms, which sometimes received Aboriginal corpses from the nearby Parkside Lunatic Asylum. Ramsay Smith took many indigenous and non-indigenous body parts from such places, including those of Tommy Walker, a well-known Ngarrindjeri man who lived in the Adelaide district at that time (*Adelaide Advertiser* 18 August 1903). Walker's story is somewhat similar to that of Lanne, particularly in regards to the public outcry that occurred when it was discovered that what had been buried, in a very public funeral, was not the full remains of Tommy Walker but instead an almost empty coffin. The story of what happened to Tommy Walker includes what may perhaps be the earliest request for the repatriation of Aboriginal remains from an overseas museum.

When Walker died in Adelaide Hospital on 4 July 1901, both major local newspapers carried long obituaries (*South Australia Register* 5 July 1901; *Adelaide Advertiser* 5 July 1901), and his popularity is evident from an account written in the *Adelaide Advertiser* (18 August 1903) two years after his death:

> He was during his life one of the best known figures in the city. A chartered libertine with a sense of humour, frequently in trouble with the police and always a vagrant, often he faced the Police Court bench on charges of drunkenness, and frequently too, has he turned a playful copper by rehearsing for the amusement of any little groups which he could draw together the scenes enacted in the solemn halls of justice. His dramatic abilities were sufficiently good to hold a whole pavilion full of people on the oval in a roar during the intervals of a game of football or cricket.

The published obituaries recorded that Walker had died of cold, exposure and neglect, a claim that was vehemently denied by the Protector of Aborigines, George Hamilton (*Adelaide Advertiser* on 6 July 1901). Hamilton's denial of any responsibility for Walker's death was corroborated by Ramsay Smith, who had seen Walker shortly before he died, and, noticing that he was very ill, and that he and his wife Ada were 'willing he should go to the Hospital', had signed the required admittance order (Ramsay Smith to Hamilton 6 July 1901, SASA GRG 52, AOF: 280).

Because of Walker's popularity, the stockbrokers of Adelaide paid for his coffin, burial and headstone (*Adelaide Advertiser* 18 August 1903), not realising that the coffin was nearly empty as his head and skeleton had been sent by Ramsay Smith to the Department of Anatomy at the University of Edinburgh. In August 1903, news of Ramsay Smith's treatment of Tommy Walker's body, as well as those of other indigenous and non-indigenous people in the hospital morgue became public and caused considerable outrage (see Plate 4). The Secretary of the South Australia Aboriginal Friends' Association reported that news of Tommy Walker's treatment had 'created anxiety amongst the natives at Point McLeay mission station, and they are manifestly disinclined to be sent to the Adelaide Hospital in case of sickness' (*Adelaide Advertiser* 25 September 1903). Presumably in response, and in what may be the first request for the return of Aboriginal remains from an overseas institution, the Friends Association wrote to the South Australian Government asking that Tommy Walker's remains should be returned for burial in South Australia. In the same letter they also requested the Government to 'consider the advisability of recovering and reinterring the skeletons which Veterinary-surgeon J. Desmond states that he obtained from Hindmarsh Island' (*Adelaide Advertiser* 25 September 1903). Desmond's grave-robbing had become public in evidence he had given at the Official Board of Enquiry subsequently convened to examine Ramsay Smith's conduct (see Chapter 4). Although Ramsay Smith was immediately suspended from civic and hospital duties, the Enquiry found him innocent of all charges. Ramsay Smith used his medical position to obtain indigenous human remains for a museum overseas, and did so in the knowledge that this risked official sanction, if not criminal charges. Almost one hundred years later, all that could be located in Edinburgh University's Anatomy Department of Tommy Walker's remains were returned to his family in South Australia and buried. The fate of the Hindmarsh Island skeletons removed by J. Desmond is unknown.

The Asylum

While Tommy Walker's remains were taken from the Adelaide Hospital morgue, other indigenous Australian remains were taken from the Adelaide University dissecting rooms, some of which had been acquired from people dying in Adelaide's lunatic asylums. For example, one inmate had been arrested in 1892 on a charge of murder. Placed on trial in Adelaide and, after a long hearing (*Adelaide Advertiser* March 1893) which sought to determine his mental state, and in which it was clear he spoke no English, the man was admitted to the Parkside Lunatic Asylum on Her Majesty's Pleasure. He stayed at this institution until his death ten years later. On the day he died, the Resident Medical Officer, Dr Cleland, requested a licence from the Chief Secretary to permit the body to be anatomised. The request was underlined in red and written on a *pro forma,* to which Cleland added the memo:

> [this] skeleton is of great scientific value and ought not to be lost. He comes from the Macdonnell Ranges and is a Governor's pleasure man having committed murder. It will be noted from the red underlining how I am trying to obtain permission for its preservation. I do not know if any better plan suggests itself to the Honourable Chief Secretary (Lunatic Asylum Office File no. 150 SASA GRG 34/72).

Despite knowing the man's mental condition and lack of English, Cleland signed the *pro forma* which stated that the deceased:

> did not, to the best of my knowledge, information, and belief, express his desire either in writing at any time during his life, or verbally during the illness whereof he died, that his body after death might not undergo anatomical examination, and the surviving wife or the nearest known relative of the said deceased has not to my knowledge required his body to be interred without such anatomical examination (LAO, File 150 SASA GRG 34/72).

The licence was granted on 3 November 1903, but the body had been removed before this, and was in the Anatomy School by 28 October. On that day, Ramsay Smith, as Justice of the Peace and City Coroner, had filled in the appropriate form which certified that, in his opinion, there was no necessity for 'holding an inquest upon the body ... and that the body ... may be buried' (PLA Admission Papers), although he must have known that there was no intention of burial. Instead, the body was collected by the undertaker and taken to Watson at the Anatomical School.

On 4 November 1903, Cleland forwarded the newly acquired licence to the Registrar at the University of Adelaide for the 'information of the Anatomical School, asking that the requisite steps may be taken for handing over the skeleton to the Adelaide Museum' (LAO File 150, SASA GRG 34/72). However, there is no record of the Adelaide Museum ever having received this skeleton and, four years later, Ramsay Smith sent it to Cunningham in Edinburgh. For Ramsay Smith, the deceased's behaviour was not perceived as 'insanity' but rather as evidence of his 'lowly' status, and which, in consequence, made his skeleton all the more valuable, as he wrote to Cunningham on 29 May 1907:

> ... you will see that [the deceased] is important. He was one of the very lowest black-fellows seen here. When he was given his food he would pick all the fat off it and anoint his body with it. If he was surprised while eating he would gather all the food in a heap and sit on it (ELSC Ms 608).

As in the example given above, it is clear that the medical officer's authorisation to use bodies for dissection was a foregone conclusion. Cadavers arrived at the Anatomy Department in Adelaide before the licence to remove them from the lunatic asylum had been signed. Involved in a professional capacity with the transfer of bodies to the dissecting rooms, Ramsay Smith, Cleland and Watson were in perfect positions to obtain any soft tissue or skeletal remains that they wanted.

Although Watson and Stirling collaborated with Ramsay Smith in supplying Aboriginal body parts to the University of Edinburgh, they also donated soft tissue and skeletal remains to other collections in Great Britain. Perhaps reflecting competition amongst curators of British collections, or an assumption that donors should remain loyal to only one institution, Ramsay Smith appears to have been uneasy about Watson supplying remains to establishments other than the University of Edinburgh. Consequently, on 29 January 1908 he wrote apologetically to Cunningham in Edinburgh:

> The skull belonging to Watson should go to you, only he says he has promised it to Macalister, who was kind to him in some matter. He has been also giving some specimens to Thomson of Oxford, whose brother is one of the best known Queensland doctors. I think one can hardly grudge such men a few good specimens (ELSC Ms 621).

Certainly, Watson is among only a very few people who donated Australian indigenous human remains to more than one collection in the UK. Unlike Stirling and Ramsay Smith, past students of Cambridge and Edinburgh respectively, Watson owed no particular allegiance to any British university, having been educated in Germany and France.

Compared to the number of Australian bones in UK museums, soft tissue remains were rare since, as has been shown (see Chapter 2), the study of comparative racial anatomy had almost exclusively concentrated upon skeletal remains. By the late nineteenth century, the lack of available specimens and an increasing interest in 'racial anatomy' (Berry 1911: 604) meant that body parts sent from Adelaide were highly valued. As Thomson wrote to Watson on 4 December 1906, acknowledging the receipt of the head of an Aboriginal person:

> You cannot see what a prize this specimen is to me. As I am much interested in physical anthropology it will be the means of providing me with a variety of rare specimens for my museum (NL 1682/33/2260).

Curators wanted to obtain soft tissue remains and wrote to their suppliers accordingly, with no evidence of concern for how remains were acquired, whether consent had been given, or even if remains had been obtained legally. Ramsay Smith replied to such a request from Cunningham on 31 October 1906:

> As for soft parts – I shall do my best, and try a few places soon. I shall make a strong effort to get a whole young subject if I can. Much material is allowed to waste for lack of somebody on the spot to secure it (ELSC Ms 599).

3. Collecting the dead

Body parts were not the only remains that were obtained prior to burial, and hospitals were not the only places from which such remains could be acquired. Some skeletal remains sent to collections overseas had not passed through funerary rights, and some of these were those of people who had met violent deaths. Obtaining the remains of people who had died in violent circumstances seems to have been an acceptable practice and was recommended by the Anthropological Institute of Great Britain and Ireland (*Notes and Queries* 1874: 142). Battlefields were common sources of human remains worldwide: in 1868 army medical officers in the United States were ordered by the Assistant U.S. Surgeon General to collect Native American human remains for the Army Medical Museum in Washington, and these included the remains of those killed in battle (Bieder no date: 36). Turnbull (1991: 115) has documented that in 1882 the Director of the Australian Museum in Sydney appears to have lamented the reduction in frontier conflict because it diminished his supply of Australian indigenous human remains.

In Australia, collectors sometimes deliberately sought out massacre sites as a source of human remains, and remains were taken from those who died in what were then known by Europeans as 'punitive raids'. One such skull (now returned to Australia) is that of Carnambeigle (or Kanabygal), which was presented to the Phrenological Society of Edinburgh by Sir George Mackenzie, some time between 1816 and 1820. According to Brook and Kohen (1991: 28-9), 'Kanabygal' belonged to one of the 'mountain tribes', presumably from the 'Callumbigles Plains (Kannabygles) near Mittagong'.

Mackenzie received the skull from a surgeon in the Royal Navy, Mr Hill, who had in turn received it from A.G. Parker, a lieutenant in the regiment which shot Carnambeigle. According to Brook and Kohen (1921: 21), after some years of relatively peaceful co-existence, hostilities between settlers and indigenous people in the Sydney area escalated in 1816. Governor Macquarie wrote in his diary that he felt 'compelled from a paramount sense of public duty' to chastise the 'hostile tribes, and to inflict terrible and exemplary punishment upon them without further loss of time' (Macquarie Diary April 1816). To carry this out, Macquarie ordered three military detachments to:

> march into the interior and remote parts of the colony, for the purpose of punishing the hostile natives by clearing the country of them entirely and driving them across the mountains as well as if possible to apprehend the natives who committed the murders and other outrages, with the view of their being made dreadful and severe examples of, if taken alive (Macquarie Diary 10 April 1816).

If the people resisted, or refused to surrender, 'the officers commanding the military parties have been authorised to fire on them to compel them to surrender, hanging up on trees the bodies of such natives as may be killed on such occasions in order to strike the greater terror into the survivors.' (Macquarie Diary 10 April 1816). Accordingly, two flank companies of the 46th (South Devon) Regiment, divided into three detachments commanded by Captain W.G.B. Shaw, Captain James Wallis and Lieutenant Dawe, 'furnished with the proper guides of European and friendly natives, ammunitions etc.' (Macquarie Diary 10 April 1816) were dispatched on 10 April, 1816.

On the night of 17 April, Captain Wallis' detachment (which included Lieutenant A.G. Parker) came upon a deserted 'native encampment', where the fires were still burning. The soldiers pushed their way through the surrounding bush to the 'precipitous banks of a deep rocky creek' where the people, alerted by the barking of their dogs, fled over the cliffs. The soldiers started firing. According to Wallis, he had ordered his troops to 'make as many prisoners as possible, and to be careful in sparing, and saving, the women and children', but:

> I regret to say some had been shot, and others had met their fate by rushing in despair over the precipice. I was however, partly successful, I led up two women and three children they were all that remained to whom death would not be a blessing (Wallis, J. to Colonial Secretary 17 April 1816. NSWSA: Reel 6045 4/1735).

Among the at least fourteen dead were Carnambeigle and Durelle. In accordance with Macquarie's orders, Lieutenant Parker hung their bodies from trees in a conspicuous part of the camp and either at this point, or some time later, Parker took Carnambeigle's skull. Carnambeigle was not the only indigenous leader in Australia whose remains were sent to the UK. The preserved heads of Pemulwoy (killed in 1803) and Yagan (killed in 1833) were also sent to Britain, as probably was that of Jandamarra (killed in 1897).[3]

There is some evidence to suggest that the lives of Australia's indigenous people may have been in danger because of the scientific value placed on their remains. For example, after he had failed to locate a massacre site near Cooktown from which he wished to obtain bones, the amateur naturalist Richard Semon (1899: 267) was told by a local settler:

> 'A pity that H. is dead, he would have procured you as many skulls as you might have wished for.' I asked how H. would have managed this, and received the cool answer, 'oh, he would have shot them.' The man in question was generally known to kill the blacks in the bush wholesale.

Certainly, those obtaining human remains could show extreme prejudice, often regarding Aboriginal people as less than human, an attitude exemplified in a letter published in the April 1866 edition of the *Popular Magazine of Anthropology,* supposedly received from a station in west Queensland:

3. Collecting the dead

I will do my best to get some blacks' skulls. I have already mentioned it to several fellows, in case they should have any accident in that way. I hear they shot two blacks at the next station, twenty-five miles off, only a day or so ago, whom they caught killing one of the working bullocks; this is the result of letting the blacks be up at the station. They are the most degraded race of beings. I cannot possibly regard them as men and brothers; in fact, I do not think they are, although I cannot elucidate the mystery of their origin (in Turnbull 1994: 17).

Oral history recorded by Sumner (1993: 5-6) suggests that the German collector, Amalie Dietrich, may have believed that obtaining Aboriginal remains justified murder. Dietrich spent ten years (1863-72) in Australia employed by the merchant J.C. Godeffroy to collect natural history specimens for his private museum in Hamburg. In January 1865, Godeffroy is supposed to have asked Dietrich to collect ethnographic objects and Aboriginal human remains during her forthcoming trip to Queensland (Godeffroy to Dietrich 20 January 1865, in Bischoff 1931: 259). However, according to Sumner (1993), Dietrich's daughter, C. Bischoff, fabricated much of the correspondence that she published in 1931 as being between Godeffroy and her mother. Nonetheless, according to Sumner (1993) shortly after Dietrich's arrival in Rockhampton, oral history records that she asked an employee of William Archer, a leading pastoralist in the area, to shoot an Aborigine so that she could obtain the remains – in particular the skin. Incensed at her suggestion, Archer is said to have ordered Dietrich to be driven back to town immediately. Whether it was obtained in this manner or not, Dietrich did acquire an Aborigine's dried skin. In addition, she also sent Godeffroy eight Aboriginal skeletons taken from funerary sites during her travels in Queensland (Sumner 1993: 3).

Those on the frontier where indigenous people were being killed certainly knew that skulls were scientific *desiderata*. Slee (1991) describes a story written in the *West Australian* (6 April 1909) in which the explorer Frank Hann had come across a group of Aboriginal people in the Warburton Ranges. According to Hann, he had dodged a spear thrust and then fired a shot at the retreating group who escaped. Hann told the journalist:

Had I shot the black ... I would have cut his head off and sent the skull to Mr F Brockman of Perth, who asked me to send him one as a friend of his in London wanted one ... I was very sorry that I could not send him the four but later on I got him a splendid one.

Apparently the article drew four letters of protest, to which Hahn responded:

I should most certainly have cut off his head and brought it in had I killed him. I hope I will have the pleasure of doing so yet and those of his three friends also.

According to Slee (1991), the matter did not end there, as the Western Australian Premier, Newton Moore, was interviewed by a journalist from the same paper who said that although Hahn had the right to act in self defence, 'there was no justification for him to obtain the head of a native and send it to a friend. The police "had taken action with a view of ascertaining how Mr Hann became possessed of the skull".'

Clearly, therefore, Aboriginal human remains were taken from all possible sources around Australia. The majority were taken from burial sites, but avid collectors, such as Ramsay Smith, took advantage of any opportunity to obtain indigenous bones and body parts. Hermann Klaatsch (1864-1916) robbed burial grounds, took brains from the hospital in Broome and, while measuring prisoners at Wyndham jail in 1906, took skeletal remains from the morgue when the prison doctor informed him of new deaths (Stehlik 1986: 63). In addition, Klaatsch acquired skeletal remains from W.E. Roth, Chief Protector of the Aborigines in Queensland, who had a personal collection of Aboriginal skulls and artefacts (Milicerowa 1955: 257). Klaatsch's collection of Aboriginal human remains, including those he received from W.E. Roth, were housed in the Department of Anthropology at the University of Wroclaw (then Breslau), where Klaatsch was Professor of Anatomy, Anthropology and Ethnology from 1907 until his death nine years later (Milicerowa 1955: 257). Other skulls collected by W.E. Roth were sent to the Australian Museum in Sydney; at least some (and possibly all) have been returned to Aboriginal communities (see Donlon and Pardoe 1991; Pardoe and Donlon 1991). Protectors, like medical doctors, were well placed to take Aboriginal human remains and were interested in anthropology; Roth was not the only member of his profession to do so. The collecting of Tasmanian Aboriginal remains by George Augustus Robinson has been documented by the Tasmanian Aboriginal Centre (2001, Attachment B). Protector Joseph Milligan also collected at least one skull in Tasmania, which he sent to Joseph Barnard Davis (1867: 269):

> An Aboriginal lad told Dr Milligan that his party, some years before, had been fired into by a white man, when a woman was injured, had her head chopped off, and was buried. Years afterwards Dr. M. took the boy to the spot and found the body in the bush. There are marks of the cutting off of the head.

Barnard Davis also received Aboriginal skeletal remains from his brother in law, Matthew Moorhouse, the first permanent Protector of Aborigines in South Australia (1867: 258-60). Ramsay Smith may also have attempted to secure the assistance of the Protector in Adelaide:

> I have interested him [the Protector] in our department of the subject. We went together to Point McLeay where there are over 200 natives, and I took the opportunity of going to the Coorong and doing some bone gathering (Ramsay Smith to Cunningham 28 April 1908, ELSC Ms 620).

3. Collecting the dead

Networks

By the early 1900s, Ramsay Smith had established a network of people across Australia to obtain human remains on his behalf. For example, in New South Wales he arranged that staff at the Government Survey should 'collect carefully all specimens they come across' (Ramsay Smith to Cunningham 20 February 1907, EADL), while in 1906 he was anxious to obtain the skulls obtained by his friends in the Northern Territory lest they were taken by Klaatsch instead (Ramsay Smith to Cunningham 31 October 1906, ELSC Ms 599).

From Blumenbach in Göttingen to Turner in Edinburgh, university collections were largely assembled by past students or staff who had, often as members of the medical profession, taken posts in the colonies or were travelling abroad. The Department of Anatomy at the University of Cambridge was no exception, and its Professor, Alexander Macalister (1893: 960), used the University's magazine to recruit potential donors:

> Our cranial collection is now the second largest in Great Britain; and, as the ethnological value of such a series depends directly on the number of comparable specimens, I am earnestly desirous of making it as complete as possible; and shall be deeply indebted to any members of the University who may be able to furnish us with additional specimens. If the members of the University who are scattered over the world were willing to aid us in this direction we should have the most perfectly equipped school of physical anthropology in Britain.

In a similar fashion, the Anthropological Society of London used its international membership to assemble a considerable collection of indigenous human remains. Thus, for example, Robert Peel, a Fellow since 1866, presented the Society with two Aboriginal crania in 1870 (*Anthropological Review and Journal of the Anthropological Society* 3: xxxi). The Anthropological Society (which, by 1871, had become the Anthropological Institute of Great Britain and Ireland) sold its collection of non-European human remains to the Royal College of Surgeons of England for £100 in 1894, except for the articulated skeleton of a Tasmanian which it had received from Morton Allport in 1871. The Institute eventually sold the Tasmanian skeleton for £100 to the British Museum (Natural History) (now the Natural History Museum) in 1898, where it is still housed today.

Curators also recruited the assistance of their friends and relatives. Professor William Turner, for instance, received three skeletons from Queensland from his friend Sir Arthur Mitchell, and Professor George Rolleston at the University of Oxford was given crania from his brother's property in the same State (Rolleston Papers, AML). Another brother, William Rolleston, lived in Christchurch, New Zealand, and supplied George with Maori skulls, those of the Moriori from the Chatham Islands, and natural history specimens, receiving essays, lectures and donations for the local museum in return. Other members of Rolleston's family contributed less directly to George's collection. For example, his niece wrote to Rolleston's sister:

> My dear Aunt Grace, I had a long letter from Uncle William the other day in which he sent a message to Uncle George so I think I ought to send it to you – it was about *bones* of course! Here it is: 'I have got a box of Maori bones and skulls for him, and a Mr Mcinalanger (this word was quite illegible so I have just copied it!) a friend of Dr Flower's is finding him a quantity from Napier; fresh killed in the Maori war'. This is all, they seem to be in a very flourishing state out there (Rolleston Papers, AML).

Without the international contacts available to universities, societies and institutional museums, private collectors, such as Joseph Barnard Davis, relied much more heavily on purchase and the efforts of 'friends in many countries' (Davis 1867: vi). If Davis' pursuit of Sir George Grey while he was successively the Governor of New Zealand (1845-53) and of Cape Colony (1854-61) is typical, considerable time and effort could be invested in cultivating such 'friendships'. This method did produce results: in response to Davis' letters, Grey sent the calvarium of a Maori and, later, those of two 'Kaffirs' and four 'Bushmen' (e.g. Davis to Grey 13 January 1854 and 27 June 1857, GGAL; Davis 1867: 214, 216, 316). Barnard Davis' collection became part of that of the Royal College of Surgeons of England. After partial destruction of the College's collections due to enemy action in 1941, what survived (and excepting the original Hunterian collection) was transferred to the Natural History Museum, London in the post-war years.

Many European institutions also profited from nineteenth-century voyages of discovery and exploration. Since the voyage of the *Endeavour*, it had become acceptable practice to include parties of scientists in the ship's company to observe, record and collect specimens of the new environment and people they encountered (Mackay 1985: 8). The French expedition to Australia (1800 to 1804) commanded by Nicolas Baudin was the first to officially include anthropology amongst its scientific objectives, Georges Cuvier (1800: 175) providing instructions on where to acquire and how to preserve the human remains that the crew were to obtain:

> Travellers should not miss an opportunity to go and visit the places where the dead were left after they have witnessed, or taken part in, combat .... These articles can, without a doubt, be prepared with no difficulty. Boil them in a solution of caustic soda or potash and clean them of their flesh, it will take a couple of hours.[4]

François Péron, appointed to the expedition as zoologist, examined and described cremation sites in Tasmania (Péron 1807-16: 267-72; see Plate 5), taking human remains from this island and Western Australia.

3. Collecting the dead

According to Wallace (1984), Péron's collections (including Aboriginal artefacts, live animals, seeds, zoological, botanical and geological specimens) were divided between the Musée d'Histoire Naturelle and the Malmaison. The latter was partly destroyed in the rioting which followed Napoleon's abdication in 1814. Later expeditions commanded by Jules Dumount D'Urville in the *Astrolabe* and *Zélée*, the second of which (1837 to 1840) included Pierre Marie Dumoutier as official phrenologist, also obtained indigenous remains, which were housed in the Musée de l'Homme in Paris (Plomley 1962: 9; Pietrusewsky to Lambert 2 December 1975, AIATSIS pMs 2976).

British expeditions were equally successful. For example, the Royal College of Surgeons of England received Australian indigenous human remains from Captain Philip King obtained during the voyage of the *Mermaid* (1818 to 1822) (Flower 1907: 333), an almost complete skeleton taken from a grave in Dampier Land and presented by George Grey, Captain aboard HMS *Beagle* (1837 to 1839) (Flower 1907: 314, Stokes 1846: 115-16), and the remains of seven Aborigines and five Torres Strait Islanders donated by Captain Blackwood and geologist Joseph Bete Jukes that had been collected on the maritime survey voyage of HMS *Fly* (1842 to 1846) (Flower 1907: 316-17). However, the scientific voyage to bring the greatest number of indigenous human remains to the UK was that of HMS *Challenger*. Charged with surveying various sections of the world's ocean floor from 1872 to 1876, *Challenger* returned to England with human remains from the Admiralty Islands, Hawaii, the Chatham Islands, New Zealand, Australia, Tierra del Fuego, Patagonia and South Africa (Turner 1886: 20). Analysed by Sir William Turner (1886), these remains augmented the collections at the Department of Anatomy, University of Edinburgh.

It is clear from the history detailed above that indigenous bodies and burial sites were almost systematically robbed throughout Australia as collectors sought to obtain remains for institutions overseas and, later, within the country. Worldwide networks were established along which indigenous remains travelled to collections in remote countries. There is no evidence that curators 'back home' felt any responsibility or concern at the circumstances in which these human remains were originally acquired, despite legislation in the UK to control the procurement of corpses by Anatomy Schools and that which made grave-robbing illegal. If curators lacked concern, the situation in the field was not so clear-cut. Documentary evidence suggests that some collectors were not so sanguine about their actions and nor was it always condoned by the wider non-indigenous population. It is also through collectors' reports, as well as other sources, that the response of indigenous communities can be heard.

4

Response and motivation

Travellers' diaries, collection catalogues and museum correspondence can be a rich source of information about individual responses, motivations and opinions about the collecting of indigenous human remains. They can provide an insight into how indigenous people reacted to the removal of their ancestors' remains and how collectors viewed their own actions. Although individuals of course responded differently, the literature shows a broad awareness by collectors of indigenous objection to the removal of remains, to the extent that many conducted their activities in secret and were wary of retaliation. Thus, the Royal Geographical Society advised caution in the procurement of remains, and anatomist Carl Vogt (1884: 8-9) wrote of the inherent dangers of this practice. In 1904 Hermann Klaatsch had to make a hasty departure from Normanton when the local community became aware of his objectives and, calling him 'Devil Devil', threatened to spear him (Stehlik 1986: 62). In September and October 1906, Klaatsch spent fourteen days on Melville Island, keen, as usual, to augment his skeletal collection:

> Luckily we remained unnoticed by the blacks during our grave violating enterprise. However they must have soon noticed what happened because, after we had finally stowed away our spoils on the boat and had continued with our journey, we wanted to stop at an appropriate place to pick up water; it had already got dark, when our blacks turned our attention to little flashes of light that started to appear in the thickets of the shore. These were the fire sticks in the hands of the natives who followed us. Cooper postponed the landing until the next morning, remarking dryly that he did not wish to give the blacks any 'opportunity' (Klaatsch 1907a: 69).

Cooper, Klaatsch's European assistant, was later killed by the Aborigines in what Klaatsch presumed to be 'vengeance for the damage done to the graves' (Klaatsch 1907a: 75). In the 1840s the crew members of HMS *Fly* and HMS *Rattlesnake* approached graves in the Torres Straits with extreme caution. In 1844, the *Fly*'s geologist, Joseph Bete Jukes (1847: 149-50) visited a grave near Port Lihou on Muralug and was 'careful not to disturb or leave any other trace of our presence than our foot prints in the sand around'. Inspecting a similar burial site a few years afterwards, the *Rattlesnake*'s zoologist, John Macgillivray (1852: 32), reported:

On the occasion of our visiting the grave in question ... Gi'om told me that we were closely watched by a party of natives who were greatly pleased that we did not attempt to deface the tomb; had we done so – and the temptation was great to some of us, for several fine nautilus shells were hanging up, and some good dugong skulls were lying upon the top – one or more of our party would have been speared.

The historical literature documents the efforts of indigenous communities to protect their dead, whether by the more direct means described above or by, for instance, asking settlers not to disturb graves, leading them elsewhere, enlisting the help of Europeans they saw as sympathetic or using the settlers' own legal authorities to object (for examples see Fforde 2002: 27-8, Turnbull 1991, 1993, 1999, 2002). Aware of the risks associated with obtaining remains, which in settled areas included the possibility of antagonising and losing Aboriginal employees, those trying to obtain human remains were often at pains to carry out their work in secret. Turnbull (1993a: 24-5) describes how the Director of the South Australian Museum, Edward C. Stirling, attempted to covertly acquire Aboriginal remains from burial sites on the property of his brother, John, at Mundi Mundi in 1892, for presentation to various British institutions. John Stirling asked the South Australian Museum to send two museum employees to obtain the remains as secretly as possible in case his Aboriginal workers left, they 'being shy of remaining where their last resting place may be disturbed' (in Turnbull 1993a: 24). In the end, Robert Kay, the Secretary of the South Australian Museum and Library Board, refused to sanction the expedition because he feared retaliation from local people.

There is a large body of literature from the latter half of the nineteenth century which describes Aboriginal burial practices (see Meehan 1971) and there is considerable historical evidence to show that settlers knew of indigenous requirements to accord their dead appropriate treatment. Turnbull (2002) has provided details of the documentation demonstrating European awareness of, and respect for, Australian funerary practices and the significance placed upon them by indigenous communities. He describes settler accounts of indigenous burial places, many of which saw in the careful preparation of sites evidence of what they described as the 'civilised' nature of Aboriginal society. Accounts also document tended burial places, regularly visited and kept tidy – clearly demonstrating their continuing significance. Others describe the reticence of Aboriginal groups to disturb graves and their respect for the dead, while still others document indigenous guides advising Europeans to avoid burial sites, or groups tactically luring the grave-robbers away. Documents record indigenous disapproval, fear and incomprehension of the actions of Europeans who sought to disturb burial places, and the knowledge by at least one Australian museum director that disinterring the indigenous dead was a punishable offence under Common Law. By 1837, in at least South Australia, funerary sites were recognised by government as evidence of

4. *Response and motivation*

indigenous proprietary title to land (see Turnbull 2002: 74-5). There can be little doubt, therefore, that most collectors were well aware of the great significance which Aboriginal people attributed to the remains of their ancestors. While anthropologist Herbert Basedow was moved by the sacredness of burial caves – 'whenever I entered these places a feeling of respect came over me, for the relatives had done their best to decorate the walls with ochre drawings of a personal and religious nature' (Basedow 1935: 237) – he still collected Aboriginal human remains.

Like Basedow and Ramsay Smith (1907a: 575, and see 1924: 209), Professor Frederick Wood Jones, the renowned anatomist and physical anthropologist, was critical of the treatment received by Australia's indigenous population. Significantly, in his Presidential Address to the eighteenth meeting of the Australian Association for the Advancement of Science in 1926, he (Wood Jones 1928: 54) placed the desecration of the dead at the top of a list of examples given to demonstrate his argument that Aboriginal people would be accorded greater respect if those responsible for their management were less ignorant of Aboriginal culture:

> If those in charge of our aborigines [sic] were somewhat more informed concerning the prejudices of primitive man we would not have an officer in charge of the native police recording in his own publication such incidents as the following: 'then we made a fire in the cave and warmed up the old warriors in the vault. I screwed two of the skulls off, but my boys shuddered at the action. They were afraid to touch them'.

Nonetheless, because of his interest in physical anthropology Wood Jones collected Aboriginal human remains. Writing in the same Address that 'although a great deal has been written concerning the ceremonials and the tribal organisation of the Australian native, we are still profoundly ignorant concerning him as a distinctive psychical and physical type', he collected at least forty-four Aboriginal skulls which in 1946 he donated to the Royal College of Surgeons of England, the year after he became its Conservator of Museums and Sir William Collins Professor of Human Anatomy. Wood Jones placed such a high value on these remains that, at least in 1926, he intended to contravene the Australian Act (1913) which prohibited the export of 'anthropological specimens' without a licence, as he wrote to Sir Arthur Keith on 5 October of that year, 'Before I leave Australia I will break the law and send you home some material which I have hoarded – but I shall have to leave a terrible lot of stuff behind – and no one may care for it' (Keith letter file, RCSEL). Whether or not the skulls were eventually exported illegally is not known. The College repatriated its collection of Australian human remains in 2002 and 2003 (see Chapter 9).

In a small number of cases, collectors describe giving goods for remains. Advantage could be taken of vulnerable communities. Knut Dahl, a Norwegian who travelled in Northern Australia in 1893 (and by 1926 was

63

Professor of Pisiculture at the Norwegian College of Agriculture in Oslo), visited a community showing symptoms of 'unpleasant diseases' such as leprosy and smallpox, writing that 'the demoralized state of the blacks' aroused his hopes 'that among these people I should be able to obtain a collection of skulls' as elsewhere he 'should only have got into difficulties by attempting to buy skulls and skeletons, but in this place conditions were obviously different' (Dahl 1926: 157-8). Hermann Klaatsch, in his quest to obtain the desiccated body of an indigenous leader in the early years of the twentieth century, was guided to surviving relatives by gold-diggers. According to Klaatsch, the diggers had earlier 'nearly exterminated the tribe' (Klaatsch 1923: 216) yet despite their presence, a senior woman argued forcefully against giving up the body. Eventually, however, Klaatsch did secure it and gave the group items from a bush store. Nonetheless, he was warned by the diggers that his 'prize' would be stolen during the night, and the next morning (perhaps when Klaatsch was no longer chaperoned by the miners) the group tried unsuccessfully to persuade him to return it. He hurried from the district and subsequently sent the body to the Berlin Academy of Science (Klaatsch 1907b; 1923: 215-16). One Australian medical officer was concerned at what had happened. In 1907, Dr Webster wrote to a colleague about Klaatsch's 'star exhibit', 'I thought at the time it should not have gone out of the country but nobody else seemed to give a damn. It would be a very small portion of reparations if it were returned' (AIATSIS Library pMs 4081).

Attitudes

Collectors exhibited a range of different attitudes towards obtaining the remains of Australia's indigenous population[1] and while many were unconcerned at the prospect of grave-robbing, others clearly felt uneasy about their involvement. Thus John Lort Stokes (1846: 115-16) did not feel 'altogether justified' in disinterring a skeleton in Cygnet Bay, and the Surveyor General of New South Wales, John Oxley, appears to have lied in his diaries about taking a skull from a burial site (Fforde 2002: 27).

Stokes and Oxley were concerned about removing Aboriginal remains from funerary sites not only because they were aware of indigenous concerns but also because of their own cultural traditions which accorded respect to the dead and recognised the sanctity of the grave. Others within the wider settler population also disagreed with removing indige-nous human remains, but this only appears to have occurred (or been recorded) when Aboriginal remains were taken from areas in which those of Europeans could also be obtained. In such cases, settlers not only reacted because grave-robbing ran contrary to their own cultural norms, but from fear that their own burial sites and those of their kin might be similarly desecrated. For example, in 1862 an Aboriginal man was shot dead whilst trying to escape from Brisbane jail (QSA Col A26/62/739). His body was buried in an area adjacent to the Church of St John's, in land 'granted to the Church of England for burial purposes, though not yet fenced in' (QSA Col A29/62/996). The Wardens of the church, Henry Buckley and Shepherd Smith, later heard that this individual's skull was on display at the house of Thomas Symes Warry, a Magistrate, Member of Parliament and amateur scientist. To confirm these rumours, they disinterred the body and, finding it headless, complained to the Colonial Secretary on 29 March:

> It has become our painful duty to report to the Government that an act alike of wanton outrage to ourselves and revolting to the good feeling of the whole community has been lately perpetrated by the violation of the sanctity of our Burial Ground, and the mutilation and part removal of the dead from within its precincts ... That the whole Colony is deeply interested in the suppression of such repulsive misdeeds we are fully satisfied; the treatment of the remains of this Aboriginal may be the treatment of ourselves, our relatives or friends: and the offence in question we submit should be made the subject of public condemnation so marked as to prevent the probability of its occurrence (QSA Col A29/62/996).

Providing an explanation of his actions to the Colonial Secretary, Warry did not deny his involvement in the incident but pleaded ignorance of any legal or moral transgression:

> I was ignorant of any law existing to protect the bodies of persons dying in the manner of this criminal and buried in unconsecrated ground and without the sites of the church. I may remark that during my residence in Queensland I have frequently had skulls of blacks given to me which have been used by me for scientific purposes in my profession and believed there was no harm in receiving them (QSA Col A29/62/1358).

The fears of men like Shepherd and Buckley may not have been unfounded. On several occasions it appears that European skeletal remains were taken under the misapprehension that they were those of indigenous people. The Rev. Joseph King, for example, was uncertain of the identity of a skull he sent to the University of Oxford in 1877, which had been discovered while foundations were being dug for an outhouse on the estate of a member of his congregation, as he wrote to Professor Rolleston at Oxford:

> I hope it is the skull of a *bona fide* aboriginal [sic] that I have sent you. I discovered the other day that some white settlers were buried about twenty years ago near to the spot were [sic] the skull was obtained. I tried to ascertain the exact spot where the Englishmen and Women were buried and my informant could give me no more definite information that that it was at, or very near, to the place where the skull was exhumed.
>   So far as I could tell it appeared to me that it was an undoubted specimen of a New Hollander. The appearance of the teeth seemed to afford conclusive

evidence, irrespective of the general conformation. You would notice that the teeth were worn down as natives teeth often are by eating gritty food (Rolleston Papers, AML).

Possibly because of the doubt surrounding the origin of the remains, the rest of the skeleton was left in the ground and the outhouse built over it.

Dissection was a procedure as detested by the public as the body-snatching with which it was associated (see Richardson 1988). Popular outrage at the procurement of indigenous remains from hospital morgues was an expression of this hatred and, once again, was presumably fuelled by apprehension that non-Aboriginal bodies might be similarly violated. The extent of public feeling against the 'indecent' treatment of Aboriginal bodies in hospital morgues was considerable, and is illustrated by the government enquiries into the mutilation of William Lanne's corpse in 1869 (see Chapter 3), and the conduct of Dr William Ramsay Smith in the Adelaide Hospital some thirty-four years later.

The Ramsay Smith Enquiry

In August 1903, William Ramsay Smith's use of the hospital morgue to obtain anthropological and medical specimens was brought to the attention of the South Australian Attorney General and Chief Secretary, and he was immediately suspended from civic and hospital duties. Growing public unease at stories of the mutilation and desecration of bodies in the hospital, combined with heated debate in the South Australian House of Assembly, as well as Ramsay Smith's intention to contest his suspension, resulted in the appointment of a Government Board of Enquiry, charged with deter-mining whether Ramsay Smith was 'guilty of conduct rendering him unfit to remain in the public service' (*Adelaide Advertiser* 5 September 1903).

As defined by the Government Prosecutor, the Board was to accept that misconduct had occurred if Ramsay Smith was found guilty of a criminal act or 'offences of a gross character that shocked public decency and outraged the public conscience' (*Adelaide Advertiser* 5 September 1903). Eighteen charges were brought against Ramsay Smith, which variously accused him of acting illegally and in violation of his duty as Coroner by: mutilating the bodies of thirteen individuals; preventing them from receiving a decent burial by removing various parts of their anatomy, and sending a number 'to parts beyond the seas'; and at times carrying out such activities in places not licensed under the Anatomy Act of 1884 (*Adelaide Advertiser* 5 September 1903). Amongst these charges, and prominent in the media coverage of the Enquiry (e.g. *Adelaide Advertiser* 18 August 1903), was Ramsay Smith's treatment of the body of Tommy Walker (see Chapter 3).

Ramsay Smith did not deny any of the charges brought against him. Instead, his defence, led by Sir Josiah Symon, argued successfully that such actions did not contravene the Anatomy Act (*Adelaide Advertiser* 16 September 1903), that they were a common and essential part of scientific research, that they were not undertaken for personal profit (but see below), and that Ramsay Smith had carried out the dissections with the necessary 'propriety and decency' (*Adelaide Advertiser* 15 September 1903). Sir Josiah also called the Board's attention to the motives of a number of the prosecution witnesses and those who had made the initial allegations, arguing that these individuals still harboured antipathy towards Ramsay Smith because of controversial events surrounding his initial appointment to the hospital in 1896. At that time Ramsay Smith had accepted an appointment at the (Royal) Adelaide Hospital that broke a strike by the honorary staff who had resigned over a dispute with the South Australian Government about the dismissal of a nurse. The Australian branch of the British Medical Association had condemned his acceptance of the post as 'highly dishonourable and unprofessional', and subsequently expelled him from the association, to which he was never readmitted (*Australian Dictionary of Biography* Vol. 2: 674). For this he was reportedly ostracised by many in the Adelaide medical community (*Adelaide Advertiser* 19 September 1903).

The Report submitted by the Board of Enquiry to the House of Assembly on 22 September 1903 found Ramsay Smith innocent of all eighteen charges. However, the Board could not entirely dismiss Ramsay Smith's treatment of the body of Tommy Walker; yet even in this case it was accepted that scientific considerations largely excused Ramsay Smith's actions, and the Board only admonished the accused for being 'indiscreet in removing the specimen under the circumstances, and allow[ing] his zeal in the cause of science to outrun his judgement' (Buchanan *et al.* 1903: 2). Acting on the recommendations of the report, the Government swiftly reinstated Ramsay Smith as Coroner and Chairman of the Board of Health but suggested that he resign his posts as Inspector of Anatomy and Vaccination Officer. Deemed unnecessary, the post of Physician to the Isolation Wards at the Adelaide Hospital was abolished, and its salary added to that already received by Ramsay Smith as Coroner.

Ramsay Smith's acquittal was achieved largely because the relevant authorities upheld the needs of science over the concerns of the public that the dead should be accorded respect and receive a proper burial. But despite the findings of the Enquiry being almost entirely in Ramsay Smith's favour, he remained cautious when acquiring human remains from the hospital morgue. He was careful not to accept any payment for remains shipped to Edinburgh, as previous refusal of monies was, he believed, 'what knocked the bottom out of the accusation I was doing wrong in collecting and exporting pathological specimens' (Ramsay Smith to Cunningham 18 December 1907, ELSC 617). Nonetheless, it is clear that he had obtained Tommy Walker's remains clandestinely, as in a letter to Professor Cunningham in Edinburgh (14 August 1901, EADL) he wrote that the body he sent: 'belonged to one of the best known of all Australian aboriginals: and how it came into my possession need not be told'. In a separate incident Watson may also have been at risk for sending Aboriginal remains overseas. Shortly after the preserved body of an Aboriginal woman had arrived at the Royal College of Surgeons of England, Sir Arthur Keith received a cable from its donor, Watson, instructing him not to dissect the corpse. Keith noted in his diary: 'is [Watson] in some kind of political trouble?' (Keith Diary Entry 29 December 1909, RCSEL).[2]

Doctors who obtained human remains were aware of the popular feeling against dissection as they took elaborate measures to hide incriminating evidence from the public, ensuring that the corpse looked complete when viewed by family and relatives. As Joseph Barnard Davis wrote to the artist Alfred Bock in Tasmania, asking him to find a local medic who would be willing and able to obtain Tasmanian remains:

> Were I myself in the colony I could with very little trouble abstract skulls from dead bodies *without defacing them at all,* and could instruct any medical gentleman to do it (Davis to Bock 4 October 1856, quoted in Ellis 1981: 133, my emphasis).

European sensitivities about taking remains from the morgue were brought home to Davis when in 1859 his medical contact (Dr Guyton Athertone, medical officer of the jail) in Graham's Town, South Africa, was unable to obtain the remains of indigenous South Africans because of a recent order issued by the Lieutenant Governor that prohibited interference with bodies lying in the jail morgue. In an attempt to have the order rescinded, Davis wrote to Sir George Grey, then Governor of Cape Colony, complaining that the order would slow the progress of science and that 'if the minds of the natives be not sufficiently enlightened to allow of any use being made of the lifeless body, surely those of Europeans, settled in South Africa, should overcome such prejudices', adding that, if carried out discreetly, dissection need not injure public feeling – 'in carrying on anatomical investigations there is no need to shock the prejudices of anyone. They are best conducted without any special notice' (Davis to Grey 5 January 1859, GGAL). If the scientific value of remains could overcome European cultural mores that upheld the sanctity of the grave, and if in the cases where collecting was brought before a court the 'law so readily deferred to science' (Turnbull 1991: 118), it is unsurprising that indigenous concerns for their dead would be ignored and overridden.

Motives

Obtaining indigenous human remains in Australia could involve considerable time, effort and financial expense. Those taking body parts risked official sanction, and those donating to overseas museums after 1913 required a permit to do so. The actual procurement of bones at times placed collectors at significant personal risk. Furthermore, many collectors were aware that their actions went against the cultural traditions of their own society and those of Australia's indigenous population. What, then, led people to engage in this activity?

The scientific importance placed on indigenous human remains, coupled with their relative inaccessibility to scholars in Europe and the belief that the Australian 'race' was on the verge of extinction, meant that remains were rare and valuable commodities that could be exchanged for a variety of goods and services. As noted by Bowes (1914: 153), '[the Australian Aboriginal] is today, so to speak, the most valuable product in the human market for scientific purposes; for he may fairly claim to be the most primitive living representative of prehistoric man among the surviving tribes'. The bones of Tasmanians were particularly highly prized, as Macalister (1893: 960) commented:

> Another remarkable addition [to the Anatomy Department at the University of Cambridge] is the skull of a Tasmanian which has been presented by J. Bonwick esq. As this race is extinct the difficulty of obtaining any of their crania is very great; and as they have been supposed by Dr Tylor to have been in some sort the last representatives of palaeolithic man, they are as interesting as they are rare.

Macalister was referring to the work of E.B. Tylor, who was shortly to publish his theories on 'The Tasmanians as Representatives of Palaeolithic Man' in the Journal of the Anthropological Institute 1894 (XXIII: 141-52).

The value placed on human remains could be translated into financial worth, leading at least one settler to investigate using the burial site on his property as an economic resource. In 1914, a pastoralist in Western Australia wrote to the British Museum (Natural History):

> I take the liberty of addressing these few lines to you with the object of ascertaining whether you, by any chance, desire to secure any skulls of the Australian aboriginal [sic].
> This particular portion of the South West Coast of Western Australia was, in the old days, a favourite haunt of the natives, who established themselves in the coast hills or such places as provided good water in the shallow sand hills. Their favoured burying grounds were presumably in and around the drift sand hills which, in course of time, have been blown away thus exposing the remains of natives so buried.
> I am not a 'professional' collector of such relics but hold this portion of the country for pastoral and grazing purposes, and have stumbled across these human remains during my rounds amongst the stock.
> It is not possible to obtain complete skeletons as the bulk of the small bones have become re-covered or been carried away by crabs. The three or four skulls I have are in a very fair state of preservation and should you feel inclined to negotiate with a view to purchase, I shall be most happy to

forward same to your care. Could you give me any idea of the possible value? (Farrar to Fleuyon, Pycroft Papers, NHM).

Although most institutions relied on donations, at the turn of the century Aboriginal skulls appear to have fetched anything up to £5 in the UK, and the remains of Tasmanians were worth considerably more. Thus in 1898 the Anthropological Institute of Great Britain and Ireland sold the Tasmanian skeleton it had been given by Morton Allport in 1871 to the British Museum (Natural History) for £100, the same amount that the Royal College of Surgeons of England, had paid for the rest of the Institute's non-European human remains collection four years earlier. In 1912, Tasmanian skulls were sufficiently in demand for one man to offer, albeit unsuccessfully, his small collection to the British Museum (Natural History) for £200 each (Anon. to Pycroft 12 August 1912; Pycroft Papers, NHM).

Nonetheless, relatively few remains were purchased and, when this did occur, it was usually when institutions bought entire collections or when remains were offered for sale by auction houses. J.C. Stevens in Covent Garden, London, plied a significant trade in natural history specimens and, on several occasions, the skeletal remains of indigenous peoples, particularly *moko mokai* from New Zealand and 'shrunken heads' from South America (see Allingham 1924). In March 1866, Stevens advertised for sale:

a REMARKABLE SPECIMEN of a Native Australian found in a limestone cave, on Mosquito Plains, South Australia, and brought to this country at great trouble and expense. It is the only specimen of its kind known to the scientific world, and is besides of considerable value as a curiosity. It is believed to be of great antiquity, and is almost perfect in every detail (*The Athenaeum* March 1866: 352).

Stevens omitted to inform the public that the 'mummy' had been taken from the Naracoorte Caves in South Australia and exhibited around Europe by a showman named 'Craig'. The theft of this 'mummy' was remembered by those in the Naracoorte area and nearly a century later, on 11 June 1952, acting on a rumour that it had been seen at the British Museum, the then Curator of Naracoorte Caves Reserve, W.G. Trotman, wrote to this museum enquiring whether the 'mummy' was indeed amongst its collections, keen to be enlightened on 'a subject that has been clouded in mystery since 1859' (Fraser Papers CL 1952/55, NHM). The Deputy Keeper answered on 21 June 1952 that the only 'mummies' in the collection were from the Torres Strait, New Guinea and Peru, and suggested that Trotman's informant had mistaken one of these as Aboriginal (NHM Fraser Papers CL 1952/55).

The auction of indigenous human remains did not cease at the beginning of the nineteenth century. In 1988 Bonham's advertised a Maori *moko mokai* preserved head to be sold at its London auction in May of that year. The proposed sale aroused controversy and anger in New Zealand and Britain. The President of the New Zealand Maori Council, armed with a High Court of New Zealand Order stating that he was the legal administrator of the deceased warrior's estate, successfully obtained a British High Court injunction against Bonham's to prevent the sale. A subsequent agreement was reached to return the head to New Zealand, where it arrived in July 1988 for burial on the Karikari Peninsula (O'Keefe 1992: 393-4).

As the majority of European collections were assembled predominantly by donation, it follows that most individuals were not supplying museums for economic gain. Those who donated human remains to institutions in the UK were usually members of the medical profession and/or had an interest in anthropology. Consequently, most donors appreciated the scientific importance placed on such items and the perceived necessity of gathering an adequate number together for comparative analysis. Most collectors donated human remains to their *alma mater*, or to an institution or curator to whom they owed some allegiance or friendship (see Chapter 3). By supplying European institutions, collectors were contributing to one of the most prestigious areas of scientific enquiry – the field of human origins – but this was not the only incentive to donate Aboriginal human remains to overseas museums. The appropriation of Aboriginal remains and their subsequent donation to museums held further considerable and diverse advantages for curators and collectors alike.

Until the latter half of the nineteenth century there were few, if any, collections of Aboriginal human remains in Australia. However, even after Australian State museums and university anatomy departments had began to collect the bones of the indigenous population (see Turnbull 1991, 1993a, 1994), many colonists continued to supply museums in Europe. An important contributory factor was the peripheral role played by the colonies in nineteenth-century science. The colonies were invariably regarded as no more than a source of data for scientists residing in the mother countries and Europe was still widely considered the centre of scientific learning (MacLeod 1982,1988; Mackay 1985; MacLeod and Rehbock (eds) 1988; Sheets-Pyenson 1988; MacKenzie (ed.) 1990; Moyal 1993). Thus, William Crowther was critical of George Stockell's desire to retain the remains of William Lanne for the Royal Society of Tasmania. Almost forty years later, a similar opinion was expressed to Professor Cunningham by Ramsay Smith (18 November 1908, ELSC Ms 625), who considered most Australian scholars both uninterested in, and largely ignorant of, the science of physical anthropology:

> Spencer was saying it was a pity to let such specimens leave Australia. I told him that all I had collected had been going to waste for want of someone to gather and describe them, and that where specimens were given to museums

in Australia nobody took any interest in them until some German or other foreigner came along with scarcely a 'thank you'. Spencer showed me a 'rare condition of the tooth in the lower jaw' which he has never seen referred. It was one of our old and common friends – 'dislocated tooth'. He had not seen a third trochanter in the aboriginal until I directed his attention to a beautifully marked instance in the femur of a skeleton which he used for teaching purposes. Now what can one do in anthropological work with such people?

Although living on the sidelines of the scientific world, interested colonists were in control of the major source of data. Consequently, Aboriginal remains were precious commodities that could be used as a means of gaining entry into scientific circles in the West. For example, Morton Allport, Vice-President of the Royal Society of Tasmania, used Tasmanian skeletons to help establish and maintain links with various scientists in the metropolis. In 1873 he wrote to the British craniologist Joseph Barnard Davis:

> The skeleton was such a perfect one that I could scarcely make up my mind to part with it at the last moment but my better feelings predominated and I shall now be very anxious to hear of its safe arrival and to learn what you think of it.
>
> I hope our correspondence may not cease altogether now that the main object of it is so far fulfilled as I am still much interested in collecting every record of the lost Tasmanian race and may from time to time learn something worth communicating (Allport to Davis 24 February 1873, ALH).

Donation of Aboriginal remains not only commanded the attention of influential patrons, but sometimes facilitated entrance into prestigious scientific societies. Upon election as a Corresponding Member of the Anthropological Society of London, Allport assured the Secretary that 'no effort shall be wanting on my part to forward the interests of the society' adding that 'before the receipt of your letter I had forwarded a skeleton of a Tasmanian Aborigine to the society' (Allport to Pim 29 January 1871, ALH). However, the most common and tangible rewards that donors received in exchange for human remains were items of scientific literature, and these would have been difficult to obtain by other means in the colonies. Thus, the second Tasmanian skeleton which Allport sent to Davis was accompanied by the following instructions:

> Please accept this as a present and expend anything you would have been willing to give for it in the articulating and figuring [of] it, our only bargain being that I am to have three copies of any publications referred to it, one for myself, one for our Royal Society's library and one for our public library (Allport to Davis 23 July 1873, ALH).

Donations to the University of Edinburgh enabled Ramsay Smith to discuss anthropological matters with Professors Turner and Cunningham, leading and influential scholars in the field of physical anthropology at that time. In addition, Cunningham edited and arranged at least six papers by Ramsay Smith for publication in leading British scientific journals, supplying him with two hundred reprints of each, along with various other relevant publications (Ramsay Smith to Cunningham 11 September 1907, ELSC Ms 615; 29 May 1907, ELSC Ms 608). At Ramsay Smith's request, Cunningham successfully proposed his membership of the Royal Society of Edinburgh, and later arranged his Fellowship of the Royal Anthropological Institute (Ramsay Smith to Cunningham 28 May 1906, ELSC Ms 598; 11 September 1907, ELSC Ms 615). The exchanges between Ramsay Smith and Edinburgh University continued after Cunningham's death in 1909. Responding to the receipt of more human remains and a hint from Ramsay Smith, Professor Arthur Robinson (Cunningham's successor) wrote:

> You say you lack some good books on anthropological measurements and methods. If you will tell me what you already have and give me the titles of those you want I will see if I can advise anything to fill the blanks and as I am in touch with one or two people who know where to look for older editions I may be able to get the volumes you wish to have, if so it will give me great pleasure and I will let you have them as soon as they come to hand. I need scarcely say, as custodian of the Museum, how very much I am indebted to you for the last and previous consignments nor how gladly I shall receive any other specimens you send (Robinson to Ramsay Smith 7 March 1911, EADL).

Thus while Ramsay Smith could argue in court (see above) that he did not obtain money for the remains he sent to Edinburgh, he nonetheless did profit in other ways from this practice. By the beginning of the twentieth century, Ramsay Smith had donated a sufficient amount of human remains to the University of Edinburgh for its indigenous Australian collection to be the largest in Britain. On occasion Ramsay Smith appears to remind Cunningham of this fact (e.g. Ramsay Smith to Cunningham 18 December 1907, ELSC Ms 617) as well as the hardship he had endured on the University's behalf:

> Many of these specimens have been collected in the most trying circumstances – thermometer at 110 degrees or above, winds hot as a furnace, sand over everything, camping out for days in adverse circumstances miles upon miles from humanity, food mixed with grit, water – none or dirty or hot, eating and drinking done in darkness on account of the flies and mosquitoes that convert bread into 'meat meal'. A chapter on the romance of collecting would prove interesting. The only consolation one has in all this work is that if it is not done now it can never be done at all. No one living at home, which means England or Scotland, can possibly have the least conception of what scientific work, that is original work of collecting, involves in this country. Distance here really means distance. My district extends two thousand miles north and south, and I believe I have collected

from most parts of it for one purpose or another (Ramsay Smith to Cunningham 23 October 1907, ELSC Ms 616).

By 1908, Ramsay Smith wished the collection to stand as a monument to his contribution to science:

> This collection is getting so large now, beyond anything even in Australian museums, that I begin to think it might be well to keep it as a separate 'contribution' to the museum along with what I shall send in the future. I have done something as a collector and suffered much as an investigator, and the collection might be associated with my name as some testimony to the fact that nothing has stood in the way of my working in this particular field despite all persecution and opposition (Ramsay Smith to Cunningham 28 April 1908, ELSC Ms 620).

Indigenous human remains were also used as exchange specimens. Curators of colonial museums used indigenous remains as currency to enlarge their own collections. Thus, for example, the Curator of the Australian Museum, E.P. Ramsay, offered to trade Aboriginal skulls for Moriori remains from the Chatham Islands with the Colonial Museum of Auckland in 1882 (Turnbull 1991: 115), and twenty-one Maori skulls were received in 1879 by the Royal College of Surgeons of England, 'in exchange from the Auckland Museum, through the courtesy of the Curator, T.F. Cheeseman, Esq.' (Flower 1907: 252). In the 1880s, in a push to increase the size of Auckland Museum's collections, Cheeseman offered Maori human remains (as well as other items unique to New Zealand, such as moa bones and tuatara lizards) to major museums worldwide.

Certainly by the late nineteenth century, curators of European collections were approaching their Australian colleagues for Aboriginal remains. George Rolleston of Oxford University unsuccessfully attempted to obtain some from E.P. Ramsay of the Australian Museum in 1881, but Enrico Giglioli of the Zoological and Vertebrate Museum at Florence's Institute for Higher Study may have been more fortunate, perhaps because he promised to obtain Ramsay a knighthood for his efforts (Turnbull 1991: 115-16). Giglioli had received numerous Maori crania from Cheeseman at the Auckland Museum, sent in exchange for various specimens from Southern Europe. He also approached E.C. Stirling at the South Australian Museum, looking to form a 'small collection of types of *modern* stone implements and weapons or ornaments, specimens which illustrate the modern stone age' for which he could supply in exchange 'specimens of the vertebrata of south Europe or other parts of the world' or other items that Stirling might require. Although human remains were not within his stated *desiderata*, Giglioli appended his letter:

> Could you give me any information on the drinking vessels made out of human skulls used by some of the native tribes of South Australia. If you can

you will greatly oblige me. Have you any specimens of such? (Giglioli to Stirling 31 July 1890, Stirling Papers, SAM).

There existed, therefore, many reasons why colonists donated human remains to museums 'back home'. The interest of collectors in the study of human origins, the value placed on such research and the prestige associated with contributing to it, as well as simply the requests for assistance from old friends and teachers were all incentives that partly account for the majority of remains in European institutions. But there were also other advantages to supplying remains. While it rarely seems that financial gain was a motivation, instead, remains were themselves used as currency, sometimes in exchange for museum specimens, but often for scientific literature and assistance in gaining entry into prestigious societies. Such gains were at the cost of Australia's indigenous population, whose funerary practices and cultural beliefs were overridden unless communities were in a position to defend their own burial sites. While concerned at the desecration of their own graveyards (and also at the treatment of the bodies of well-known Aboriginal people), unless these too were under threat, there is little sign of any mass objection by the non-indigenous public to the widespread collecting of Aboriginal human remains. Owing to the actions of bodysnatchers, who robbed graveyards for corpses to sell to anatomy schools, by the nineteenth century anatomists were not widely renowned for caring about how their subjects were acquired. Nonetheless, the fact that few anatomists donated their own bodies to medical science (Richardson 1988: 185-6) shows that while they may have been willing to ignore the concerns and beliefs of others, they did not dismiss them as invalid. Thus, in 1931 the aged Professor Archibald Watson, who had, during his career, obtained the bodies of many indigenous and non-indigenous people for dissection and dispatch to overseas museums, was particularly anxious to ensure that his parents' burial place (in which he also wished to be interred) was not disturbed by the construction of a road. His complaints were not appreciated by the relevant authority, who was annoyed at Watson's 'desire to have [his] parents resting place made sacred' (NL 1682/38/2454).

5

Implications and context

The previous chapter documented attitudes towards, and reactions to, the removal of human remains at the local level. But did this mass movement of human bones around the globe have other effects? In what way, for example, did the appropriation and study of human remains fit within larger historical processes that negotiated the relationship between indigenous Australians and the colonising culture? One way of approaching this question is to examine how the procurement and analysis of human remains contributed to how Europeans perceived themselves and others, for of central importance to the colonial experience in Australia was how European society viewed and valued the indigenous population.

Over the past fifteen years there has been an increase in literature devoted to examining the Western practice of collecting and the nature of the collected object (e.g. Stewart 1984; Stocking 1985; Clifford 1985, 1988; Benedict 1990; Pomian 1990; Hooper-Greenhill 1992; Pearce 1992, 1994a). These texts have largely concentrated on the collecting of artefacts and, as a general rule, have been less concerned with other types of collected material. Ten years ago Pearce (1994b: 1) pointed out that although their nature does not preclude them from being analysed in the same manner as other collected items, there was a distinct shortage of literature that focused on the collecting of natural history specimens. And, while there has been considerable interest in the collecting of ethnographic objects, little attention has been paid to human remains obtained for the purposes of anthropological study.

It has been argued (e.g. Baudrillard 1994: 8; Pearce 1992: 48-50) that collections of any sort *articulate* identity, a characteristic derived from the way in which the predominant meaning of collected objects is extrinsic, determined and imposed by the collector. Divorced from its previous social context, the object now exists within a new one that is 'framed by the selectivity of the collector' (Stewart 1984: 152) and almost always organised according to a particular system of classification chosen by the collector. It is therefore a feature of collections that they physically represent the collector's conceptualisation of the order of the objects amassed and the relationship which exists between them.

Collections of human remains were arranged according to various systems for classifying humankind. How collections were arranged represented how those responsible for their organisation perceived the order of humanity, and they in turn supported (and mirrored) the general perceptions of human diversity held by society as a whole. For example, human remains in the Museum of the Army Medical Department at Fort Pitt, Chatham, were arranged according to a system in which skull shape was used as a basis for distinguishing between four different races:

> first, the oval shaped skulls [which included Europeans, Egyptians, Afghans, Hindu, and Singalese]; second, skulls with projecting alveolar processes, or with nasal bones on the same plane [which included the 'Negroes' from the west coast of Africa, 'Kaffirs', 'Hottentots', and 'Bushman']; third, skulls with very prominent superciliary ridges [which included only the Sandwich Islanders]; fourth, skulls with broad and flat face [which included the Burmese, Malays, Chinese, 'Esquimaux', and North American Indians] (Williamson 1857: 5).

The late nineteenth-century confusion about human taxonomy was also sometimes a reason for *not* organising human remains according to racial origin. As William Flower (1879: viii) explained about the collection at the Royal College of Surgeons of England, with which he was associated from 1861-4, first as Conservator and then as Hunterian Professor of Comparative Anatomy:

> the arrangement of these specimens is one of considerable difficulty, partly owing to the present state of uncertainty as to the true classification of the varieties of species ... it has therefore been thought that these difficulties will be best overcome ... without committal to any theoretical view of the origins or affinities, by adopting a geographical arrangement, and placing all specimens according to the countries of which they are presumably native.

Although the geographical organisation of the College's collection illustrated Flower's early distrust of racial taxonomies, the later exhibition of human remains in the public galleries at the British Museum (Natural History), where Flower became Director in 1884, may represent a change in attitude. These cases were arranged according to the tripartite system ('white', 'yellow' and 'red', and 'black' races) that Flower had adopted by 1885 (Flower 1885; Harmer 1912). The very existence of collections of human remains articulated key nineteenth- and early twentieth-century Western assumptions about the nature of human diversity, not only the idea that morphology was the primary criterion for distinguishing between different human groups, but also that morphology determined racial hierarchy.

Identity through measurement

The 'metric torrent' described in Chapter 2 was the product of a desire to define human diversity scientifically and quantitatively and, in so doing, define human 'worth'. The identity of races was constructed through measurement, and, once defined, these same measurements were used to assign peoples to separate rungs on a hierarchical and, later, evolutionary ladder. Science compared Aboriginal remains with those of ancient European people, to support the contention that Aborigines were a distant lower rung on an evolutionary ladder that placed Europeans firmly at the top. Thus Klaatsch's 1908 study of Aboriginal skulls focused on comparing Australian skulls with those of ancient fossil Europeans, based on T.H. Huxley's 1864 assertion that an Australian skull from Western Port in South Australia (then housed in the Royal College of Surgeons of England) was similar to that of a Neanderthal. This type of comparison was common (e.g. Dahl 1926: 10).

Notions of European superiority pervaded the colonial era and were central to its ideology. Colonisation was often viewed as a 'natural' and therefore fitting and justifiable, process. Darwin's theory of 'survival of the fittest', underpinned much contemporary comment on the decimation of indigenous populations at the hands, directly or otherwise, of the colonisers. Thus, according to Wallace (1864: clxv), Caucasians would displace the 'savage' races: 'just as the weeds of Europe overrun North America and Australia, extinguishing native productions by the inherent vigour of their organisation, and by their greater capacity for existence and multiplication'. Unsurprisingly, therefore, the racial identity prescribed for Australia's indigenous population is a central theme in historical literature that documents prejudicial and violent treatment received by Aboriginal people (for examples, see Evans *et al.* 1993: 67-84). Such treatment could be condoned because of a belief in the 'lowly' status of Australia's indigenes, and the inevitability of their extinction, or subjugation, by a 'superior' culture. It appears that so common was the perception of Aboriginal people as sub-human at this time that it led the British High Commissioner to observe to his friend, Prime Minister Gladstone, in 1883:

> The habit of regarding natives as vermin, to be cleared off the face of the earth, has given the average Queenslander a tone of brutality and cruelty in dealing with 'blacks' which is very difficult for anyone who does not *know* it, as I do, to realize. I have heard men of culture and refinement, of the greatest humanity and kindness to their fellow white, and who when you meet them here at home you would pronounce to be incapable of such deeds, talk, not only of the *wholesale* butchery (for the iniquity of *that* may sometimes be disguised from themselves) but of the *individual* murder of natives, exactly as they would talk of a day's sport, or having to kill some troublesome animal (Gordon, 1883, in Evans *et al.* 1993: 78).

The scientific view that placed Aboriginal people on the lowest rung of the evolutionary ladder reflected and supported prejudicial perceptions (echoed in contemporary journalism, political speeches and popular writing) of Australia's indigenous population. This stereotyping helped both to justify and to rationalise the way in which they were treated by the dominant culture. As noted by Evans *et al.* (1993: 67) regarding race relations in Queensland:

> A detailed and denigrating racial stereotype of the tribalized Aborigine arose out of the direct experience of the violent frontier. Backed by ingrained ethnocentric conceptions, traditional as well as scientific beliefs and emotive second hand evidence, this stereotype emerged as the major *raison d'être* for racially prejudiced attitudes and responses towards the libeled native. Both the negative stereotype and the aura of prejudice surrounding it were then utilized in turn as a 'bridging' explanation for the violence, exploitation and discriminatory behaviour to which the 'civilized' European was 'forced' to stoop in his dealings with the 'savages'.

Scientific interpretation of human remains therefore provided authoritative 'truths' about Aborigines – and these influenced how the dominant society perceived and acted towards Australia's indigenous population. Through media such as museum displays organised to illustrate the ranked order of the races (such as that described by Regan (1921) in the British Museum (Natural History)) those considered to have authority in these matters confirmed these 'facts' to the general public. More directly, while social and physical anthropologists rarely played a role in the forefront of colonial administration (despite the belief of many that they should do so (e.g. Flower 1898: 236, and see Kuklick 1991: 27-74)), their studies influenced, or affirmed, how those in power perceived indigenous people – and these perceptions led to definitions of Aboriginal people that were central to the legislation developed to 'manage' them. Sutton (1986: 47) has observed that in Australia there is a 'long and continuous thread connecting old-fashioned ethnographic fact collecting, professional anthropology, corporate and public policy, and administration'. Notions of race were increasingly used in the later nineteenth and early twentieth centuries to develop definitions of Aborigines that were enshrined in Australian legislation; Aboriginal people were categorised by their 'genetic' inheritance, with a focus on how much 'pure' Aboriginal blood ran in their veins (see Marcus 1988, Kennedy 1985). The impact of such legislation was far reaching (Cowlishaw 1986; Sutton 1986: 47; Beckett (ed.) 1988; Beckett 1988: 195-212; Edwards and Read 1989; Lattas 1993; Thomas 1994: 6; Cove 1995: 70-139; Commonwealth of Australia 1997; Wolfe 1999; Weatherall 2000). These legal definitions had little to do with how Aboriginal people saw and defined themselves – the process was a 'top-down' imposition designed to control a subordinate population.

Nineteenth- and twentieth-century scientific analysis of Aboriginal human remains can be seen as part of the lens through which the colonising culture viewed Australia's indigenous population. It influenced how Aboriginal people were perceived and valued, yet it in turn was upheld by pre-conceived notions of racial hierarchy. Viewed in this way it can be seen as part of what Attwood (1992) has described as 'Aboriginalism' (influenced by Said's 1978 work on *Orientalism*), a mode of discourse that constructs, guides and constrains European knowledge about the 'Aborigines'. According to Attwood (1992: i), Aboriginalism encompasses several interrelated practices but in particular: the production of knowledge about Aborigines; a way of thinking that is rooted in a distinction between 'Us' and 'Them'; and a corporate institution that 'exercises authority over Aborigines by making statements about them, authorising views of them and ruling over them'. Supported by colonial bureaucracies, scholarship, social thought and other aspects of European culture, Aboriginalism is a 'hegemonic system of theory and practice' (Attwood 1992: iii) that pervaded colonial power structures and had profound implications for Australia's indigenous population.

In Attwood's (1992: ii) analysis, Aboriginalism's critical role in the colonial enterprise derived largely from its construction of an identity *for* 'the Aborigines'. Central to this contention is the observation that prior to European settlement, the people who lived in Australia defined themselves not as 'Aborigines', but by their own group names. Rather, they were defined in common as 'Aborigines' 'only in the context of colonisation and their ensuing relationship with Europeans who, conversely, came to be 'Australians' (Attwood 1989: x; and see Cowlishaw 1986, 1987; Hollinsworth 1992; Myers 1994: 681). What Attwood (1989) has called the 'making of the Aborigines' was therefore a process determined more by the West than the people who were the object of definition. How Europeans imagined 'the Aborigines' had little to do with how Australia's indigenous population, in all its diversity, saw themselves (and see Weaver 1984). The construction of an 'Aboriginal' identity by outsiders led to a situation in which, 'much European knowledge of the autochthonous people is peculiarly dependent on representations which construct "the Aborigines" in their absence' (Attwood 1992: ii, and see Beckett 1988: 191-2). Such representations were, according to Attwood (1992: v), 'inseparable from the colonists' exercise of power'.

Imposing an outside identity onto Australia's indigenous population had wide-ranging implications. Not only did it mean that the self-identity(ies) of indigenous communities which were developing in relation to the colonial experience were undervalued – both at the time and in later analysis of this period (see Reynolds 1981, 1990; Cowlishaw 1986, 1987, 1992; Keefe 1988; Weaver 1984), but also it influenced the relationship between Europeans and 'Aborigines'. The identity prescribed for Australia's indigenous population thus constrained the colonisers' perceptions of them. Analysis of Aboriginal human remains was part of this process, particularly the way in which it quantified and valued *difference*.

The European conceptualisation of an 'Us' set against a non-European 'Them' is a division which has been seen as forming the 'core of cultural thought during the era of Imperialism' (Said 1994: xxviii).

Both Orientalism and Aboriginalism are particularly reliant on, and productive of, this conceptualisation. However, although they are perceived as opposite to, and radically different from, one another, it is important to recognise that fundamentally 'Us' and 'Them' are not separate, isolated entities. Instead, they are intricately linked and inter-dependent – one cannot exist without the other – and they both ultimately derive from the European perception of 'Self'. Races were defined by the comparison of their remains and as the European skull was 'perfect' so, therefore, the skulls of other peoples had to differ, negatively. So, for example, Lumholtz (1889: 282-3) wrote:

> The features distinguishing the cranium of the Australian from that of the European are, in the first place, the projecting jaws (the prognathous character), which are very rare and never marked among Europeans; in the second place, the low forehead and the small capacity, which among Europeans would be called microcephalus, and would indicate a weak mind; in the third place, the flat nose, which is also very rare in Europe; and finally, the large Daubenton's angle.

Studying human remains did not create the notion of racial inequality. The identity constructed by science for 'Aborigines' would never have been realised without the adherence of nineteenth- and early twentieth-century anthropology to the concept of biological determinism. European preconceptions of racial hierarchy were instead 'mapped' onto human bodies, to be 'objectively' analysed as if they existed 'in nature'. As Urla and Terry (1995: 3) have observed, science does not simply interpret bodies but constructs them, and nineteenth-century physical anthropology effectively constructed the Aboriginal body as 'different' and 'inferior' to that of the 'normal' and 'superior' European. The propagation of scientific knowledge about the Aboriginal body was instrumental in sustaining relations of inequality that lay at the core of the colonial experience. These relations not only derived from the way in which Aboriginal remains were analysed to produce knowledge, but also because during this process Aborigines themselves became objects *of* knowledge. Turnbull (1991: 110) has argued that it led 'professional scientists, scientific institutions, amateur naturalists and some ordinary colonists, to treat Aborigines as if they were endangered, though crucially important, scientific specimens'.

Exhibition

The process of objectifying the 'Other' was already apparent in the exhibition and display of a significant number of indigenous people in circuses and parades, ethnographic exhibitions and anthropological societies. Stewart (1984: 109-11) and Bennett (1995: 83-4) have shown that in the display of indigenous peoples in the various fairs, expositions and circuses of the eighteenth and early nineteenth centuries, the exotic body of the Other took on an identity comparable to that of the side show freak. Indeed, Stewart (1984: 109) notes that the freak has often been a cultural as well as natural aberration ('the Little Black Man, the Turkish Horse, the Siamese twins ... the Irish giants'). As in the exhibition of carnival freaks, the display of exotic humans 'normalised' the observer as it also constructed the cultural Other as both different and inferior (Stewart 1984: 109; Bennett 1995: 79; Stallybrass and White 1986: 198-9). As Bennett (1995: 84) has observed:

> In their interrelationships ... the expositions and their fair zones constituted an order of things and of peoples which, reaching back into the depths of prehistoric time as well as encompassing all corners of the globe, rendered the whole world metonymically present, subordinated to the dominating gaze of the white, bourgeois, and ... male eye of the metropolitan powers.

In some cases, exhibited people themselves came to be part of museum collections, thus seamlessly continuing the objectification process. Saartje Baartman's remains became part of the collection in the Musée de l'Homme (see Chapter 2).[1] Similarly, the indigenous Uruguayan leader Vaimaca Pirú was part of an exhibition which toured France in the 1830s and when he died his bones were also placed in the Musée de l'Homme (Barbosa 2002).[2] In Argentina in the mid-1880s, following eighteen months of imprisonment for their resistance to the settlement of their territory in Patagonia, chief Inakayal and other Mapuche were, at the request of the museum's director, given accommodation in La Plata Museum. Although some were allowed to return to their homeland, Inakayal was not, and, when he died in 1888, his brain, bones, scalp and death mask became part of the museum's collection (Endere 2002).[3]

The story of Tambo provides an example of how, through display, the body of a Manbarra man was made an object in both life and death. In 1883 Tambo and eight other indigenous people from Palm Island and Hinchinbrook Island off the tropical coast of Queensland were 'recruited' by Robert Cunningham, an Agent of P.T. Barnum, to form a stage troupe that would tour overseas. They were exhibited in New Zealand and the Pacific Islands and then in North America, as part of Barnum, Bailey and Hutchinson's Greatest Show on Earth. As Poignant describes (1993: 49):

> the essence of the circus was a Grand Parade of the animals and a great variety of humankind, led by a Beauty Queen who was sometimes described as the Circassion Princess, rescued from the infidel. Together these star performers represented Tamed Nature, Savagery, and the Captive Maiden with her attendant company of jugglers, clowns and trick performers. The show itself was marked by simultaneity of action, both in the three circus rings and the surrounding side-shows of 'Living Curiosities' and marvels.

When the circus season ended, Cunningham exhibited the group in various dime museums across North America. On 23 February 1884, the group arrived in Cleveland and, that night, Tambo died of pneumonia. Cunningham stopped Tambo's companions from carrying out any appropriate funerary customs, took his body and had it embalmed (Houzé and Jacques 1884: 140; Palm Island 2002). For the next thirty-six years, Tambo's preserved body was displayed in the Cleveland Dime Museum. When the museum closed down, the body was kept in a succession of funeral parlours until it was eventually transferred to the Cuyahoga County Coroner's Office in 1993. In October of that year, Tambo's body was claimed by his great-great-nephew, Walter Palm Island and returned to Palm Island shortly afterwards (see Chapter 9).

The circus was designed to present to the public the various races of humankind. In the circus Tambo and his Aboriginal companions were only part of a larger troupe that included 'Bushmen', 'Zulus', 'Nubians', 'Sioux Indian Savages' and 'Fijian Cannibals' (Poignant 1993: 49).[4] Tambo's group was represented as members of an inferior race – pamphlets advertising the Aborigines emphasised their savagery and brutishness by descriptions of cannibalism, infanticide and body mutilation; they were 'distorted' in form and 'with but a glimmering of reason and gift of speech' (promotional flier reproduced in Turnbull 1993c, and see Poignant 1993: 49). The show space mirrored through display of the living what scientific analysis accomplished by measurement of the dead. By March 1884, without Tambo and another of the group who is also believed to have died in America (Poignant 1993: 40), Cunningham had taken the troupe to Europe. Here they were displayed to the public, being described as 'ranting man eaters', 'veritable blood thirsty beasts' and 'the lowest order of mankind' (reproduced in the *Townsville Bulletin* 30 October 1993). By 1888, those who survived had been exhibited before, at least, the anthropological societies of Great Britain and Ireland, Berlin, Paris, Brussels and Russia (Houzé and Jacques 1884; Topinard 1885; *Journal of the Anthropological Institute* 1888, XVII: 83-4; Poignant 1993).

In the circus, Tambo's living body was a thing of curiosity, a spectacle disempowered and made object through display (Poignant 1993: 37-9, and see Rydell 1984; Stewart 1984; Bennett 1995). In the dime museum, whether Tambo was living or embalmed, the same processes were in play. As observed by Stewart (1984: 110-11), as circus 'freaks' were regarded as objects, it made no difference whether they were alive or dead. Once he had died and his preserved remains were placed on display, Tambo's body continued to be an object of curiosity. His body was also made into an object because it was a commodity; as people paid to see Tambo alive, so they gave a dime to see his preserved remains in the museum.

Objectification

The work of Michel Foucault on the objectification of the body through techniques of power and knowledge suggests an alternative perspective for examining collections of human remains, which is related to, but indepen-

5. Implications and context

dent from, the scientific interpretation of their contents. Foucault has brought into focus various interrelated modes by which relations of power and knowledge construct the body as an object. He has, for example, considered the role of scientific classification and the scientific gaze in the objectification of the human subject (e.g. 1970, 1977). Of greater relevance to the present analysis is Foucault's (1977) contention that since the seventeenth century the body has increasingly become an object and target of power through a technique which employs scientific classification in conjunction with regulation and confinement.

According to this suggestion, the body as an object became the target of a new set of procedures – 'disciplinary technologies' – which aimed to produce 'docile' bodies, or those which might be 'subjected, used, transformed and improved' (Foucault 1977: 136). 'Docility' was achieved in a number of related ways, an important component of which was the organisation of bodies in space. Such organisation enabled 'meticulous control of the operations of the body ... assured the constant subjection of its forces and imposed upon them a relation of docility – utility' (Foucault 1977: 137). Although they existed before the seventeenth century, in, for example, monasteries, armies and workshops, Foucault (1977: 136-7) contends that disciplinary technologies became the 'general formulas of domination' during the course of the seventeenth and eighteenth centuries, occurring in such institutions as the prison, the asylum and the hospital (Foucault 1977: 135-69).

Disciplinary technologies organised individuals in an enclosed area – each individual must have its own specific place, and, equally, each place must have its own specific individual: 'disciplinary space tends to be divided into as many sections as there are bodies or elements to be distributed' (Foucault 1977: 143). Enclosed and partitioned, the disciplinary space was essentially cellular. In this way, at any moment, the conduct of each individual was under surveillance, and could be supervised, assessed and controlled. The disciplinary procedure was therefore aimed at 'knowing, mastering and using' the subject. Organised as an 'analytical space', the cell could also, therefore, provide a 'useful space' (Foucault 1977: 143, 144).

According to Foucault (1977: 145-6), the location of each individual space is defined by its position in a series. Guided by classification, therefore, the space occupied by each cell is based upon rank. In organising the distribution of individuals into cells, places and ranks, disciplines therefore created 'complex spaces that are at once architectural, functional and hierarchical'. In essence such spaces and their distribution physically embodied and enlivened the classification tables which were of such central concern to the 'scientific, political and economic technology of the eighteenth century' (Foucault 1977: 148). However, as well as methods of rational arrangement, these 'tableaux vivants' transformed 'the confused, useless or dangerous multitudes into ordered multiplicities'. Disciplinary technologies therefore stood at, and emerged from, the congruence of techniques of power and procedures of knowledge.

Even though the bodies they contain are not living, collections of human remains do share many similar features with Foucault's 'disciplinary technologies'. First, that the body of the Other is expropriated and held within the walls of an institution; second, that within the institution collections of human remains are partitioned, each one occupying its own place through having been assigned unique numbers and recorded and catalogued individually; third, that the position of each remain is determined by its place within the collection as a ranked series in accordance with the system of classification that was used to order and organise the collection. Similar to other 'disciplinary technologies', collections of human remains can therefore be seen to be composed of complex spaces. Occupied by bodies, these spaces are 'architectural', because of the physical manner in which they are imposed, 'functional' and 'useful', because they allow and reflect systematic and ordered scientific analysis, and 'hierarchical' because they are determined by systems of classification implicitly or explicitly constructed within the race paradigm. By classifying the skeletal remains of colonised peoples, having appropriated these items to do so, collections also demonstrate a confluence of power and knowledge.

Collections of human remains therefore appear to be similar in structure, practice and outcome to the disciplinary technologies identified by Foucault as objectifying the living body. To take the analogy further, collections and Foucault's carceral institutions often targeted exactly the same bodies, as those of Aboriginal people dying in prisons and asylums sometimes became part of collections. Today, collections themselves have sometimes been described as prisons by those who request the return of human remains. Museums have been referred to as places that incarcerate the ancestors, unco-operative museum curators have been equated with jailers and campaigns for the return of remains have frequently employed language which implicitly or explicitly relates repatriation to liberation (e.g. *Melbourne Morning Daily* 23 November 1985; *The Advertiser* 10 May 1989, *Melbourne Sun* 11 November 1991).

The concept that collections inflict eternal torment is not confined to the indigenous groups most vocal in their wishes to have human remains returned. Europeans could also see collections as a mechanism of punishment. The skull of an Aboriginal elder of the Shoalhaven district appears to have been donated to the British Phrenological Society in 1825 in part as an exercise in retribution:

> although this man escaped punishment and died in peace, yet mark eternal justice his bones have not been allowed to rest in their grave and it is to be hoped that his skull will throw such light on science as may sufficiently expiate the crimes which he committed (A. Berry, quoted in Turnbull 1993a: 21).

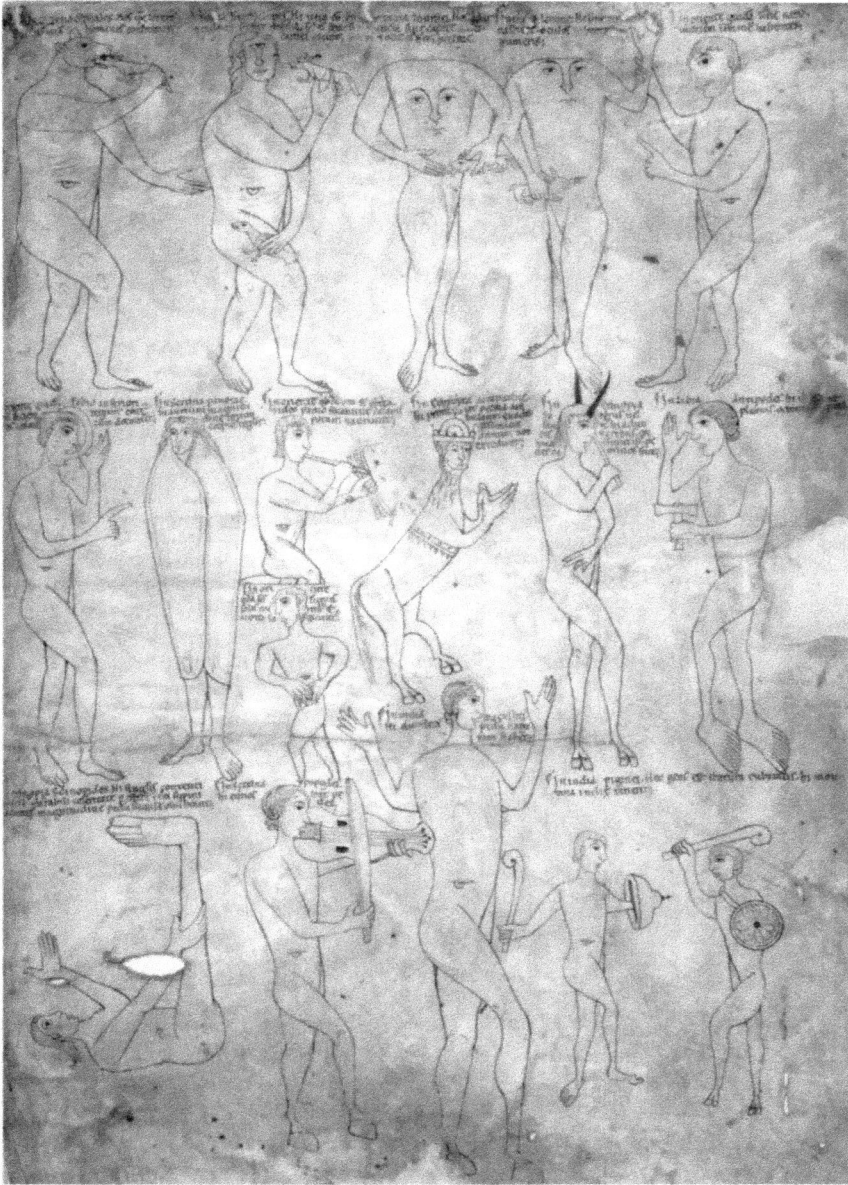

1. Drawings of the seventeen monstrous races, including Giants, Pygmies, Blemmyae and Donestre, from the Arnstein Bible, 1172.

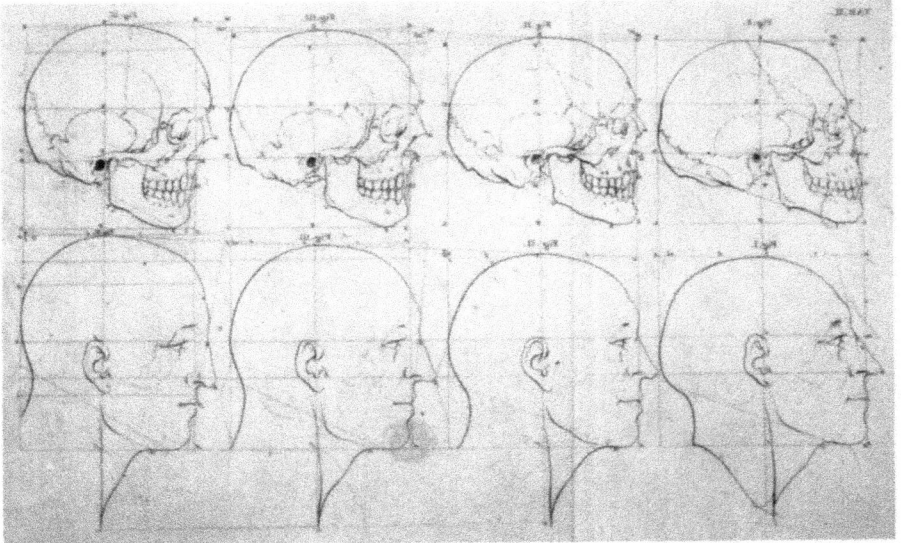

2. Petrus Camper's illustration of the facial angle.

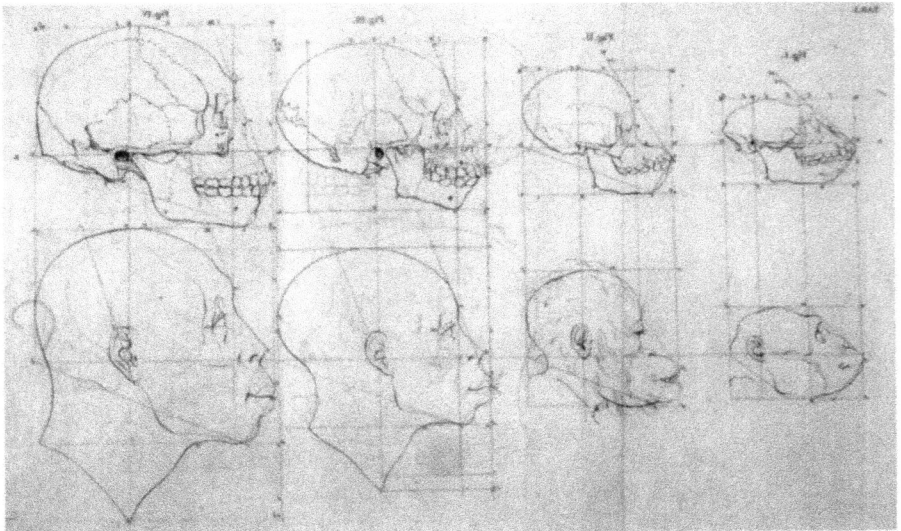

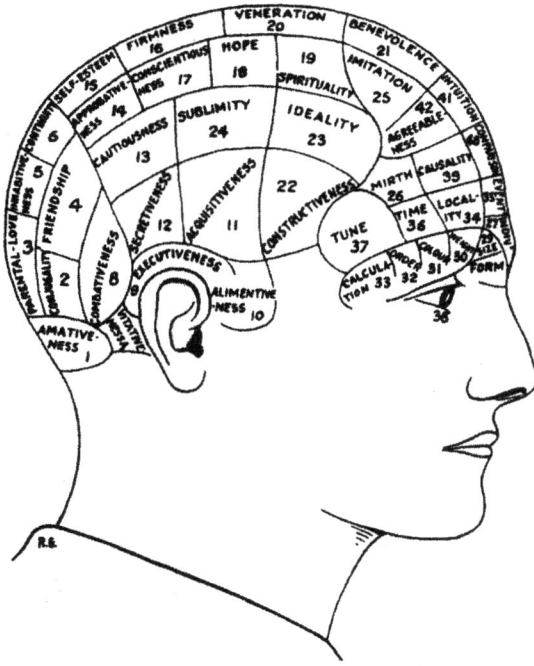

**HEAD SHOWING THE LOCATIONS, NAMES
AND NUMBERS OF PHRENOLOGICAL ORGANS.**

3. The phrenological organs.

TOMMY WALKER.

HE RESTS IN PIECES.

A SCIENTIFIC INTERMENT.

In the south-eastern corner of the West-terrace Cemetery stands a neat marble slab bearing this simple inscription—

IN MEMORY
of
TOMMY WALKER,
A Dusky King,
Died 4th July, 1901.
A tribute from Stock Exchange.

The grave over which this headstone has been erected is freshly planted with flowers, and it looks as neat and as well kept as though loving hands were continually tending it. Indeed, the last resting place of Pollpalingda Booboorowie—for that was the impressive and picturesque native name of the aboriginal vagabond whom Adelaide knew as Tommy Walker—is too symmetrical and orderly altogether. And thereby hangs a tale.

4. Newspaper headline in the *Adelaide Advertiser*, 19 August 1903.

5. Disturbance of Tasmanian Aboriginal graves during the French scientific expedition to Australia, 1800-04.

6. The reburial of Native American human remains
at Wounded Knee in South Dakota, 1989.

7. Memorial to Kappitipola Nilama in Kandy public park, Sri
Lanka. His skull is believed to be buried at its base.

8. The Edinburgh collection in process of repatriation, 1991.

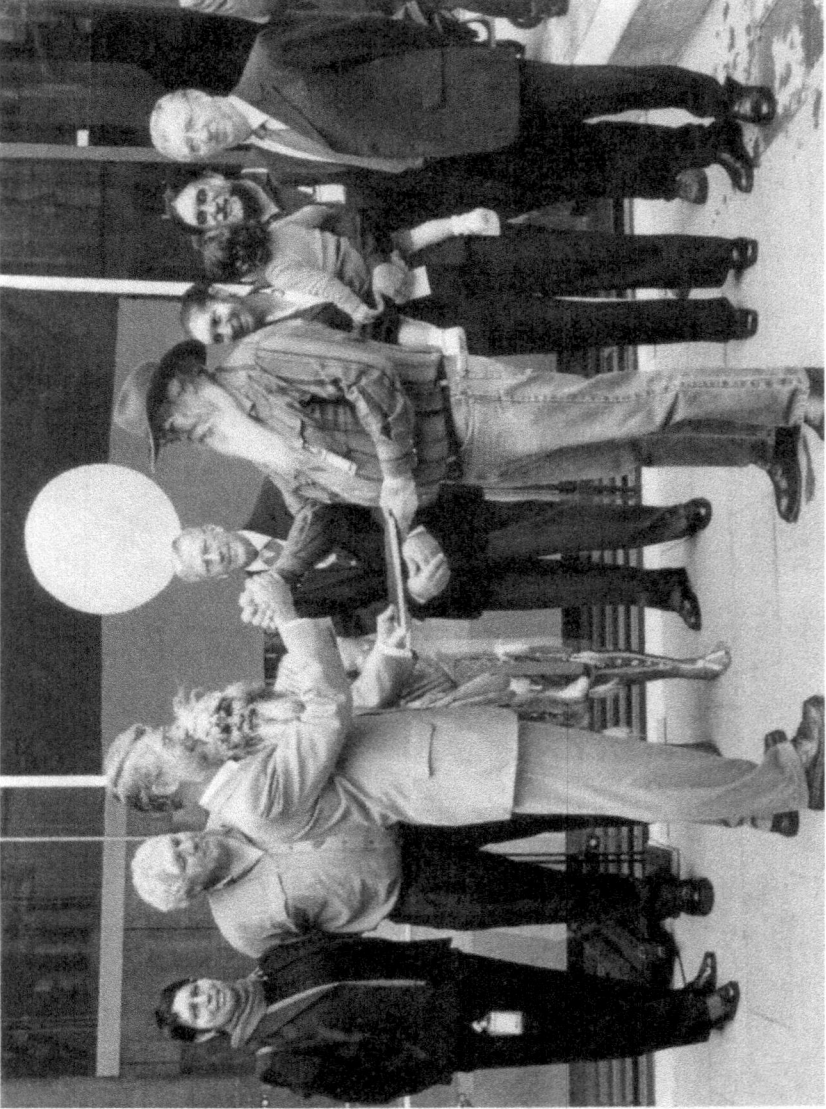

9. The hand-over ceremony at Manchester Museum, 2003. Director Tristram Besterman and Bob Weatherall of FAIRA in the foreground.

5. Implications and context

Another example is provided in Scotland where, in January 1829, William Burke (of Burke and Hare, the infamous murderers who sold the bodies of their victims for dissection at the Department of Anatomy, University of Edinburgh) was sentenced to public execution and public dissection with his skeleton being preserved for posterity (Richardson 1988: 131-43). It is still held by Edinburgh University today.

The Western notion of retribution being exacted from the criminal body after death derives from the historical relationship that existed between dissection and punishment. Prior to the Anatomy Act of 1832, anatomists could officially acquire only the corpses of the condemned. Since the sixteenth century, medical schools had been allowed, by royal grant, to obtain a limited supply of bodies from the scaffold (see Richardson 1988: 30-2). Richardson (1988: 32) notes that such grants represented the inception in Britain of 'a relationship between the medical profession, the ruling elite and the judiciary on the one hand, and between dissection and exemplary punishment on the other'. The link between dissection and criminality was further established by the Murder Act of 1752, which enabled dissection to be served as a post-mortem form of punishment that could be substituted, at the discretion of the judge, for gibbeting in chains (Richardson 1988: 35-7). Sawday (1995: 55) has observed that the Murder Act was:

> designed specifically to evoke horror at the violation of the body and denial of burial to the offender. The denial of burial, in particular, was intended to evoke an added dimension to capital punishment, in that it drew upon widespread belief that lack of a proper burial was not merely a disgrace to offenders and their families, but involved the posthumous punishment of the criminal's soul which would not rest whilst the remains lay ungathered within sanctified ground.

Enshrined in law, the relationship between dissection and punishment was direct and, as argued by Richardson (1988: 32) and Sawday (1995: 55), central to the history of the practice of anatomy in Europe. Although the Anatomy Act subsequently repealed the legislation that brought executed bodies to the anatomy table, the popular association of dissection with punishment persisted for many years afterwards (Richardson 1988: 159-92).

In his analysis of the collecting of ethnographic objects, Stocking (1985) observed that because most collections contain items that were once those of others there are associations inherent in the constitution of collections that can be identified as relations of power. These derive not only from the expropriation of material objects but also from the way in which they and their meaning are appropriated by the collector. While perhaps at their most conspicuous when bones were removed despite objections from the local community, or are the remains of people killed during battle, relations of power are also an integral feature of the appropriation of human remains. The practice of collecting is not only associated with relations of power on a local scale, but has a more wide-ranging significance because it was embedded within the larger historical process of colonialism. Colonialism enabled collecting to take place, but there is also to be found a more fundamental interrelationship between the interpretation of these remains and colonial ideology. Collecting, and the analysis of human remains that followed, supported, and was entangled within the relations of power that existed between the colonisers and the colonised. This was not only because remains were appropriated, but also because they were analysed to produce facts about the order of humankind, and concepts of racial hierarchy that were a fundamental facet of colonial ideology. Taken together, the collecting and interpretation of human remains was part of a complex system of theory and practice that both helped sustain, and was the product of, the unequal relationship between Europe and Australia's indigenous population. Through study and analysis Aboriginal people were objectified and, consequently, further dehumanised – creating yet more distance from the 'normal' Europeans who looked at Australia's indigenous population down the colonial microscope. Yet despite this unequal balance of power, the history of the appropriation of human remains is also one of indigenous resistance. As has been shown, communities sought to protect their dead. Turnbull (2002: 82) has argued that such protection can be traced up until the late 1960s, when indigenous groups started a concerted effort to have their ancestors' remains returned to them, and what became known as the 'reburial campaign' began.

6

Reburial: the development of an issue

The number of indigenous human remains received by UK institutions declined greatly during the first half of the twentieth century and had largely ceased by World War Two. As collections were no longer used, institutions which had once invested so much time in gathering remains from around the world now placed them in storage or sought to transfer them to other museums. Thus, Edinburgh University's Anatomy Department cleared the workroom in which it had kept most of its collection of post-cranial remains and removed its contents to the basement where they were largely forgotten. The majority of the anthropological collections at both Oxford University and the Royal College of Surgeons of England, were transferred to the British Museum (Natural History) after the war, the latter following partial destruction of its museum by enemy action in 1941.

However, museums continued to receive human remains in those countries with indigenous populations. Thus in New Zealand, Maori remains continued to be acquired by museums after World War Two, usually via archaeological excavation, donation from the public or when found through construction work. In North America and Australia also it was common for indigenous remains found in the course of construction to be placed in local museums or other collecting institutions, rather than to be reburied as would have been European remains discovered in similar circumstances. In the USA it was an example of the differential treatment accorded to white and Indian remains which has been identified as the beginning of the reburial campaign in that country (Zimmerman 1989a: 60-1).

In Australia, the campaign for the return of human remains to their communities of origin began in the late 1960s. Indigenous groups claimed remains in institutions and museums, but also those newly disturbed through construction. Over the past fifteen years, requests for museums to return human remains have increasingly been heard from indigenous people outside Australia and the USA, from, for example, the Arctic, Norway, Argentina, Uruguay, South Africa, Botswana, New Zealand and Irian Jaya.[1] In some of these countries the reburial debate is in its early stages, while in others campaigns have prompted significant changes in museum policy and archaeological practice. Some museums have accommodated the concerns of indigenous communities in relation to this issue. For example, New Zealand's new National Museum, Te Papa Tongarewa, was built with a special vault within its foundations to house human remains, and this was blessed for the purpose by Maori elders. Te Papa has received Maori remains repatriated from overseas museums, including those returned from the University of Edinburgh in 2000.

Requests for the return of remains from such diverse indigenous groups worldwide arise from local cultural beliefs and historical experiences but are united in a common concern to accord their dead appropriate treatment. The significance of the reburial issue to indigenous groups globally is reflected in the attention paid to it in the United Nations Draft Declaration for Indigenous Rights of 1985, and in the 1990s it was a topic of discussion at the UN's Working Group on Indigenous Populations (e.g. Tickner 1994: 88). In 1993 the UN's Sub-Commission on the Prevention of Discrimination and Protection of Minorities requested its 'Special Rapporteur' to draft principles and guidelines for the protection of the heritage of indigenous peoples. These principles recognise indigenous ownership and control of their cultural property (including human remains) and state that governments and international organisations should assist in the recovery and restitution of indigenous heritage. Article 21, for example, reads:

> Human remains and associated funeral objects must be returned to their descendants and territories in a culturally appropriate manner, as determined by the indigenous peoples concerned. Documentation may be retained, displayed or otherwise used only in such form and manner as may be agreed upon with the peoples concerned (Daes 1995: 130).

The UN is not the only international forum that has debated the issue of indigenous peoples' rights to their heritage. As Ormond Parker (forthcoming) has documented, various international instruments are now available to assist indigenous peoples in gaining control over, and protection for, their heritage, including their ancestors' remains.

Indigenous requests for the repatriation of their ancestors were (and are) opposed by many who curate and study human remains. Those opposing return believe that the scientific importance of collections outweighs indigenous concerns. They point to the importance of human remains as a source of potential information about, for example, human origins, disease and past environments (see Grupe and Peters 2003). The Natural History Museum in London's Policy on Human Remains (2001) states that this institution is:

> committed to the scientific study of humans as part of its mission to promote the discovery and understanding of the natural world. Such scientific research may include: studying human origins and evolution; identifying patterns of variation within and between human populations in time and by geographical area; determining the impacts of diet and disease on particular populations; and exploring the nature of human interaction with the environment at different times in our past.

6. Reburial: the development of an issue

By the 1980s the reburial issue had become the subject of intense debate, to the extent that, as one observer later commented, it had 'grasped archaeologists in some areas of the world firmly by the throat – and [showed] no sign of letting go' (Hubert 1989: 131). The issue was debated at archaeological forums; the World Archaeological Congress (WAC), an international organisation, was unique in proactively seeking discussion with, and the involvement of, indigenous groups worldwide (see Hubert 1992: 107). Of the archaeologists who did attend the WAC meetings, some were 'frankly shaken' by the strength of indigenous concerns (Doumas 1989: 21 and see Layton 1989). Perhaps because of the indigenous involvement, these meetings were attended by relatively few scientists who had been outspoken against reburial, despite efforts by WAC conference organisers to ensure their participation (Zimmerman 1989b: 26, Zimmerman 2002). Here perhaps was an early and clear indication of the difficulties of bringing at least one side of the contesting parties to discussion. Nonetheless, proving that common ground could be attained between indigenous people and archaeologists (and these groups are obviously not mutually exclusive), WAC adopted the Vermillion Accord at an Inter-Congress in 1989 (similar versions were later adopted by the Canadian and Australian archaeological associations). After the meeting, conference delegates (archaeologists, Native Americans and indigenous peoples from many parts of the world) took part in the reburial of Native American remains at Wounded Knee in South Dakota (see Plate 6).

The Vermillion Accord (*World Archaeological Bulletin* 4, 1989: 18-19), is a series of statements according respect to the wishes of the dead, their biological and/or cultural descendants and the legitimate concerns of science, with the belief that:

> the express recognition that the concerns of various ethnic groups, as well as those of science, are legitimate and to be respected, will permit acceptable agreements to be reached and honoured.

In Zimmerman's analysis (2002) the Accord contributed to an atmosphere of change in the USA that helped to facilitate the enactment of repatriation legislation (see below) in 1990. The Accord did not cause the legislation to be passed, but it put pressure on the scientific community to accept change, 'Congress saw that a world archaeological organization could reach an agreement, and wondered why much of the US scientific community could not' (Zimmerman 2002: 93).

WAC's commitment to the issues at hand remained after Vermillion as it continued to seek common ground in the reburial debate and related topics. In 1990, it adopted the 'First Code of Ethics (Members' Obligations to Indigenous Peoples)' (*World Archaeological Bulletin* 5, 1991: 22-3) which introduced principles and rules to govern archaeological investigation of the indigenous cultural heritage 'including sites, places, objects, artefacts [and] human remains'. The Code acknowledged indigenous ownership of their cultural heritage and disallowed interference or removal of human remains without permission from the appropriate indigenous authority. The Code was later adopted, in a slightly modified form, by the Australian Archaeological Association and others.

The Native American Graves Protection and Repatriation Act (NAGPRA)

In 1990, following increasing pressure from Native American groups, and after unsuccessful attempts to secure the enactment of appropriate legislation in the late 1980s (see Raines 1992: 646-9; Gerstendblith 1995: 627), the United States passed NAGPRA. This was landmark legislation as for the first time anywhere in the world a nation's indigenous population(s) have been recognised in law as the rightful owners of their ancestors' remains. NAGPRA protects from removal and sale all Native America human remains, funerary and sacred objects and those of cultural patrimony discovered on federal, Native American and Hawaiian lands. Under the legislation, the former are to be returned to 'specified native claimants when the agency or museum does not have right of possession', while the latter are to be returned, on request, to culturally affiliated tribes or native groups (Monroe and Echohawk 1991: 6). It has been estimated that the total number of Native American or Native Hawaiian human remains in collections covered by NAGPRA amounts to approximately 200,000 (McKeown 2002: 116).

Under NAGPRA, the intentional excavation (i.e. planned archaeological removal) of Native American or Hawaiian human remains or cultural items from Federal lands can be undertaken only after consultation with the appropriate indigenous organisation(s) and in accordance with the Archaeological Resources Protection Act (ARPA). On tribal lands intentional excavation can occur only with the consent of the appropriate Indian or Hawaiian authority. If Indian or Hawaiian human remains or cultural items are discovered inadvertently on Federal lands, NAGPRA legislates that the responsible Federal land manager must be notified immediately by telephone, followed up by written confirmation. If remains or cultural items are inadvertently discovered on tribal lands, these must be reported to the responsible Indian official without delay. The discoverer must cease any further activity and 'make a reasonable effort' (McKeown 2002: 129) to protect the items uncovered (for civil cases relating to discovery and excavation provisions in NAGPRA see McKeown 2002: 117).

NAGPRA requires federally funded museums and Federal agencies (see McManamon 2002) to inform Native American and Hawaiian organisations of their holdings of human remains and cultural items. Summaries (simple written descriptions of collections containing sacred objects, objects of cultural patrimony and unassociated funerary goods) were to be presented to Indian tribes and Hawaiian organisations (with a copy to the National Park Service) within three years of enactment. Inventories (item-by-item descriptions of human remains and associated funerary objects) were to be completed within five years of enactment, and provided to appropriate Native American and Hawaiian organisations and the National Park Service by 1996. Unlike the summaries, the completion of inventories must be undertaken in consultation with Native American and Hawaiian organisations and 'represent a decision by the museum or Federal Agency official as to the cultural affiliation of particular human remains or funerary objects' (McKeown 2002: 116).

Many museums (such as the Peabody at Harvard – see Isaac 2002) found themselves unable to meet these deadlines, and requested extensions. After 1993, an increasing number of museums and agencies had completed their required inventories (*Federal Archaeology* Fall/Winter 1995: 41-2, Fall/Winter 1996: 34). Funds to assist museums and indigenous groups in undertaking NAGPRA's requirements were not made available until 1994, but since then over $15 million has been awarded in grants, a sum which has been criticised as inadequate (see Isaac 2002, Anyon and Thornton 2002). According to McKeown (2002: 116), by the middle of 2001, summaries had been received from 1058 Federal agencies and museums and inventories had been received from 850. Although it is a decade since NAGPRA's enactment, both the size of collections and the fact that many, if not most, Federal museums and agencies had insufficient records of their own collections to meet summary and inventory requirements, means that the total number of holdings of relevant institutions and agencies is still unknown. Culturally unidentifiable remains are also regulated under NAGPRA. Inventories of these remains are provided by the National Park Service to a Review Committee so that it may make recommendations as to the disposal of such items. McKeown (2002: 117) suggests that up to 25% of the total number of human remains under NAGPRA's jurisdiction may be culturally unaffiliated.

As long as none of the statutory exemptions apply, Federal agencies or museums must return human remains and cultural items expeditiously if so requested by a Native American or Hawaiian group with standing under the Act and where cultural affiliation to those items has been established. A total of 758 Indian tribes and two Native Hawaiian organisations currently have standing to make requests under NAGPRA. NAGPRA also provides criteria to determine if other Native Hawaiian claimants have standing (Mckeown 2002). In the USA, repatriation has thus been the law for over a decade, although it is important to remember that NAGPRA has no jurisdiction over human remains and cultural items held by private individuals or found on private land. It also has no jurisdiction over holdings of human remains in the National Museum of the American Indian (which is part of the Smithsonian Institution). However, these collections are controlled by the National Museum of the American Indian Act (1989), which requires the Smithsonian to 'inventory, document, and, if requested, repatriate cultural affiliated human remains and funerary objects to federally recognised Native groups' (The Repatriation Laws, www.nmnh.si.edu/anthro/repatriation/repat.htm accessed 7 August 2001). In 1996, the Act was amended and brought definitions of categories of objects subject to repatriation and the deadlines for provision of inventories generally in line with those of NAGPRA.[2]

Australia

Australia has no legislation regarding the return of human remains to compare with that of the USA. However, through State legislation and museum policy Aboriginal people may now successfully claim the remains of their ancestors kept in Australian museums. Of primary concern is that the dead must be returned to their place of origin and be accorded appropriate funerary rites:

> Indigenous law holds that the deceased will not enjoy spiritual rest until they are returned to their ancestral home and given the last rites in accordance with tradition. For this reason, indigenous people feel a deep responsibility to their ancestors to respect their remains and to repatriate them, if necessary, to their rightful burial grounds (Aboriginal and Torres Strait Islander Social Justice Commissioner, quoted in Janke 1998).

Thus, at the official handover ceremony of the first part of the Edinburgh Collection to Aboriginal representatives on 31 September 1991, a Ngarinyin elder spoke of the intimate attachment of each Aboriginal person with one area of land and the absolute necessity of that individual being buried there (and see Poignant 1992).

The removal of human remains, whether before or after appropriate ceremony, has been described as causing the ancestors great anguish, whose consequent unrest can be highly dangerous and may cause misfortune within a community. It is believed that there are potentially severe consequences if human remains are inappropriately handled and/or not accorded appropriate funerary rites. Fundamental to these concerns is the belief that human remains are not material objects but people who exist in the present and must be accorded appropriate treatment.

Respect for the wishes of the dead is a primary consideration of those who have advanced the campaign for the return of Aboriginal remains. For example, the Foundation for Aboriginal and Islander Research Action (FAIRA), asserts the fundamental rights of the dead 'to receive their customary last rites and have their remains left in peace as dictated by custom' (Weatherall 2000). The responsibility to ensure that these rights are fulfilled lies with the descendants of the dead, who thus are obligated to retrieve their ancestors' remains from museums and other holding institutions.

The necessity of according the dead appropriate treatment is fundamental to requests for the return of human remains, but other ethical considerations also play a significant role. Collections of Aboriginal human remains symbolise the past subjugation of Aboriginal people, not least because of the manner in which much of their contents was obtained. As recognised by the Australian Institute for Aboriginal and Torres Strait Islander Studies (AIATSIS):

> Past unethical or insensitive treatment of Aboriginal human remains by collectors, researchers or institutions and general lack of consultation on these matters with the Aboriginal community has added to legitimate Aboriginal concerns in this area (Aboriginal Human Remains: Draft Policy Statement 1988).

The Aboriginal and Torres Strait Islander Commission's (ATSIC's) 2001 submission to the UK's Working Group on Human Remains (see Chapter 9) explained the importance of repatriation in the following terms:

> The repatriation of Indigenous human remains is of paramount importance to the traditional owners/custodians and relatives who are seeking a sense of closure to this period of history.
> There are personal and spiritual feelings of attachment to remains as well as their cultural and historical significance. This emotion underpins the sensitivity of this issue to Indigenous peoples. Once the human remains are returned, a community can satisfy its spiritual needs and cultural imperatives to see that the dead have been treated with due respect and ceremony. In many cases the human remains are buried according to custom in a place designated by the community.

One reason that knowledge of the existence of collections has sometimes been traumatic for Aboriginal people (e.g. West 1987: 1-2) is because collections are seen as evidence of the oppression endured by past generations. Indigenous Australians have also objected to the differential treatment which has, until relatively recently, been accorded to the newly uncovered remains of Aborigines and Europeans (the former having been automatically assigned to museums, and the latter reburied). Indigenous groups have criticised such double standards and questioned why European society, which respects its own dead, should accord such minimal respect to the human remains of other cultures (e.g. *Australian Financial Review* 25 October 1991).

The assumptions about race which surrounded, and were supported by, past scientific research on Aboriginal human remains have been highlighted by campaigners in today's demands for the return of remains. The contribution made by past research to the construction of an inferior identity for Aboriginal people and the role that this played in the justification of their oppression by settlers and government, have formed key elements in many arguments for repatriation (e.g. Mansell 1990). Turnbull (1993: 14) has pointed out that, 'in demanding control of remains Aboriginal people were articulating a politics which stressed the degree to which their identity had been forged through the historical experiences of colonialism', while Weatherall (2000) has written:

> We are all too aware of the fact that who owns the past, controls the past and dictates in some ways the social position of the present. Our everyday living reality is a testament to this fact. We are also all too well aware of the fact that one of the spoils of conquest as a necessary part of maintaining political and social control over the vanquished is the power of definition – not only over personal identity but cultural identity as well.

The reburial issue is one facet of a wider indigenous drive to regain control of their heritage (e.g. Langford 1980) that also finds expression in Land Rights and campaigns for the return of cultural objects. Securing control of ancestral remains has been articulated as a matter of empowerment and self-respect (e.g. Mansell in AAP News Report 23 September 1985). As Des Morgan of the Echuca Aboriginal community was reported to have commented: 'We are trying to take some control over our lives. After all this time we have to. But ... if you can't control your destiny in death, how can you do it in life?' (*Canberra Times* 8 September 1990). Recognising indigenous rights to their ancestors' remains is often viewed as important for the social health of communities, and influential in the ability of groups to heal past wounds (see Thornton 2002) and thus move forward. Without addressing past wrongs, injustices remain unresolved, to the continuing detriment of communities. Thus ATSIC has written:

> The removal of Indigenous human remains strongly contributed towards an overall feeling of dispossession amongst Indigenous peoples of Australia. This along with the continuing unjust treatment of Indigenous people in Australia, up until the early 1970s, contributed towards the further alienation of the traditional owners/custodians of this land from the rest of the population. It is strongly felt that collecting institutions which continue to hold onto these Indigenous human remains as part of their collections perpetuate this feeling of dispossession and unjust treatment and cause Indigenous peoples further spiritual torment and pain (ATSIC 2001 Submission to the Working Group on Human Remains).

The development of the reburial issue in Australia

In the early 1970s, responding to the requests of Aboriginal people (see Hemming 1985; Jones 1985; Anderson 1986, 1990) some Australian museums began to change their policies governing the accession and curation of Aboriginal human remains. For example, in 1972 the Queensland

6. Reburial: the development of an issue

Museum resolved no longer to accept newly discovered Aboriginal bones (which, in most cases, had been the subject of police investigation) save in 'exceptional circumstances and with the permission of the relevant Aboriginal community' (Queensland Museum Pamphlet, no date). Previously such material had been automatically accessioned into the museum's collections. Although the Australian Museum was legally obliged to accept remains found in New South Wales according to the National Parks and Wildlife Act (1974), it resolved to return all recently excavated material on request. In addition, this museum removed Aboriginal human remains from display and placed them in secure areas with access restricted to approved scholars only (see Lampert 1983: 20 and Specht and MacLulich 1996: 34-6).

An increasing awareness and acceptance by some scientists of indigenous concerns for the appropriate redisposition of their ancestors' remains was illustrated in 1976 by the Australian Institute of Aboriginal Studies (AIAS – now the Australian Institute of Aboriginal and Torres Strait Islander Studies, or AIATSIS) which took the initiative in returning the skeletal remains of a known individual, then recently found in Melbourne, to the appropriate community on Groote Eylandt. After ceremony, these remains were placed in a rock shelter (Hubert 1989: 154). However, probably the most significant single development in the 1970s was the successful campaign for the return of the remains of Truganini. This campaign contained nearly all of the elements of those which were to follow in the 1980s and 1990s – the successful lobbying of government by Aboriginal groups, press coverage, debate, and the wide support of the non-Aboriginal public. The eventual cremation of Truganini's skeleton was also the first sign that indigenous demands for the return of remains obtained in the past and believed to be of continuing scientific value could gain the support of influential scientists and politicians. Moreover, it showed for the first time the power of the reburial issue to unite the Aboriginal community.

Truganini

Unlike any other reburial campaign in Australia that was to follow, demands for the return of Truganini's remains could cite the recorded wishes of this individual. Shortly after the death of William Lanne in 1869, Truganini had asked her friend, the Reverend H.D. Atkinson, to take her by boat to 'the Shepherds', the deepest part of the D'Entrecasteaux Channel. When they arrived at the spot, she broke down in tears and told Atkinson that, 'all were dead excepting herself, and the people in Hobart had got all their skulls' and then implored, 'bury me here. It's the deepest place. Promise me!' (account by H.D. Atkinson, quoted in H.B. Atkinson to the Tasmanian Museum 16 December 1950, in Ryan 1974: 2). Seven years after her death, unsubstantiated reports also surfaced that

Truganini had requested that she be buried behind one of the Hobart Mountains (see Ryan 1974: 4). Whatever the detail of her last wishes, Truganini did not want her remains taken by scientists, and had a terrible fear that they might be so.

The day after Truganini died on 8 May 1876, the Royal Society of Tasmania requested that it be given her body, since its efforts to obtain the skeleton of William Lanne had been 'frustrated' (see Chapter 3) and it was anxious that 'a type of a race just passing away should be secured for the Colony for all future time' (Agnew to Gilmore 9 May 1876, AIATSIS Library pMs 1774). The request was denied, the Colonial Secretary believing that Truganini should receive a decent burial free from the 'unseemly proceedings which took place subsequently to Lanne's interment' and Truganini was buried two days later. However, following two further requests from the Secretary of the Royal Society of Tasmania, the Governor in Council authorised the exhumation and transfer of Truganini's body to the Royal Society 'on the understanding that the skeleton shall not be exposed to public view, but be decently deposited in a secure resting place where it may be accessible by special permission to scientific men for scientific purposes' (Moore to Agnew 6 December 1878, AIATSIS Library pMs 1774). However, Ellis (1981: 153-5) notes how one account describes Truganini's skeleton being secretly and illegally exhumed by the Royal Society long before they had been given permission to do so. If so, by the time of the 'official' exhumation in December 1878, Truganini's skeleton had already been in the Royal Society's museum for some months. Contrary to the terms of the initial donation, Truganini's skeleton was put on display at the Melbourne Exhibition in 1888, but otherwise remained in the vault at the Museum of the Royal Society of Tasmania until 1904 when her remains were again taken to Melbourne (where her skeleton was articulated and a plaster cast taken), this time by anthropologist Baldwin Spencer. On return to the Royal Society of Tasmania, Truganini's skeleton was again placed on public display until 1947.

In the 1950s two attempts were made by the Church to persuade the museum (which had by then become the Tasmanian Museum) to reinter Truganini's remains. The first approach was made in 1950 by Rev. H.B. Atkinson, Archdeacon of Launceston, who asked the museum to honour the request which Truganini had made to his father, H.D. Atkinson. The Museum replied that its Trustees had 'no power to dispose of the body' (Pearson to Atkinson 6 April 1951 in Ryan 1974: 8). In 1953 the Bishop of Tasmania requested a meeting with the museum to discuss the possibility of reburying Truganini's remains. Before the meeting, the Director of the Museum sought the opinion of a number of eminent scientists, all of whom strongly rejected the Bishop's proposal (Ryan 1974: 8 and see Cove 1995: 143-5). In an argument similar to those which would be expressed by scientists opposing the reburial of other Aboriginal skeletons some thirty years later, Professor A.A. Abbie wrote that, to his mind:

any disposal of this unique material as suggested would be a scientific crime of the worst order and would receive world-wide condemnation as such. The commission of a crime of this nature could not in any way atone for the original crimes committed against the living Tasmanians (Abbie to Bryden 7 September 1954 in Ryan 1974: 8-9).

The museum decided to retain Truganini's skeleton, intending that it be placed in a specially constructed chamber which would form part of a planned Aboriginal section of the museum (Ryan 1974: 9). According to Ryan (1974: 11) there was little scientific analysis of Truganini's skeleton in all the years that it had been available for research.

In the late 1960s an Aboriginal law student, Harry Penrith (who later took the name of his great grandfather, Burnum Burnum) began a long campaign to have Truganini's skeleton removed from what was now the Tasmanian Museum and Art Gallery and be accorded appropriate funerary rites. Penrith wrote to the Trustees and the Director reasoning that the retention of her skeleton in their institution was not only against Truganini's wishes and the traditions and beliefs of her kin, but represented the continuing European oppression of Aboriginal people. Although recognising the importance of scientific research, he argued that the bones of 'Queen Truganini' had been available for analysis for long enough and questioned whether 'in the wildest flights of imagination' the bones of an English monarch would be allowed to 'lie in a room of the British Museum marked "for the genuinely scientifically curious only"' (*Origin* 1970, 2 (7): 8). To reinforce his argument Penrith organised a demonstration outside the Museum on 8 May 1970, the ninety-fourth anniversary of Truganini's death. Although these initial efforts were unsuccessful, the next four years witnessed increasing interest from the media and continuing pressure on the museum from Aboriginal groups such as the Aboriginal Information Centre (an organisation later to be replaced by the Tasmanian Aboriginal Centre (TAC)) which demanded her remains for her descendants (see Ryan 1974: 9-10; Cove 1995: 146-50).

In September 1974, following a letter from the Director of the Tasmanian Museum to the Principal of the Australian Institute of Aboriginal Studies (AIAS) which proposed that Truganini's skeleton be housed in a 'mausoleum' accessible to scientists, the issue of Truganini's remains was discussed at length by the Institute's Prehistory Advisory Committee, comprising many leading archaeologists in Australia at that time. Acting on recommendations from this committee, the Institute's Council instructed its Principal to inform the Director of the Tasmanian Museum that AIAS believed Truganini's skeleton 'should be disposed of immediately in accordance with her own wishes or those of her descendants' (Minutes of Council 11 October 1974-12 November 1974, HL A928/14.2). Demonstrating a significant change in attitude towards Aboriginal skeletal remains, the Institute's decision was a reversal of its stance of only a few years previously, and in many cases it was the same scientists who had revised their opinions (Ellis 1981: 159; Hubert 1989: 150). Although the debate surrounding Truganini's remains had prompted considerable, but inconclusive, discussion by the Institute's Prehistory Advisory Committee about the 'digging of bones in general' (Minutes 9 September 1974, HL A928/14.1), the Principal made it clear that Truganini's skeleton was an exceptional case and that, by implication, the Institute was not necessarily committing itself to supporting the blanket return of all Aboriginal remains (see Ucko 1975: 7).

In response to continuing pressure from the Tasmanian Aboriginal community and the Commonwealth Government, and in accordance with advice from AIAS, the Tasmanian Cabinet overruled the objections of the museum. Following an amendment to the Tasmanian Museum Act (1950), possession of Truganini's remains was transferred to the Crown in order that they should be 'decently interred' (Tasmanian Museum Act 1974 5A(3)). In 1976 the Government arranged for Truganini's remains to be cremated and on 1 May the State Secretary of the Aboriginal Information Service, Roy Nichols, in the presence of the Acting Premier, government officials and twenty-one representatives of the Tasmanian Aboriginal community, scattered Truganini's ashes in the D'Entrecasteaux Channel. In a tribute to Truganini at the cremation ceremony, Rosalind Langford, the former Secretary of the Aboriginal Information Service in Tasmania, addressed the participants and was reported to have talked, amongst other things, of how 'the degrading of [Truganini's] body has brought the Aboriginal race together for one cause – to have her rest in peace' (*Aboriginal News* 1976, 3 (2): 8).

The return of Truganini's remains demonstrated that by the mid-1970s, some physical anthropologists and archaeologists were beginning to revise their views about the reburial of named individuals, and politicians were signalling their support of Aboriginal demands and their readiness to pass relevant legislation if necessary.

The Crowther Collection

The next major step in the development of the reburial issue within Australia was the campaign fought by Tasmanian Aborigines for the return of the Crowther Collection. In 1909, William Crowther (grandson of W.L.H. Crowther, who had removed the skull of William Lanne in 1869), accompanied by other medical students, had dug up a number of graves in the Christian cemetery at Oyster Cove, a settlement on the D'Entrecasteaux Channel which, from 1847 to 1868, had been the final home for many of the 'last' Tasmanian Aborigines (Ryan 1981: 182-221). Crowther bequeathed these remains to the Tasmanian Museum and Art

Gallery which, after housing them for some years, officially received them in 1963 (Clark 1983: 18).

The Tasmanian Aboriginal Centre (TAC), an organisation which would also play a leading role in later national and international campaigns for the return of Tasmanian, and other, Australian indigenous human remains (see TAC 2001), became aware of the existence of the Crowther Collection in the early 1980s. Incensed that the museum had not previously informed Tasmanian people of these remains, especially considering the sentiments publicly expressed by them at the time of Truganini's cremation (*Sunday Evening Mercury* 29 May 1982; Langford 1980: 2-3), TAC asked that the collection be returned to the community for cremation at Oyster Cove. As one of the campaigners later explained to the *Hobart Mercury* (17 April 1984), only then would the spirits of the dead be finally put to rest and the responsibilities of their descendants fulfilled.

Initial attempts in 1982 by TAC to persuade the museum to return the Crowther Collection failed and approaches to the newly elected Liberal government in Tasmania were equally unsuccessful. In September 1982, TAC filed criminal and civil complaints against the museum, but these were dismissed by a Hobart Court (see Clark 1983: 18). The museum continued to argue that the collection must be retained for scientific purposes, but indicated that although it was not willing to relinquish control over the remains, it was prepared to share responsibility for them with Aboriginal people. This offer was rejected with derision by Langford (*Hobart Mercury* 11 August 1982), who called on the Church and all Tasmanians to back TAC's requests. Significantly, TAC had the support of the Australian Archaeological Association (AAA) which, at its general meeting in Hobart in 1982, adopted the following motion:

> The Australian Archaeological Association strongly urges the Tasmanian Government to hand over unconditionally to the Aboriginal people the collection of human remains known as the Crowther Collection, to be disposed of as they see fit. The Association is of the opinion that ethical considerations of the manner in which the collection was obtained far outweigh any potential scientific value (in Meehan 1984: 124-5).

At the beginning of 1984, faced with continuing pressure from Tasmanian Aborigines, who by now had gained the support of the Church and many non-Aboriginal people (Errey to the Editor, *Canberra Times* 1 February 1984; *Launceston Examiner* 18 October 1982), the State Government agreed to legislate for the return of the Crowther Collection. However, the Government was to be responsible for both the cremation (in a municipal crematorium) and the subsequent disposal of the ashes, as it had been for Truganini's remains. This course of action was rejected by TAC who insisted that the bones must be accorded a traditional funerary ritual and be cremated at Oyster Cove. Eventually, after extensive lobbying, the Tasmanian Government backed down and, having surveyed Tasmanian Aboriginal opinion, agreed that the remains should be handed over to representatives of the Tasmanian Aboriginal community (*Hobart Mercury* 18 July 1984; Cove 1995: 156-9). By August 1984 the Tasmanian Government had also agreed to return remaining Tasmanian Aboriginal skeletal remains in both the Tasmanian Museum and Art Gallery in Hobart and the Queen Victoria Museum in Launceston (*Hobart Mercury* 10 August 1984).

In May 1985, the Crowther Collection was finally cremated at Oyster Cove by members of the Tasmanian Aboriginal community. The Chairperson of the Tasmanian Council of Aboriginal Organisations commented that, for the first time in years, the community had been able to put the spirits of their ancestors to rest (*Hobart Mercury* 8 May 1985). The rest of the Tasmanian human remains housed in the Tasmanian Museum and Art Gallery were returned to the Tasmanian Aboriginal community in 1988 and have since been cremated. The Queen Victoria Museum in Launceston returned its collection of Tasmanian Aboriginal skeletal remains in 1985 and 1988 (Clark 1990).

The pressure required to persuade the Tasmanian Government to allow Tasmanian Aborigines to receive the Crowther Collection unconditionally shows how difficult relinquishing control of such items could be, and how central they were to the political relationship between these two parties at that time. By returning remains in this way, the Government had to recognise the Tasmanian Aboriginal community at a time when it was fighting against admitting their very existence (and see Cove 1995). For archaeologists, their support of the Tasmanian Aboriginal community demonstrated that, almost a decade after the cremation of Truganini's remains, the bones of individuals obtained in 'unethical circumstances' had been added to the list of those that this discipline would agree to returning. However, the fact that the Australian archaeological community would not contest ownership of some Aboriginal remains did not mean that they unanimously agreed to the reburial of all of them. The decision to return *all* Tasmanian Aboriginal remains in the collections of the Tasmanian Museum and the Queen Victoria Museum was heavily criticised. The Australian Archaeological Association expressed its concern to the Tasmanian Minister for Education and the Arts (Meehan to Beswick 13 August 1984 in Meehan 1984: 134). The *Bulletin* (4 September 1984), a magazine which consistently opposed the reburial campaign throughout the 1980s and early 1990s, contended that 'bone rights have apparently become a substitute for land rights' and quoted eminent Australian archaeologists in condemning the Tasmanian Government's decision. Arguing for the 'tremendous international scientific significance' of human remains such as those discovered at Eagle Hawk Neck and Mount Cameron West, the *Bulletin* reported that scientists believed such ancient material had little connection to the modern indigenous population of Tasmania, which was 'overwhelmingly of mixed race'. As it had been for more recent remains, the issue of present day Tasmanian Aboriginality was a primary reason for invalidating requests for the return of ancient remains. It would be repeated, and rejected, many times in the future.

7

Fossils and ancestors

In the mid-1980s reburial developments in Australia began to attract more attention overseas as archaeologists became increasingly concerned at the potential international implications of the success of indigenous Australian requests. Thus, despite the return of a significant number of human remains to Aboriginal communities in the previous decade, it was not until the mid-1980s that the debate surrounding reburial and the scientific use of Aboriginal human remains escalated to become a major international issue. Scientists' assumptions about scientific authority, ethical practice and the nature of their disciplines' relationship with indigenous peoples were to be challenged again and again over the subsequent decade, and continue to be in many countries today.

In Australia, campaigns for the return of Truganini's remains and the Crowther Collection had shown that Aboriginal concerns were beginning to be placed before those of archaeologists who opposed repatriation. In the second half of the 1980s, changes in Victorian legislation and the campaigns for the return of the Murray Black Collection and the Kow Swamp fossils continued the trend towards recognition that Aboriginal people had pre-eminent rights to determine the future of all Aboriginal human remains. By the late 1980s, the unconditional return of ancient remains to one community in New South Wales, and their decision to place these remains in a 'Keeping Place', illustrated that even for the most contentious remains, a compromise between archaeologists and indigenous groups was possible.

Victorian legislation and the Murray Black Collection

In 1984, Alan Thorne of the Australian National University was preparing to take fossil Australian remains housed at the Museum of Victoria to the 'Ancestors' conference in New York (*Melbourne Age* 6 April 1984, 12 April 1984). Primarily to stop this from happening, Jim Berg, then head of the Aboriginal Legal Service in Victoria and an Inspector under the Victorian Archaeological and Aboriginal Relics Preservation Act (1972), obtained a Supreme Court injunction against the museum which required that it take steps to recall all Aboriginal human remains currently on loan and to cease lending any relic without Ministerial approval (*Melbourne Herald* 17 April 1984). Thorne went to New York without the remains. A month later, reportedly in response to its inability to prosecute the perpetrators of an auction of Aboriginal artefacts the year before (*Melbourne Age* 14 September 1984), the Victorian Government amended the 1972 Preservation Act, making it an offence to hold Aboriginal skeletal remains unless written consent had been obtained from the Secretary for Planning and Environment. In so doing, the Victorian Government asserted its authority over Aboriginal remains in the State, and took control away from the institutions that had housed them for so many years.

Within two days of the amendment, Berg had approached the University of Melbourne about its holdings of Aboriginal skeletal remains. The University's Department of Anatomy housed over eight hundred remains, most of which had been collected by George Murray Black between 1931 and 1951 from Aboriginal cemeteries along the Murray River. Black had initially donated remains to the Institute of Anatomy in Canberra, whose collections became the responsibility of the National Museum of Australia in 1982. After 1939, he began to send Aboriginal bones to the University of Melbourne instead, including the late Pleistocene remains of some seventy individuals discovered at Coobool Creek, described as 'one of the most important collections of this type in the world' because they formed a representative sample of an ancient population.[1]

Berg obtained a Supreme Court injunction which impounded the University's collection. When the Vice-Chancellor, as now required by the new legislation, attempted to obtain the consent of the Secretary for Planning and Environment to house the remains, his request was refused. The Supreme Court then ordered the University to transfer its collection to the Museum of Victoria and Berg announced that he hoped that the entire collection, and other remains housed in the museum, would be returned to the appropriate Aboriginal communities for redisposition (*Melbourne Age* 19 June 1984). As Berg was later reported to have said:

> the desecration of burial sites and the locking away in museums of our ancestral remains has shown a complete lack of respect for the Aboriginal community ... it causes us great anxiety and stress (in Lewin 1984: 393).

Although there was no reaction to Berg's announcement from the Victorian Government, it provoked condemnation from scientists in Australia and overseas who argued that many of the remains, in particular the fossils, were so unique and of such international scientific importance that they must be preserved for future generations of scholars, both Aboriginal and non-Aboriginal (e.g. Brown to Jones 29 June 1984 reproduced in Meehan 1984: 139). The Victorian Opposition spokesman for Planning and the Environment warned the Government to be cautious, reportedly supplying his opposite number with correspondence from Australian and overseas scholars which stressed the scientific importance of the remains. There was a general rejection of Aboriginal claims to ancient remains, and thus the beliefs on which they were founded; the opposition spokesman echoed the opinion of many scientists by reportedly stating that, 'we are certainly aware of the significance Aboriginals attach to skeletal remains, particularly when they are of recent times. But there can be very little emotional attachment to remains which are up to 13,000 years old' (*The Herald* 23 July 1984). As will be discussed in Chapter 10, how fossil remains were perceived in western cultural beliefs therefore played a significant role in opposition to their return.

Academic organisations also showed their apprehension. The Australian Archaeological Association and the Australian Vice-Chancellor's Committee both expressed deep concern that the Victorian collections might be lost to science (Meehan 1984; *Canberra ANU Reporter* 12 October 1984). As well as its concern for the loss of scientific material, the AAA appears to have been particularly distressed at how antagonistic and destructive the controversy itself was becoming. 'Dismayed ... by the negative and socially divisive nature' (Meehan 1984: 124) of media reports, and seeking to address and defuse the situation, the AAA formed a small sub-committee which hastily prepared a document outlining the scientific and heritage value of all collections of Aboriginal human remains, and those housed in Victoria in particular (Meehan 1984: 122). This document was sent to the Victorian Minister for Planning and Environment, with copies to the Victorian Aboriginal Legal Service and the Tasmanian Government, accompanied by a covering letter from the then President of the AAA (see Meehan 1984: 127). The letter showed that archaeologists had changed their views since the return of Truganini's remains, although the blanket return of all remains was still opposed. It also demonstrated that the AAA was not going to support the vilification of Aboriginal concerns voiced by some archaeologists:

1. The AAA congratulates the Victorian Government for the initiatives it has taken to accommodate Aboriginal requests to exercise significant control of Aboriginal skeletal material in the State of Victoria.
2. The AAA supports the disposal of Aboriginal skeletal remains of known individuals according to the wishes of the deceased, where known, and if not, by being transferred to the appropriate Aboriginal community to dispose of as they see fit.
3. The AAA believes that all other Aboriginal skeletal remains are of scientific importance and should not be destroyed by being reburied or cremated.
4. The AAA believes that the Aboriginal community and the archaeological profession share a common concern to protect and preserve prehistoric sites and material of significance.
5. The AAA believes that it is possible for Aborigines and archaeologists to reach a compromise about what should happen to Aboriginal skeletal remains. The employment and training of Aborigines as museum curators, the construction of Aboriginal Keeping Places and joint projects

carried out by Aborigines and archaeologists are examples of such compromises.

6. The AAA urges the Victorian Government to instigate a programme enabling the construction of Aboriginal Keeping Places and the training of Aboriginal people in the skills necessary for employment in these Keeping Places as well as in the State's museums.

Although the AAA's approach to the Minister questioned neither the validity of Aboriginal demands nor the Victorian Government's motive for agreeing to them, others attacked both, reflecting not only a fear for the future of archaeology and physical anthropology, but also a sense of disbelief that Aboriginal claims should be accorded greater consideration than those of scientists. The notion of absolute scientific authority in these matters continued to be used to justify the retention of remains despite the beliefs of indigenous groups – echoing the earlier use of scientific justification by collectors who had procured remains in the nineteenth century. In particular, some argued that Aboriginal demands for the return of ancestral remains had no basis in 'traditional' beliefs, and that the destruction of the Victorian collections was, for both the Aboriginal community and the State Government, motivated for political reasons only and stood condemned on this basis: 'sacrifice of this material in the search for short term power or political expediency is criminal and should be considered an offence against all mankind' (Brown to Jones 29 June 1984, reproduced in Meehan 1984: 139; and see K. Kennedy, Cornell University, to the Editor, *The Bulletin* 9 October 1984).

The Victorian Government was accused of using the collections to make token gestures of atonement for its past mistreatment of Aborigines (Lewin 1984), and merely providing them with a 'sop' of power without addressing the real reasons for the 'powerlessness and disadvantage of the majority of Aborigines'.[2] Some scientists branded the new legislation 'racist' because, they argued, only indigenous Australians could now study certain aspects of Victorian prehistory (e.g. Brown to Jones 29 May 1984, reproduced in Meehan 1984: 139; *Armidale Express* 27 August 1984). Overseas, the legislation was heralded as the extinction of archaeology and physical anthropology in Australia (e.g. Lewin 1984) and reburial was likened to book-burning (e.g. Kennedy to the Editor, *The Bulletin* 9 October 1984).

The media played a large part in fanning the flames of the controversy, representing it as a polarised conflict between Aborigines and scientists. At this time, and with some exceptions (e.g. *National Times* 20 September 1984), the media only represented the opinions of those scientists who opposed repatriation (e.g. *The Australian* 8 August 1984; *Melbourne Herald* 16 August 1984; and see the *Melbourne Age* 16 June 1989). Demonstrating how high emotions were running in the press about this issue, and how potentially damaging some articles could be, the Victorian Minister for Planning and the Environment accused *The Bulletin* of publishing an article that would 'only succeed in adding to the climate of fear being created in the community about anything to do with Aborigines and their rights' (Walker to the Editor, *The Bulletin* 11 September 1984). An editorial in the *Armidale Express* (27 July 1984), later criticised for its 'social irresponsibility' (Creamer to the Editor, *Armidale Express* 10 August 1984), demonstrated how extreme were the views of those who opposed the new legislation:

> It seems ridiculous that this prehistory could be reburied under some archaic law that will prevent the world from gaining valuable information on the world and its peoples thousands of years ago. Any government, whether in Australia or in some suppressive dictatorship, has no right to stand in the way of the search for knowledge ... [the Minister for Science and Technology] must intervene in such a vital issue. No one, irrespective of race, has the right to stand in the way of prehistory and archaeological research. It will be a criminal act against mankind to confiscate archaeological remains and rebury them. Such items should be preserved for all to see, particularly our future generations. It seems logical that political expediency is the basis of this treacherous legislation proposal. Everyone should be aware of the proposals and condemn the government on its ignorance towards mankind.

Responding to what seemed an escalating crisis, in May 1984 the Museum of Victoria placed a moratorium on any scientific research being carried out on its holdings of Aboriginal human remains and ten months later the National Museum of Australia followed suit (Webb 1987b: 1). In the subsequent year TAC successfully negotiated for the return of Tasmanian remains from the Museum of Victoria and collected them two years later (*Hobart Mercury* 24 May 1985; *Melbourne Age* 8 April 1987). In November 1985 the Museum of Victoria returned fragments and other pieces of unprovenanced Aboriginal bones to members of the Victorian Aboriginal community. Hundreds of Aboriginal people watched while the remains, wrapped in bark, were reburied in a traditional manner in a Melbourne park.

Although there were exceptions, such as the work of Colin Pardoe at AIATSIS who undertook research on skeletal remains under conditions negotiated through consultation with local communities (Pardoe 1991, 1992), by the end of 1985 the reburial issue had caused considerable antagonism between various Aboriginal groups and many archaeologists and physical anthropologists. In December, again concerned at these divisions and attempting to open an avenue of communication and discussion, the Skeletal Sub-Committee of the AAA instigated a liaison programme in which Steven Webb, a physical anthropologist, was appointed to consult with Aboriginal communities, particularly those with a direct interest in the Murray Black Collection:

the scientific community feared the permanent loss of unique data – a loss which would not only affect the present generation but those, both black and white, in the future. The consultation, therefore, focused on explaining the value of preserving such remains. Scientific value had to be emphasised, together with the long term benefits to Aborigines of such study (Webb 1987a: 293).

Webb's report (1987b) is an exceptional document as it offers a unique insight into an archaeologist's experience of discussing human remains with Aboriginal groups at the height of the reburial issue in Australia. It also provides an insight into indigenous attitudes at the community level towards the issue at this time.

Webb found that communities were highly suspicious of archaeologists and physical anthropologists, the result of an almost complete lack of information about their work from scientists who had taken remains in the past. He found that communities believed researchers to have little respect for Aboriginal people, and many commented that his own consultancy was motivated only by a potential loss of data (and livelihood), rather than any interest in really communicating with Aboriginal people. According to Webb, this lack of communication had led scientists to react only to the most extreme views of some Aborigines that were broadcast in the press, and not to communicate with the broad range of Aboriginal people in whose areas they worked. Some communities said simply 'when are you people going to stop studying us?' (1987a: 294).

The lack of communication between scientists and Aboriginal communities was demonstrated by the surprise and shock shown by indigenous Australians at the sheer numbers of remains in museums, how they had been acquired and the fact that this had been allowed in the first place. People believed that remains had been taken without consultation or approval and kept in a secretive manner – a deduction that Webb could not refute. Communities pointed out the double standards in operation emphasising that 'had white cemeteries been desecrated, the perpetrators would have been prosecuted by the full weight of the law' (1987a: 294).

Some Aboriginal people 'felt a degree of disgust for this type of research, and the people who carried it out, because it dealt and interfered with the dead'. Others commented that even if white scientists also studied their own dead, they should not treat other people's ancestors' remains with the same disrespect. Little distinction was made between those who studied the remains in the 1980s, and those who had removed and analysed them in the past. Many of those whom Webb consulted were particularly angry at the way in which some scientists had used the media to promote their viewpoint, and had gathered support from academics overseas. The failure of anthropologists to support reburial claims, something which had genuinely surprised many Aboriginal people, was considered to have shown them in 'their true colours'.

During the consultancy, Webb's own attitude towards Aboriginal claims began to change:

> After listening to why people did not want research to continue, I could find no scientific argument to balance or equate with their moral one. It is difficult to argue against the rights of any group of people to choose what should and should not happen to their skeletal remains. I found myself increasingly sympathetic to their point of view. A biological anthropologist finds this was difficult to accept, because it means, in effect, accepting destruction of the remains by reburial if Aboriginal people wished it. I could not agree with any destruction by reburial, but I understood why they might wish to carry out the act (Webb 1987a: 293).

Although Webb acknowledged that the reburial issue was sometimes used as a political platform, he rejected the common assertion that the issue was solely political in nature.

Webb (1987a: 295) had seen that for the Aboriginal people he consulted, the reburial issue represented a 'moral stance stemming from a genuine desire to protect their dead'. However, despite the anger and concern which he encountered, Webb also met with many people who had a strong interest in gaining knowledge about the past, and were in general supportive of archaeological research. He was convinced that many Aboriginal people were willing to discuss compromises regarding the future of skeletal collections. Primarily, communities wanted to be consulted about research, have control over the future of their ancestors' remains, have communication with the potential researchers and be involved in future projects (Webb 1987a: 295).

Webb concluded that the reburial issue could be overcome only with continued and considerable discussion between scientists and Aborigines. Archaeologists and anthropologists, already forced to 're-evaluate the ethics and philosophy of the study of recent skeletal populations' (Webb 1987a: 296), would have to understand (and presumably respect) differences in cultural attitudes towards research on human remains of all ages. By the time of Webb's consultancy there were already signs that such changes were beginning to occur. Pardoe's continuing work illustrated how research on Aboriginal remains could proceed with recognition of Aboriginal ownership and extensive community consultation (see Pardoe 1991: 16-17). Changes were occurring in the museum world also: in 1985 the Department of Anatomy at the University of Queensland agreed to return to the Kombumerri people both post- and pre-contact skeletal remains which had been excavated from the Aboriginal cemetery at Broadbeach in the 1960s. The Kombumerri people were successful in their claim because they could demonstrate their descent from those who had been buried at Broadbeach from the eighth to the mid-nineteenth century (Hall 1986: 1-2). In 1988, these remains were placed in baskets and reinterred on land which the Kombumerri had obtained from the local City Council near the site of the 1960s excavation (Aird 2002: 304-5).

Following continued pressure from Aboriginal groups, in 1989 the Museum of Victoria began to hand over the Murray Black Collection to communities. By this time the National Museum of Australia, which had given its holdings of Tasmanian remains to TAC in 1986 (*Launceston Examiner* 30 July 1986), had also started to give back its section of the Murray Black Collection (Wettenhall 1989: 18). The latter half of the 1980s also witnessed a number of returns from other Australian museums. For example, in 1989 the South Australian Museum gave its collection of Tasmanian remains to Tasmanian representatives (*Adelaide Advertiser* 10 May 1989) and in 1990 the Queensland Museum agreed to return remains taken from the St George area.

Kow Swamp

By the end of the 1980s, most Australian museums had adopted policies which responded positively to Aboriginal requests for the return of the remains of named or known individuals, those who had died post-contact, those whose line of descent to a modern community could be demonstrated or those which had been obtained in 'unethical' circumstances (for a list of relevant museum policies see *Australian Archaeology* 1990 31: 52-66). However, with perhaps the exception of the Australian Museum in Sydney, holding institutions rarely committed, or had access to, the resources required to identify and return the 'eligible' parts of their collections. Furthermore, museums were still opposed to the unconditional return of fossil remains, the future of which continued to be a hotly debated issue. Thus, in 1990, when the Victorian Government announced that it would hand over the Kow Swamp fossils to the indigenous people of Echuca, prominent archaeologists, both in Australia and overseas, condemned this decision. The view that fossils could be legitimately claimed as ancestors of living populations was roundly rejected as either ignorance or political manipulation.

The Kow Swamp fossils are the remains of some forty individuals dated to between 9,000 and 15,000 BP. Some of the fossils had been found by Alan Thorne in store at the Museum of Victoria in 1967 and the rest were uncovered during his later excavations at Kow Swamp in northern Victoria between 1968 and 1972. The fossils represented the world's largest collection of late Pleistocene/early Holocene human remains from a single site, and contributed information to the debate about human evolution in Australia (Thorne 1971; Thorne and Macumber 1972).

Faced with the return of the Kow Swamp remains, archaeologists once more heralded reburial as the 'death' of archaeology (e.g. Mulvaney 1991: 12, Piggott to the Editor, *The Australian* 9 August 1990). Despite indigenous beliefs to the contrary (and see Yunupingu to the Editor, *The Times*

10 September 1990), many archaeologists continued to argue that there was a clear difference between recent bones and fossils, and that the international significance of the latter should take precedence over Aboriginal concerns. As Les Hiatt, a past President of the Australian Institute of Aboriginal Studies, wrote to the Editor of *The Australian* (2 August 1990), he applauded the return of recent remains but human fossil material was 'another matter entirely' and was:

> surely the heritage of all humankind. It would be ludicrous to suggest that remains of Homo sapiens neanderthalensis should be returned to the people of Düsseldorf for ritual burial or destruction. If such a proposal was made, we would quickly dismiss it as the product of misplaced sentimentalism, philistinism or political opportunism.

With very few exceptions (e.g. *Canberra Times* 8 September 1990), the media supported the opinions of those who opposed reburial (e.g. *The Times* 6 August 1990; *The Bulletin* 7 August 1990). *The Australian* (29 July 1990), for example, informed the public that, 'Australia is poised to sanction the destruction of a priceless, irreplaceable piece of its national heritage, an enormous part of our human past'. However, demonstrating that there had been some changes since 1984, some archaeologists were now publicly sympathetic to indigenous opinion and highly critical of the views expressed by their colleagues (see O'Brien and Tompkins to the Editor, *The Australian* 5 August 1990; McBryde to the Editor, *Melbourne Age* 1 September 1990; and see Bowdler 1992). Thus the Professor of Archaeology at the University of Western Australia wrote to the editor of *The Australian* (3 August 1990) disassociating herself from the views expressed in the paper a few days before, noting that:

> If archaeologists do indeed 'face refusal to excavate any more Aboriginal sites' ... it will be because of the attitudes reported in your front page article which sees those sites as part of the general Australian heritage before it recognizes them as Aboriginal sites.

From July 1990 a few eminent Australian archaeologists became involved in what they termed a 'vain public and behind-the-scenes campaign to save the [Kow Swamp] collection' (Mulvaney 1991: 12), and attempted to approach unresponsive Ministers to explain the scientific viewpoint. Aware that it was unlikely that the remains would ever be retained in a museum environment, these scientists unsuccessfully sought the 'prudent compromise' of a Keeping Place – 'a ritual centre under absolute community custodianship' – which would have 'kept future options open and did not place the burden of reaching a final solution upon a small community' (Mulvaney 1991: 19). In 1991 the Kow Swamp remains were returned to the Echuca Aboriginal community, demonstrating that scientists' claims to fossil remains were no longer perceived as pre-eminent by those in government (for an analysis of the return of the Kow Swamp remains see Lahn 1996). Approaching the Kow Swamp issue from a different angle, Isobel McBryde (Department of Prehistory and Anthropology, Australian National University) wrote of her discussions with members of the Echuca community about the possibility of a Keeping Place, that she had 'appreciated the sincerity in their considered response that to them reburial seemed the culturally appropriate course of action', noting that:

> We should be sensitive to the genuine concerns of Aboriginal people for knowledge of their past and for involvement in the custodianship of their cultural heritage. We should also be ready to accept that for local communities archaeological sites and collections may hold values and significance that differ from, or are additional to, those accorded them on scientific criteria (McBryde to the Editor, *Melbourne Age*, 1 September 1990).

The concept of Keeping Places for the storage of Aboriginal human remains had been debated since at least the mid-1970s (see Webb 1987b, Cove 1995: 155) and had been established for the storage of secret/sacred (and other) objects within various communities since at least the 1980s (see Atkinson 1985; Duroux 1985; Sampson 1988). Since developing its Draft Policy Statement on Aboriginal Human Remains (1988) AIATSIS suggested Keeping Places (either at museums or at the original burial site) as a possible option (of many) that might be considered for the future management of Aboriginal human remains. Notwithstanding its recognition that 'the potential significance of [human remains] to Aborigines has been neglected in the past ... [and] is of particular present relevance because of the historical and political situation of Aborigines', the Institute recommended that the ideal management strategy for such material is that which 'pays due regard to the multi-faceted value of the material and attempts to provide for the proper acknowledgement of all these values, and provision for their conservation'. Thus, the Institute considered that:

> Acknowledgement of Aboriginal custodianship leads to the conclusion that the provision of Keeping Places is the most effective way of articulating this custodianship, while allowing for, and encouraging, appropriate research by Black and White scholars (Aboriginal Human Remains: Draft Policy Statement 1988).

Mungo Woman

Although a Keeping Place was not favoured by the Aboriginal community at Echuca, such an arrangement was established for the storage of 'Mungo Woman' – probably the most famous Late Pleistocene remains in Australia – when they were returned to the local community by Alan Thorne on 11 January 1992. The remains of Mungo Woman (or Mungo I), the oldest known cremation in the world, had been discovered in 1968 at Lake Mungo in the Willandra Lakes, New South Wales. Of exceptional scientific importance (see Bowler *et al.* 1970; 1972), these remains are also of immense spiritual significance to the local and national Aboriginal community. Along with the remains of nearly a hundred and fifty other individuals excavated in the surrounding area, Mungo Woman had been kept initially in the Department of Anatomy at the University of Sydney and subsequently in the Department of Prehistory at the Australian National University in Canberra.

After the return of the Kow Swamp remains, Thorne had become aware of increasing pressure to address the issue of the future of the remains excavated at Lake Mungo. Aware not only of the great significance of Mungo Woman to Aboriginal people but also that the return of her remains might facilitate an atmosphere of trust in which future archaeological research in the Willandra Lakes could be possible, Thorne offered unconditionally to return her remains.

Acknowledging the scientific value of her remains, the local community decided that Mungo Woman should be kept in a Keeping Place (e.g. *Sydney Morning Herald* 6 August 1991). As hoped for by Thorne, and stated repeatedly by those who participated in the handover ceremony, the return of Mungo Woman and the community's historic decision to use a Keeping Place were believed to symbolise a new, co-operative relationship between Aboriginal people and the archaeological profession (e.g. Thorne to the Aboriginal Tribal People of Western New South Wales 11 November 1991; *Melbourne Age* 13 January 1992). The media coverage of the event reflected this new, positive, attitude:

> it is precisely through the study of these ancient remains that we are able to know objectively what the Aboriginal people have always said – that they have been in this land for a very long time. The decision by archaeologists at the Australian National University to give Mungo Woman back is a sign that reconciliation, and negotiation, between Aboriginal beliefs and science may be possible (*Melbourne Age* 18 January 1992).

The co-operative relationship is demonstrated by recent work on the extraction of DNA from other fossilised remains from Lake Mungo in the same collection at the Australian National University which acknowledges the support of the local community (Adcock *et al.* 2001).

In the 1990s many other Aboriginal communities have obtained their ancestors' remains from Australian museums. For example, in 1991 the Australian Museum in Sydney and the Queensland Museum in Brisbane returned remains to the Darambul people near Rockhampton. In 1992 the Australian Museum returned remains to Gunganjii people at Yarrabah in North Queensland, and the Queensland Museum returned remains to the Aboriginal community in Springsure (see Aird 2002). In 1993, the Australian Museum and the Queensland Museum again collaborated and returned remains taken from the Keppel Island group to the Woppaburra people. Sydney University's Macleay Museum has returned seven sets of remains, the latest in June 2001 to Bunuba people in the Kimberley, and these have now been interred in Bunuba country. Aboriginal organisations such as FAIRA, TAC and the New South Wales Aboriginal Land Council continue to work to facilitate the repatriation of remains to Queensland, Tasmania and New South Wales communities respectively. Both FAIRA and TAC also continue to negotiate for the return of indigenous Australian human remains from overseas institutions. FAIRA's Ancestral Remains Project, funded by ATSIC, has increased the available information about holdings of Australian indigenous human remains in Australian and European museums (Ormond Parker 1997a).

Developments in relevant legislation and policy

In December 1990 discussions took place at the AAA annual conference in Townsville about the adoption of a Code of Ethics for Australian archaeologists involved in studying and managing Aboriginal heritage. Although based upon the Code of Ethics formulated by the World Archaeological Congress two months previously, the AAA Code – finally adopted in 1991 – contains slight alterations suggested by participants at the 1990 AAA conference (see Davidson 1991: 64).

With the exception of the initial resistance of the Tasmanian Government to returning the Crowther Collection, Australian Governments have not opposed Aboriginal demands for the right to determine the future of Aboriginal human remains, and have frequently amended or developed legislation to force museums to respect Aboriginal wishes. The Federal Aboriginal and Torres Strait Islander Heritage Protection Act (1984), for example, enables the 'satisfactory disposal of remains held contrary to expressed Aboriginal wishes' by empowering the Minister for Aboriginal Affairs to order the delivery of Aboriginal human remains to himself or Aboriginal people 'entitled to them, and willing to accept responsibility for them, in accordance with Aboriginal tradition' (*A Guide to How the Act Works* 1984: 13).

In more recent years there have been various attempts by the Australian Government to develop a national policy on the return of cultural material from Australia and overseas (and see Fforde and Ormond Parker 2001). In October 1993 the Australian Aboriginal Affairs Council (AAAC), comprising the Federal Minister for Aboriginal Affairs and his State and Territory counterparts, adopted a set of National Principles which recognised indigenous rights of ownership over Aboriginal cultural property (including human remains) housed in museums and other holding institutions, and asserted the pre-eminent role of Aboriginal people in the recovery of Aboriginal cultural property. However, these Principles do not commit the Commonwealth, State or

Territory Governments to allocating the required funding. By contrast, the Aboriginal and Torres Strait Islander Commission's (ATSIC's) Policy on Protection and Return of Significant Cultural Property (1993, and endorsed by the ATSIC commissioners in April 1998), which it adopted less than a month after the National Principles had been approved by the AAAC, is more binding, committing ATSIC not only to provide financial resources for research to locate and provenance sensitive cultural material and to inform relevant communities accordingly, but to carry 'primary financial responsibility for the identification, negotiation and return of significant cultural property held overseas'.

From the early 1970s, the reburial issue forced Australian museums to develop individual policies towards their holdings of Aboriginal human remains. However, in December 1993, the Council of Australian Museum Associations (now Museums Australia) adopted principles and policies to direct the future management of Aboriginal and Torres Strait Islander cultural material on a national scale. The policy states that a museum's role is custodial, and that decisions regarding the future of collections of human remains are the responsibility of the relevant Aboriginal and Torres Strait Islander community:

> Museums recognise the potential value that human remains may have to the scientific advance of knowledge. Where it is considered that there are valid scientific interests in some remains, claims to that effect must be established to the satisfaction of Aboriginal and Torres Strait Islander people. Age by itself does not establish scientific importance. Before scientific research of any kind is carried out on human remains the relevant community, having been able to consider all appropriate information available to the museum, must give permission for that research. The results of any scientific research must be communicated effectively to that community (*Previous Possessions, New Obligations* 1993: 12).

Giving priority to the wishes and concerns of indigenous Australians, Museums Australia's policy on scientific research demonstrates how far Australian museum attitudes towards Aboriginal human remains had changed since the early 1970s. Nonetheless, this policy has been criticised for its ambiguous approach to Aboriginal ownership and its failure to 'seriously address issues of administration, funding and management of the repatriation of those items covered by the policy' (Ormond-Parker 1997b: 10). Ormond-Parker (1997b: 10) also noted that there are many Australian institutions that house Aboriginal human remains which are not members of Museums Australia and are therefore not bound by this policy.

Apart from the Museums Australia document, and ATSIC's *Policy for the Protection and Return of Significant Cultural Property*, an additional national policy existed which sought to govern the return of ancestral remains. This was the Australian Aboriginal Affairs Council's draft interim policy on the *Return of Aboriginal and Torres Strait Islander*

Cultural Property and Its Return to Aboriginal and Torres Strait Islander Ownership (1998). Also in 1998, a *Strategic Plan for the Return of Indigenous Ancestral Remains* was developed by the Australian Cultural Ministers Council. This plan sought to co-ordinate the repatriation efforts of governments and museums at all levels, although it focused on government-funded museums and did not apply to overseas collections.[3] The plan intended to provide a framework whereby Aboriginal and Torres Strait Islander people could become informed of all ancestral remains and secret/sacred objects from their community held in Commonwealth and State museums around Australia. The main objectives were the identification, where possible, of the origins of ancestral remains held in museums; the notification of all communities who have ancestral remains held in museums; and [to have] repatriation arranged where culturally appropriate and when requested (Fforde and Ormond Parker 2001). In August 2000, the Australian Cultural Ministers Council committed funds over three years to implementing the *Strategic Plan* via the *Return of Indigenous Cultural Property Programme*. Two grant programmes were developed to facilitate arrangements for the return of ancestral remains and secret/sacred objects, where requested: the Community Support Programme, to assist communities with the return of ancestral remains and secret sacred objects, and the Museums Support Programme, to assist museums to identify ancestral remains and secret sacred objects.[4]

8

The repatriation issue in the UK

By the 1980s, demands for the return of Aboriginal human remains were beginning to be heard outside Australia, and particularly in the UK. British institutions had also been approached by Maori and Native Americans to discuss the future of human remains in their collections (Simpson 1994: 31) and towards the end of the decade Aboriginal people were beginning to achieve some success in persuading museums to remove remains from public display or to return them to their homeland.

One of the first campaigns to receive public attention occurred in the early 1980s when the Tasmanian Aboriginal Centre (TAC) asked the University of Edinburgh to return the skull of William Lanne (see below). This approach was unsuccessful, but received sympathetic coverage in the British press. Although it was assumed to be the first time that a request for the repatriation of an indigenous human remain had been made to Edinburgh University, and indeed one of the first to have been faced by any institution in the UK, this was not in fact the case. Edinburgh University had speedily repatriated a skull to Ceylon (Sri Lanka) some thirty-five years previously, demonstrating that indigenous requests for the unconditional return of remains have not always been opposed by those in control of collections.

Keppitipola Nilama

The skull was that of Keppitipola Nilama, the Dissave of Uva, who had been a leader of the 1817 Ceylon rebellion, for which he had been subsequently tried for treason, and beheaded (Brohier 1933). In 1947, Professor Brash of Edinburgh University's Anatomy Department received a letter from the British Colonial Office:

> The Governor of Ceylon has written to say that the Vidyalankhara Students' Association are asking for the return to Ceylon of the skull of Keppitipola Nilama, which is alleged to be at the Museum of the Phrenological Society of Edinburgh.

The letter continues:

> The Ceylon Government can find no record of the removal of the cranium from Ceylon, and think that it was probably the unauthorised act of Dr Henry Marshall, FRSE, an army officer, who was Deputy Inspector of Army

119

Hospitals at the time and was present at the death of Keppitipola. In this connection Dr Marshall himself, in his book 'Ceylon' (published in 1846) records that 'Keppitipola's cranium was presented by the writer to the Museum of the Phrenological Society of Edinburgh'.

I apologise for having to trouble you with this matter but we should be grateful to know if the skull is in the Anatomy Museum and, if so, we should be glad to have your comments on the request of the Students' Association for its return (Webber to Brash 1 July 1947, EADL).

In his response, Brash confirmed that the skull was in the University's collection, and wrote:

There being no doubt about the identification the question is whether we should accede to the request conveyed to you by the Governor of Ceylon. The specimen itself is of no very particular interest except for its place in the Anthropological collection. Presumably there is a political aspect of this request and as Conservator of the Museum I am entirely in your hands. If you think it advisable that the skull should be returned to Ceylon as requested then I shall be very pleased to let you have it in due course (Brash to Webber 3 July 1947, EADL).

After photographs and a report were made of the skull (which concluded that 'the general inference denotes a skull with a rather large proportion of primitive features, suggesting considerable mixture of Veddah blood in the possessor – a not unusual feature in Kandian Sinhalese'), and following a formal request to the Colonial Office from the Governor of Ceylon for the return of the skull for the proposed purpose of placing it in the National Museum in Kandy, Brash dispatched the skull to the Colonial Office. He enclosed the photographs and information about the skull suggesting that these could accompany it to Ceylon (Brash to Armitage Smith 29 October 1947, EADL).

The return of Keppitipola Nilama's skull to Ceylon is the earliest example yet found of the repatriation of indigenous human remains from a UK institution. It illustrates that decisions about repatriation, at least of a named individual, could be made swiftly and easily, and that a blanket refusal to repatriate any human remains because all skeletal material had an enduring scientific significance simply was not the fundamental argument that it would come to be in later decades. In this example, the request for the return of the skull of an historical individual was considered of such importance that it was made through high diplomatic channels, foreshadowing the involvement of government in repatriation issues over forty years later.

In his decision to return the skull of Keppitipola Nilama, Brash deferred to the Colonial Office, acknowledging that the importance of the repatriation, perhaps for UK–Ceylon relations, outweighed any scientific arguments to keep it in Edinburgh. In this early incidence therefore, politics were an openly accepted reason as to why remains should be returned, as opposed to a focus of criticism by many opposed to repatriation in later years. The Governor's proposal to place the skull in the National Museum in Kandy was not a factor in decisions as to whether or not to return it to Ceylon, as it was made after Brash had responded to the Colonial Office indicating his agreement to the request. What is yet unknown is the background to the Vidyalankhara Students' Association's original request for the skull, and whether the Association agreed to its placement within a museum. Today, Keppitipola Nilama's skull is believed to be buried at the base of a pillar erected to commemorate him in a public park in Kandy (see Plate 7), and the story of his decapitation is the subject of at least one popular Sri Lankan song (by Nanda Malini) (personal communication from J. Weerasinghe).

The 1980s and 1990s

Almost forty years later, securing the repatriation of indigenous human remains from UK institutions, even of those of historic named individuals, was not achieved nearly so easily. In 1985, TAC sent Michael Mansell, then a solicitor with the Aboriginal Legal Service, to Europe and the USA in order to gather information about collections of Tasmanian Aboriginal remains, and to negotiate for their return. Mansell's assignment (dubbed the 'Journey of Dignity' (*Melbourne Age* 5 October 1985)) was endorsed by the Tasmanian State Government and arose out of discussions which followed the cremation of the Crowther Collection at Oyster Cove when the Tasmanian Aboriginal community had expressed its concern that Aboriginal human remains were held in overseas institutions. Mansell met with a number of European museums, returning to Tasmania with the belief that a considerable amount of further work would be required if human remains were to be returned even by those museums which appeared sympathetic to his requests. The 'Journey of Dignity' highlighted Aboriginal concerns, attracting media attention within Tasmania and, to a lesser extent, throughout the rest of Australia (e.g. *Hobart Mercury* 9 July 1985, 10 July 1985, 6 August 1985, 23 August 1985; *Launceston Examiner* 31 July 1985, 6 September 1985; *Melbourne Age* 5 October 1985; *Sunday Tasmanian* 27 October 1985).

With a few exceptions, attempts to secure the return of remains from overseas museums ceased during the late 1980s, although it was actually during this time that the first repatriation of Aboriginal human remains from the UK took place. In 1989, three Aboriginal skulls, one articulated post-cranial skeleton and a wooden club from St Thomas's Hospital were transferred to the Australian High Commission, in perhaps the only example of a UK institution returning human remains to Australian authorities without a direct request, but, rather, in acknowledgement of Aboriginal concern. The repatriation of these remains was facilitated by Michael Day, Professor of Anatomy at St Thomas's Hospital and President of the World Archaeological Congress. Day had chaired WAC's discussions leading to the development of the Vermillion Accord (see Chapter 6). These remains were repatriated to Australia and placed in the custody of the National Museum of Australia in Canberra, which, according to Section 21.1.c. of the Aboriginal and Torres Strait Islander Heritage Protection Act 1984, is the only prescribed authority for the safekeeping of Aboriginal remains returned from overseas.

In 1990 Tasmanian Aborigines approached the Royal College of Surgeons, Dublin with a request to return the preserved head of a known Tasmanian man who had died in 1830. Soon afterwards, Mansell and Bob Weatherall of FAIRA came to the UK, where their campaign was the subject of a BBC television documentary. While in the UK, they visited and demonstrated outside a number of institutions to request the return of Aboriginal remains. They also presented a petition to Mrs Thatcher which called for the return of all Aboriginal human remains held in British institutions. Although Mansell and Weatherall returned to Australia empty-handed, shortly afterwards the Royal College of Surgeons, Dublin transferred the preserved head to the Australian Embassy in Dublin, on the understanding that it would be sent to the National Museum of Australia. However, initial plans by ATSIC to freight the head to this museum, from where it would be returned to the originating community, brought heavy criticism from Aboriginal groups who argued that to do so would be disrespectful and inappropriate, and his remains should be accompanied home by an appropriate authority from his own community. A campaign by TAC ensured that the head was collected by Mansell and brought back to Tasmania in March 1990.[1] In June the same year, a small number of Australian remains were returned by Peterborough City Museum, Bradford University and the Pitt Rivers Museum, Oxford. Accompanied back to Australia by indigenous representatives, all of these remains were transferred to other Aboriginal people in Sydney who undertook to deliver them to appropriate communities.

While in England, Mansell had also contacted the Glasgow Art Gallery and Museum to ascertain whether it held any Aboriginal human remains and, if so, whether it would be willing to repatriate them. The museum responded that it had located four Queensland remains – three skull fragments from a cave near Mount Morgan and one skull from near Bowen. After a meeting with Mansell, the Curator of Anthropology discussed the request with her museum colleagues who agreed that the 'views of contemporary descendants concerning the display and disposal of the remains should be respected' (Lovelace 1994: 30). At the Curator's request, the Glasgow City Council agreed to de-accession these remains and, in September 1990, a delegation consisting of FAIRA representative Bob Weatherall, Monty Prior (a Birri Gubba elder and Catholic Deacon), and William Toby (a Gangulu elder and Chaplain) travelled to the UK to collect them. At the official handover, attended by the Australian Consul in Edinburgh and officials of the museum and City Council, Toby conducted a short ceremony for the Mount Morgan remains and presented the museum with a decorated scroll signed by members of the Gangulu community which identified Toby as their representative. This scroll was accessioned into the museum's collection, 'as a material momento and affirmation of the repatriation' (Lovelace 1994: 30).

On return to Australia, Toby reburied the skull fragments on Mount Morgan. More than sixty people attended, and Toby was quoted in the local press as saying:

> The feelings that have been generated by this historical burial will not be known for some years .... The things that have been told to people here today, and the things that they have seen, they will never forget .... In 20 or 30 years time the younger people who were here will be able to look back at the traditional side of the burial – it would have been a learning experience for them (*Rockhampton Morning Bulletin* 12 November 1990).

The skull from Bowen was taken to Townsville by Monty Pryor, who subsequently placed it in the Material Culture Unit, James Cook University, for safekeeping. It remained there until it was reburied in the late 1990s. The early 1990s therefore witnessed a number of UK institutions returning Aboriginal human remains to Australia, although none had large collections of such items, with the exception of the University of Edinburgh.

The University of Edinburgh

Throughout the 1990s, Edinburgh University was the only UK institution with a major collection of human remains to respond positively to requests for their return. The University developed its policy in 1991 in response to a campaign by Aboriginal people that had begun in the early 1980s. In December 1982, the Manager of TAC had asked the Department of Anatomy to return the skull of William Lanne. The then Professor of Anatomy refused TAC's request reportedly on the basis that research would suffer if the skull were returned (*Sydney Daily Telegraph* 23 December 1982). TAC's request to have Lanne's skull repatriated received largely sympathetic press coverage in the UK, which drew attention to the history of the treatment of William Lanne's body after death and the violence received by Tasmanian Aborigines during the early years of settlement (e.g. *The Scotsman* 27 December 1982, 18 January 1983, 29 January 1983; *The Observer* 19 December 1982).

In 1985, Mansell again approached the University on behalf of TAC during his visits to museums in Europe and the USA, but this time he talked with the Secretary of the University, as opposed to the Professor of Anatomy. Although Mansell returned to Tasmania confident that positive steps towards the return of these remains had been taken, no repatriation was forthcoming (*Australian Associated Press News report* 23 September 1985; *Melbourne Age* 5 October 1985).

Further representations were made to the University in February 1990, this time by Mansell, Bob Weatherall (FAIRA), and Ricki Shields (an Aboriginal man living in the UK who had campaigned for the repatriation of indigenous Australian human remains), who also staged a demonstration outside the University Medical Buildings. Although they were unsuccessful in their attempts to persuade the University to return the remains at this time, and they then returned to Australia, their campaign was maintained by Edinburgh students led by the University's members of Survival International who, by March, had begun to lobby University officials, sending letters of protest and gathering signatures for a petition which demanded 'the return of all Aboriginal remains to the Aboriginal people of Australia without further delay' (*The Student* 1 March 1990). As reported in the *Times Higher Educational Supplement* (23 March 1990), the University of Edinburgh admitted that, 'the issue is not a closed question. Obviously we are aware of the concern that has been expressed, and the feelings of those who are seeking the return of these items'.

In September 1990, a delegation comprising Weatherall, Monty Pryor and William Toby (who were in the UK to collect remains from the Glasgow Art Gallery and Museum – see above) met with the Secretary of the University to request the return of the University's entire holdings of Aboriginal remains, but returned to Australia empty-handed. However, in response to these ongoing requests, on 23 October and 5 November 1990 the University Court reviewed the issue of the Anatomy Department's holdings of human remains, and in particular the Tasmanian items in its collection. The University Court[2] is the highest decision-making body in the University and, by reviewing this issue, it was asserting its authority to determine the future of the Anatomy Department's collection rather than leaving the decision in the sole hands of the Anatomy Department.

Although the Court acknowledged the collection's potential importance to scientific research, and some members voiced their concern that the University might be seen as 'washing its hands of its legitimate custodial responsibilities towards future scholars' (Court Minutes 5 November 1990), it decided by majority vote that 'the University should adopt a policy of returning all human remains, when so requested, to appropriate representatives of cultures in which such remains had particular significance' (Court Minutes 5 November 1990). Because of the possible implications of this decision for academic research within the University, the Court invited comments from the *Senatus Academicus* before a final decision would be taken. The Senate is the University's academic body, comprising the Principal (or Principals) and all Professors at the University.[3]

8. The repatriation issue in the UK

On 5 December, the Senate debated the Court's proposal. The involvement of the Senate threw the decision-making process to the wider University community, demonstrating that the collection was perceived not as the property of one department, but as that of the establishment as a whole. A debate followed which is remembered vividly by many of those who attended. To introduce the motion, the University's Vice Principal outlined the argument that had prevailed at Court. He explained that as nineteenth-century attitudes towards other cultures, based upon notions of racial superiority which might have justified exploitation and the appropriation of indigenous cultural property, were now discredited and unacceptable, it was therefore unsustainable to claim both to respect the rights of other cultures and, at the same time, to abuse these rights in the name of scientific progress. He noted that although some Aboriginal people supported scientific research on Aboriginal human remains, the right to decide whether such research was carried out did not lie with the University. The Professor of Anatomy argued in opposition that the future scientific potential of the remains should not be underestimated, and that, if these were returned, invaluable information of use to scientists and Aborigines alike would be irreversibly lost. The Professor of Social Anthropology dismissed this argument as it did not address the ethical and moral considerations which he believed should be pre-eminent in deciding the future of the collection. It was argued that continued possession and scientific use of the remains denied Aboriginal rights and both expressed and perpetuated the oppression to which they had been, and were still, subjected. After a lengthy debate, the Senate decided almost unanimously to support the Court's proposal, and to reject the suggestion of the Professor of Anatomy that the Tasmanian crania should be retained for a finite period of time in order that scientific analysis could take place. The Senate's decision demonstrated that the wider University community placed the wishes of indigenous claimants above arguments in support of retention.

In 1991 representatives from TAC travelled to the UK to collect the Tasmanian remains in the Edinburgh collection and to accompany them directly back to Tasmania. Shortly afterwards, remains from the rest of Australia were returned to the National Museum of Australia in Canberra (see Plate 8) accompanied by a Ngarinyin elder and Bob Weatherall of FAIRA. Up until very shortly before these remains were returned, no comprehensive documentation about the collection was available – only a list (which accounted for approximately half the collection) of how many remains could be provenanced to each State or Territory. In such circumstances, ATSIC decided to send the remains to the National Museum of Australia in Canberra with the aim of transferring remains to communities subsequently.

In the mid-1990s substantial documentation about the collection was uncovered in Edinburgh University, which included extensive provenance information. This, in turn, led to the discovery of a large amount of additional post-cranial Aboriginal remains still housed in the University's Anatomy Department. Amongst these remains was the partial skeleton of Tommy Walker (see Chapter 3), whose skull had been returned to Australia in 1991. Tommy Walker's family, represented by the Aboriginal Legal Service, engaged consultants to search for the still missing remains of their relative, a project which resulted in a detailed catalogue of the entire collection. The second part of the Edinburgh Collection was repatriated to Australia in 2000 and Tommy Walker's remains have since been reburied by his family.

Remains from the Edinburgh Collection were returned to various communities from 1991. However, the process was initially slow in some cases not only because of the absence of provenance information but also because of the lack of funding available for communities to retrieve their remains, as neither the State nor Federal authorities would take financial responsibility for this process. With the return of the second part of the collection in 2000 (and the increase in available provenance information), a repatriation unit at the National Museum of Australia was set up specifically to facilitate the return of remains to communities. As part of this process, the hundreds of remains taken from numerous burial sites in the Coorong area of South Australia (mostly by Ramsay Smith) were collected by Ngarrindjeri people and reburied on the Coorong in May 2003.

UK Museum Policies

Until 2002, the University of Edinburgh was the only institution with a large collection of human remains to adopt a pro-repatriation policy. The other main collections, at the Natural History Museum, London, the Duckworth Laboratory at Cambridge University, and the Odontological Museum in the Royal College of Surgeons of England, refused requests for return. The Natural History Museum in London states that it is bound to retain its collections under the British Museum Act (1963) and considers that the present and potential future scientific value of its collections outweighs any local concerns. According to its policy, the Museum has:

> very limited power to return human remains to their countries of origin on a permanent basis, owing to the constraints on disposal of items from the collection. This is combined with a presumption against disposal that arises from the recognition of the scientific value of maintaining a collection of human remains as a resource for active research (NHM Policy on Human Remains, November 2001).

The Director of the Natural History Museum explained:

> We have a duty to the scientific international community to use them as a very valuable scientific resource. We would find it extremely difficult to return any such objects if there was any doubt at all about their continued

safety and accessibility. If they were to be buried or cremated then that would not at all be a possibility for us (House of Commons 2000: para. 162).

On the matter of the constraints on disposal, the Tasmanian Aboriginal Centre (2000) has argued that the British Museum Act does not restrict the de-accessioning of human remains, and that such a decision would be possible under its current statutes as it could be made at the discretion of the Trustees. The British Museum has itself de-accessioned items in the past (Simpson 1997: 34) and is currently investigating its position under the Act in this regard:

> The British Museum does not commit itself to any particular interpretation of any of the provisions of its governing statute, the British Museum Act 1963, or of any of other relevant enactment, such as the Charities Act 1993. The British Museum reserves the right and power to make its own judgments about the meaning of relevant provisions on a case-by-case basis. At the time of writing, the British Museum awaits the Attorney-General's determination as to whether, as a charity, it has the power to give effect to moral claims that the trustees wish to recognize, subject to the Attorney-General's sanctioning the course that the museum proposes to take. The British Museum takes the view that the powers of the Attorney-General to sanction the relinquishment of material from the collections of the Museum should be established before other avenues to relinquishment (such as statutory amendment) are explored (WG Report 2003: 81).

Moreover, the power of the British Museum Act to stop the de-accessioning of human remains will be removed by Clause 49 of the Human Tissue Bill (introduced into the House of Commons in December 2003) should it be passed (see Chapter 9).

During the 1990s, many institutions had no written policy relating to the repatriation of human remains, despite the continuing high profile of the reburial issue, and the considerable changes in legislation and museum policy that had taken place in other countries over the preceding decade (for a summary of current policies see the Report of the Working Group on Human Remains 2003). Those that did have a policy frequently placed conditions on what types of remains they were willing to return. Thus, by 1990, the University of Cambridge would return human remains to close kin, although its restrictions on access to information about the collection mitigated against identification of named individuals. In a recent statement, its position on repatriation was clarified:

> Because of the scientific importance of the collection and its inherent potential, the Duckworth Laboratory does not accept requests for repatriation simply on the basis of geographical origin or cultural association. Only requests arising from next of kin for remains of named individuals within the collection, or for the remains of individuals for whom a biological relatedness can be established, will be considered. These will be treated on a case by case basis, and all effort towards a satisfactory outcome to all parties will

be made. We consider the onus of demonstration of biological relatedness the responsibility of the claimant (WG Report 2003: Appendix 6 p.267).

Until May 2001, the Royal College of Surgeons of England's policy regarding repatriation also related only to close relatives:

> So far as human material derived from named individuals is concerned, the museums will consider requests for its return received from close relatives sympathetically, provided that (i) they can furnish legal evidence of the relationship, (ii) the wishes of the named individual are not contravened and (iii) provided the return does not involve contravention of any relevant British regulation (including the Anatomy Regulations 1988 and the Anatomy Act 1984) or of any international legal regulation regarding the exportation and importation of human remains. Any decision to return such material can be taken only after due consideration by the governing body of The Royal College of Surgeons of England.

The College's policy was clearly written from the position of a medical institution abiding by legislation relevant to the treatment of bodies donated to the school for dissection, but this was not necessarily readily applicable to the remains in its anthropological collection. For example, the policy gave weight to the wishes of named individuals, providing that these wishes were *against* repatriation, without consideration that few, if any, of the individuals in its collection had consented to the use of their remains in this manner in the first place. In May 2001 the College augmented its policy with the following section:

> So far as human remains and other artefacts of indigenous inhabitants of North America, Australia and New Zealand are concerned, the College Council will consider sympathetically requests for the return of material for which accurate geographical provenance exists provided that:
> – The request originates from a representative body recognised as such under relevant regional, state or national legislation covering the return of human remains
> – Ownership of the remains is not contested between two or more recognised representative bodies
> – Return does not involve contravention of any relevant local or British or international legal regulation regarding the treatment or transport of human remains.
> In the event of such a request being received, the College Council, and in the case of any material from the Hunterian Collection, the Board of Trustees of the Hunterian Collection, will seek opinion of the scientific and historical value of the specimens concerned, together with the views of the indigenous community from whom the request is made. This information will be taken into consideration when deciding whether to grant any such requests (Royal College of Surgeons of England, Acquisition & Disposal Policy 2001).

In light of this policy, the College decided to respond positively to outstanding requests for the return of Aboriginal human remains, and its Australian holdings were repatriated in 2002 and 2003.

Organisation guidelines

Until 2000, one of the only sets of museum guidelines in the UK relating to repatriation was that approved by the Museum Ethnographers Group (MEG) 'for the storage, display, interpretation and return of human remains in ethnographical collections in UK museums' (*Museums Journal* July 1994: 25). This was non-binding and, while the guidelines stressed that respect and sensitivity must be accorded to requests for the return of human remains and that all curators should make themselves aware of the relevant issues, the MEG did not take up any position as to whether or not remains should be returned to relevant communities. Instead, the guidelines stated that 'the rules and governance of the museum or institution will dictate the parameters for any action', and that requests should be resolved on a case-by-case basis, with consideration of:

> ownership, cultural significance, the scientific, educational and historical importance of the material, the cultural and religious values of the interested individuals or groups, and the strength of their relationship to the remains in question.

In the 1990s, the UK Department of National Heritage held the opinion that repatriation was a matter for each individual museum, an opinion shared by the Museum and Galleries Commission (Simpson 1994: 31). In 1996 the Museum's Association stated that it 'intend[ed] to issue some guidance on the subject' (*Ethical Guidelines, Advice from the Museums Association Ethics Committee* June 1996), and meanwhile referred its members to the guidelines of the MEG.

In the second half of the 1990s, the prolonged campaigns for the return of indigenous human remains began to provoke discussion of repatriation issues by the main museum professional bodies in the UK (Simpson 2002; Fforde and Ormond Parker 2001). Two projects were commissioned by the Museums Association to examine the experience of its members 'in relation to the handling, display and repatriation of human remains and objects' (Simpson 2002: 205). Limited to Museums Association members, the surveys are not exhaustive and indeed do not include those institutions housing the major collections of human remains, but both provide an important window into the experiences of, and attitudes towards, repatriation within the UK museum profession at this time.

Results of the first project, which had twenty-four respondents, included the finding that seventeen out of nineteen museums which had human remains on display had removed those belonging to Native

American, Aboriginal, or Maori people, but that only eight of the respondents had written policies in relation to the repatriation of human remains, and ten had unwritten policies (Simpson 1994). The second project (Simpson 1997) concentrated on material other than human remains (except for when human remains formed part of a cultural artefact) and results included the finding that of 123 responses from individual members of the Museums' Association, only three were categorically opposed to repatriation. However, despite the over-whelming consensus from museum staff that, in some circumstances, repatriation was an acceptable course of action, hardly any institutions had a written policy on the matter. Any policies that did exist were almost exclusively focused on human skeletal remains. Furthermore, as Simpson (2002: 210) notes, while staff may have been sympathetic to the issues motivating repatriation in principle, few had had these sympathies tested in practice. Significantly, few of the big museums, or those which had received the greatest number of repatriation requests, took part in the survey. One outcome of the Museums Association projects was a set of guidelines commissioned by the Museums and Galleries Commission, in association with the Museums Association and the National Museum Directors' Conference. These guidelines were published, as *Restitution and Repatriation: Guidelines for Good Practice,* in 2000 (Leggett 2000) and seek to advise museum staff on how to handle repatriation requests for any object, not exclusively human remains. The guidelines, for example, set out suggested proce-dures for responding to requests as well as common arguments in favour of retention and return.

Access to archives

A significant, and informative, facet of the repatriation issue and the reburial campaign is the difficulty that indigenous groups have had in finding out what museum collections actually contain. For indigenous groups, information about collections and, particularly, access to the museum records themselves is needed, not only to help compile inventory listings of remains, but also to find out as much information as possible about where remains were taken from. Such information is important as without it the location of appropriate communities, descendants, burial locations and other details cannot be determined.

Most institutions in the UK which hold significant collections of indige-nous human remains are, or have been in the past, extremely reluctant to divulge details about their collections, and have generally been unrespon-sive to indigenous requests to obtain such information. As the then Secretary of World Archaeological Congress informed its members in an editorial to *World Archaeological Bulletin* 6 (1992), an issue dedicated, at the request of indigenous members of WAC's Executive Committee concerned at the paucity of available information, to placing such details in the public domain:

> Those responsible for collections of human remains in England vary greatly in their response to the suggestion that the details of their holdings should be made public. Most exhibit extreme defensiveness in discussing their holdings; almost all admit that their collections are badly catalogued and that they are not able to say definitively whether or not their catalogues match their holdings (Ucko 1992: 1-2).

No such barrier exists to those wishing to study the human remains themselves, while indigenous groups have been disallowed access not only to archives, but also to ancestral remains for religious purposes. Until 2000, for example, the Natural History Museum, London, refused to provide information about its human remains collection to any but those undertaking scientific analysis of the remains themselves, despite consistent argument from indigenous groups, archaeologists and museum professionals that its position was untenable. Responding to this pressure, in 1999 the Natural History Museum had begun to compile an inventory of the human remains from Australia and New Zealand in its collection. Completed in the summer of 2000, access to information about the collection was, at that time, guided by the following policy:

> An accurate catalogue of holdings from these areas will be accessible on request, subject to the approval of the Head of the Department of Palaeontology, to all *bona fide* academic researchers affiliated to universities, governments and associated institutions.
> Access to the humans remains themselves (as well as to other documentation and records) continues to be given only to *bona fide* scientific researchers in human variation and origins, subject to the approval of the Head of the Department of Palaeontology (Natural History Museum Statement to the World Archaeological Congress January 1999).

By 2001, the Museum had changed its position. In its Policy on Human Remains (November 2001) the Museum dropped its requirement that those requesting information should be *bona fide* academic researchers and that access was only permitted to the recently compiled inventory. The policy states that the museum is:

> committed to the principle of access to its information resources, and will respond positively to those requesting information on the human remains in the collection. The Museum will work with the enquirer to determine how their needs may be best satisfied, particularly where requests are general, or where a response may demand considerable resources. The Museum operates under UK Government guidance on access to information.

It had also adopted a new policy on access to remains by non-scientists:

The Museum will consider requests for access to specific remains for non-scientists with established traditional links to the remains. Such access will only be granted after mutual agreement on the terms and nature of access requested. Requests for such access should be made in the first instance to the Keeper of Palaeontology.

In 2000, the Director of the Natural History Museum, Sir Neil Chalmers, was asked to explain his institution's history of lack of provision of information to requesting parties to the Department of Culture, Media and Sport's Select Committee on *Cultural Property: Return and Illicit Trade*:

If you look at the various ways in which the material was acquired over a long period of time, often over very indirect routes, it is not surprising that many museums find themselves uncertain as to the provenance and the identity and the nature of the material they hold. It took us about two years of very hard and expert research work to go through the holdings from our Australian and Torres Straits holdings to clarify that. We are now able to make that information available to the Australian Government and to anybody who requests it.

The Director clearly recognised the implications of such lack of provision, for when asked by a member of the Committee what could be done to solve the uneasy relationship between indigenous groups and museums holding human remains, he responded:

There are two things that can be done. One is in terms of information about collections. I think there could be and should be more done to make that information more readily available such that one knows clearly what is available. In the case of the Natural History Museum we have not been able to make that information available in the past because the information has simply not been good enough quality. We have put in a lot of effort in the last two years to make sure that we now do have very good quality information and that is now in the public domain.

Yet the relationship between Aboriginal authorities and the Natural History Museum continues to be 'uneasy'. In 2003, following a meeting with the Natural History Museum, an Aboriginal delegation in the UK to collect human remains from other institutions accused the museum of 'hostility' – an accusation which was strongly denied (AAP 30 July 2003). Shortly afterwards, the delegation picketed the Natural History Museum in protest at its continuing refusal to return remains or to allow the delegation access to the Aboriginal remains in its collection.

In the 1990s, restrictions on access to museum documentation were not always condoned by others in the museum community (e.g. Jones 1994: 29) and, as Simpson (1994: 29) noted, were 'surely contrary to the Museums Association's code of ethics – and the spirit of knowledge and education on which museums are founded'. On this issue, the Museum Ethnographers

Group Guidelines on Management of Human Remains stated that 'museum collections are in the public domain and *bona fide* enquirers have the right of access to data on holdings' (*Museums Journal* July 1994: 25). The lack of transparency and the way in which museums appeared to gate-keep information did little to foster relationships of trust between indigenous groups and museums. Refusal to provide listings of human remains was seen as obstructive, as well as undermining museum claims to be holding human remains for 'all humanity'. As exemplified by Chalmers' admission, it was clear that many museums simply did not know what was in their human remains collections – a situation which, as indigenous campaigners pointed out, further undermined any arguments for retention.

By the late 1990s there had, therefore, been a number of returns of Aboriginal remains to Australia. With the exception of the University of Edinburgh, most had occurred at the beginning of the decade and were from institutions in which human remains did not form a significant part of their collections. With the exception of the second return of Australian remains from the University of Edinburgh, Aboriginal authorities or their agents had not been directly involved in the organisation of repatriations, but had travelled to Britain to collect their ancestors and bring them home. While many museums continued to disagree with repatriation, the Museums Association survey showed that an increasing number of the museum community were at the very least open to the possibility. By the end of the twentieth century there was a distinct possibility that some change might not be far away. The first evidence that this was the case was the convening of a House of Commons Select Committee under the Department of Culture, Media and Sport to consider issues relating to *Cultural Property: Return and Illicit Trade*. This committee was the first step in a series of significant developments that were to occur in the repatriation debate in the UK in the first years of the new millennium.

9

Recent developments in the UK

Initially, the issue of human remains in UK institutions was not to be a specific concern of the House of Commons Select Committee. However, as its enquiry progressed, and evidence was heard from a wide range of interested parties,[1] including some indigenous organisations, the Committee became convinced that human remains, as a category of return claims, deserved separate analysis.

In a section of its report specifically devoted to human remains, the Culture, Media and Sport Select Committee (CMSSC) noted that 'existing guidance for museums on *Restitution and Repatriation* [did] not give sufficient weight to the particular issues relating to requests for the return of human remains' (CMSSC 2000: para. 163), and recommended that the Department of Culture, Media and Sport (DCMS) initiate discussions with appropriate authorities, to 'prepare a statement of principles and accompanying guidance relating to the care and safe keeping of human remains and to the handling of requests for return of human remains' (CMSSC 2000 para. 163). This recommendation, endorsed by the Government, is of great significance in the history of the reburial debate in the UK because it included claimant communities, as well as museum and government representatives, within its listing of those with whom discussions should be initiated. By recommending indigenous participation, the Committee signalled not only its acceptance of the validity of indigenous claims, but also, and perhaps more importantly, its recognition that the repatriation issue could not be progressed unless originating communities were part of the process. For the first time, a UK Government authority was suggesting that meaningful discussions about the repatriation of indigenous human remains should not be undertaken exclusively within the museum community. The new millennium was thus witnessing events that had occurred almost fifteen years previously in North America and Australia – the involvement of government in the reburial debate, and the erosion of the position that the scientific community had the authority to determine the future of the contested human remains within its collections.

Reflecting the Committee's identification of the importance of provenance information as a key finding of its broader enquiry, it noted that, as in Australia and the USA, identifying the origin of ancestral remains in UK collections and providing this information to interested parties was of crucial importance, and that it should be used as a starting point for initiating discussions, and for promoting the strengthening of relations and mutual understanding between holding institutions and indigenous claimants. To this end, the Committee recommended that the DCMS 'seek commitments from all holding institutions in the United Kingdom about access to information about holdings of indigenous human remains for all interested parties, including potential claimants, as part of these discussions' (CMSSC 2000: para. 164). Again this recommendation, and its recognition by government, was significant. Not only did it highlight a situation which had been experienced and criticised by indigenous groups, but it positively backed the provision of provenance information as a key element in pushing the repatriation debate forward.

In March 2001, the UK Government published its final response to the Committee's report and recommendations of July 2000. Its agreement with the Committee that the issue of human remains required further and detailed attention was evidenced by its appointment in March 2001 of a Working Group to specifically consider this matter.

The UK Working Group on Human Remains

The Working Group on Human Remains was comprised of leading members of the museum and legal professions and a Professor of Social Anthropology. The group had a comprehensive brief to:

- examine the current legal status of human remains within the collections of publicly-funded Museums and Galleries in the United Kingdom;
- examine the powers of museums and galleries governed by statute to de-accession, or otherwise release from their possession, human remains within their collections and to consider the desirability and possible form of legislative change in this area;
- consider the circumstances in which material other than, but associated with, human remains might properly be included within any proposed legislative change in respect of human remains;
- take advice from interested parties as necessary;
- consider the desirability of a Statement of Principles (and supporting guidance) relating to the care and safekeeping of human remains and to the handling of requests for return. If the Panel considers appropriate, to draw up the terms of such a Statement and guidance;[2] and to
- prepare a report for the Minister for the Arts and to make recommendations as to proposals which might form the basis for a consultation document as part of the procedure required under the Regulatory Reform Bill (WG Report 2003: 1).[3]

The formation of the Working Group indicated the UK Government's commitment to further discussions on the issue of the repatriation of human remains. In particular, it was committed to considering the possibilities of legislative change in order to underpin the Select Committee's conclusion that human remains are a distinct type of cultural property and that claims for the repatriation of remains should be considered apart from the repatriation of other items.

The UK Government's interest in facilitating the repatriation of human remains voiced in its response to the Culture, Media and Sport Committee's report was unsurprising, given the UK/Australia Prime Ministerial joint statement on Aboriginal remains announced in July 2000, which stated:

> The Australian and British governments agree to increase efforts to repatriate human remains to Australian indigenous communities. In doing this, the governments recognise the special connection that indigenous people have with ancestral remains, particularly where there are living descendants.
>
> The Australian government appreciates the efforts already made by the British government and institutions in relation to assisting the return of human remains of significance to Australian indigenous communities. We agree that the way ahead in this area is a cooperative approach between our governments. Our governments recognise that there is a range of significant issues to be addressed in order to facilitate the repatriation of indigenous human remains. Addressing these issues requires a coordinated long-term approach by governments involving indigenous communities and collecting institutions. Consultation will be undertaken with indigenous organisations as part of developing any new cooperative arrangements.
>
> Significant efforts have already been undertaken by individuals and particular organisations in this area. More research is required to identify indigenous human remains held in British collections. Extensive consultation must also be undertaken to determine the relevant traditional custodians, their aspirations regarding treatment of the remains and a means for addressing these.
>
> The governments agree to encourage the development of protocols for the sharing of information between British and Australian institutions and indigenous people. In this respect we welcome the initiative of the British Natural History Museum which has catalogued 450 indigenous human remains.

By this statement, the UK Government committed itself to the repatriation of Aboriginal human remains, to increasing the availability of information about collections and establishing the requirement to involve, appropriately, Aboriginal communities in the repatriation process. The statement indicated a large step away from the Government's previous position of non-involvement and significant developments had been made in the repatriation debate in a relatively short period of time. It is perhaps not unconnected that this period also witnessed the adoption of a new policy (Jan 1999 and then Nov 2001) by the Natural History Museum enabling access to collection archives, and a new pro-repatriation policy by the Royal College of Surgeons of England (2001).

Over the past two years, the debate about the repatriation of human remains from UK collections has developed largely in anticipation of the Working Group's report. Incorrect news, in December 2002, that its publication was imminent caused the ATSIC Commissioner for Tasmania, Rodney Dillon, to issue a press statement welcoming its main findings as then reported by the UK *Independent*. At the same time, and also in response to the continuing debate about the Elgin Marbles, eighteen international museums issued a joint statement opposing the return of objects from collections, which was in itself widely criticised by organisations such as the International Council of Museums, the Museums Association (UK) and the Australian Museums Association.

Six months later, in May 2003, the media again wrongly predicted the report's publication. This time, UK and Australian newspapers ran numerous articles publicising the views of leading British scientists opposed to repatriation which reflected those publicised in Australia many years before: that repatriation would put a stop to science and ruin invaluable collections; that human remains should not be viewed as the property of one group but of the heritage of human kind as a whole; that what was now considered past unethical collection of human remains should not be a viable factor in decisions as to whether remains should be returned or not – curators today should not have to 'pay the price' for the behaviour of their predecessors. The argument was also repeated that as Tasmanian Aborigines no longer existed, it was therefore impossible for their remains to be claimed. Concern at the diverse membership of the Working Group was also voiced, with the intimation that the views of science would not thus be given the significance they deserved – '[it would be] folly to let lack of understanding of science cloud judgment to the extent of depriving future generations' (*Independent* 16 May 2003). Even in such opposition, however, there was nonetheless some stated support for the return of the remains of known individuals to close kin, if the institution was not restricted in doing so by legislation (*Sydney Morning Herald* 9 June 2003). The response of Aboriginal authorities was unequivocal, the ATSIC Commissioner for Tasmania, for example, stating that 'Aborigines were not put on this earth for British scientists to do research on' (*Observer* 1 June 2003).

Once again, the debate was largely reported by the media as one of contention, a 'furious row' (*Observer* 1 June 2003) or 'one of the hottest scientific/cultural debates on the planet' (*Sydney Morning Herald* 9 June 2003) despite the fact that in the first six months of 2003, three museums in the UK (the Manchester Museum, the Horniman Museum, and the Royal College of Surgeons of England) had returned remains to Australia voluntarily and, in the process, had involved Aboriginal people. These returns had been undertaken through discussion and negotiation with ATSIC and FAIRA and as such demonstrated a wish for inclusiveness, dialogue and partnership, a desire further illustrated by statements from the participating institutions that placed emphasis on the building of future mutually beneficial relationships with Aboriginal groups.

The Manchester Museum had initially decided to return remains to

Australia in 1992, and endorsed this decision in 2003. It returned the remains of four individuals, with the:

> recognition that it should relinquish possession of the remains of Australian Aborigines ... on the grounds that they were obtained and are retained in continued violation of the beliefs and cultural values of the originating communities. Their moral claim to the remains was therefore judged to override any scientific or interpretive value, or legal rights of possession vested in the University (http://museum.man.ac.uk/information/newsarchive.htm).

At the handover (see Plate 9), Tristram Besterman, Director of the Museum, and a member of the Working Group on Human Remains, described the museum's intentions:

> The return of the remains of the ancestors of living indigenous Australians is an act that recognizes our common humanity. These remains were removed during the colonial era at a time of great inequality of power. Their removal more than a century ago was carried out without the permission of the Aboriginal nations, and they have been held in the Manchester Museum ever since, in violation of the laws and beliefs of indigenous Australian people. The Manchester Museum cannot atone for the wrongs of our own forebears at a time when different values prevailed. Nonetheless, by returning these remains now, we hope to contribute to ending the sense of outrage and dispossession felt by Australian Aborigines today, and trust that we can begin to build a more rewarding relationship based on mutual understanding and respect between our peoples in the future (http://museum.man.ac.uk/information/newsarchive.htm).

On 5 November 2003 (two days before the eventual release of the Working Group's report) the Royal College of Surgeons of England issued a press statement (*Press Notice 2003/0010*) relating to the return of its substantial collection of human remains, without wide media coverage, to Australia in the preceeding eighteen months. In May 2002 the College had returned remains to Tasmania through the Tasmanian Aboriginal Centre (TAC) and in April 2003 it had returned the last of its Australian Aboriginal human remains. Staff had worked with representatives of TAC, ATSIC and FAIRA to identify and provenance the remains in its collection. Like that from Manchester Museum, the repatriation of Australian human remains from the Royal College was collaboratively undertaken. The statement of Sir Peter Morris (President of the Royal College of Surgeons of England and a member of the Working Group on Human Remains) delivered on the occasion of the return of its mainland Australian human remains made the College's position clear:

> Today sees the culmination of a very fruitful and positive dialogue between the Royal College of Surgeons of England and the Aboriginal and Torres Strait Islander Commission (ATSIC) and its recognized agency the Foundation for Aboriginal and Islander Research Action (FAIRA). In May

last year the College returned human remains to Tasmania through the Tasmanian Aboriginal Centre and this handover completes the process. I am sorry not to be present in person to make the handover but as President of the College and an Australian I am particularly pleased to welcome representatives from ATSIC and FAIRA to the College for this significant event.

We have come to recognize that the culture of Australian Aborigines is very different to British culture. It is very important to an Aboriginal Australian that their body, and their ancestors' bodies, be returned to the land from which they arose. Staff from the College and FAIRA have been working together over the last year to identify correctly the Aboriginal remains in the Museum's holdings so that they can be returned to the right community and location. If not, the Aboriginal communities will decide where best they should be laid to rest.

When I was last in Australia I visited the new galleries at the National Museum of Australia and was impressed by the displays of Aboriginal culture planned with the involvement from the aboriginal communities. Understanding different cultures is the way forward and as our museum here in the College is currently undergoing a change of direction – I look forward to a continuing dialogue on cultural issues (WG Report 2003: 47-8).

While some UK museums have chosen a new direction, others still consider that scientific value outweighs all other concerns. Those in charge of UK collections of human remains therefore increasingly hold quite different (and public) opinions about repatriation, and such differences are reflected in the Working Group's report, finally released on 7 November 2003.

The Working Group Report

The DCMS Working Group on Human Remains had a comprehensive brief to consider the status of human remains collections (see above). Its analysis was restricted to English and Welsh collections and excluded fossils and sub-fossils, material obtained after 1948, or from biopsies or post-mortems, all of which were covered by the Retained Organs Commission. It undertook a considerable amount of research before reporting and consulted widely. In recognition of the deficiency of information available about collections, it conducted its own scoping survey. It took written and oral submissions from almost sixty parties, and consulted with Australian and New Zealand Government representatives. On several occasions the Chair visited Australia, conducting seminars on the work of the Working Group and consulted with Aboriginal, Government, and museum authorities. Members spoke at the Museums Associations conference and on various occasions the Chair met his counterpart on the Retained Organs Commission[4] and Department of Health officials to discuss matters of common interest. Individual members conducted research into key aspects such as 'information and other gains from retention of human remains', 'arguments for and circumstances favouring restitution or relocation', 'UK institutional treatment of contemporary human remains', 'alternatives to compelled physical location' and the 'size and distribution of collections, measurement, resource [and] implications'. Legal advice was sought on the implications of the Human Rights Act 1998 for the handling of requests for return (WG 2003: 5). Its members read widely on associated issues and considered relevant museum, organisation and other policies and agreements both within the UK and internationally (WG Report 2003: 53-6, 64-79). The report is therefore the result of three years of discussion, information gathering, consultation and debate with a wide range of authorities by leading professionals and, as such, is a very significant body of evidence in the repatriation debate in the UK. The report formed the basis of a consultation document which the DCMS is to issue in 2004, the results of which will inform the Government's response.

The views of science and originating communities

Throughout the report, the Working Group recognises that scientific analysis of human remains has made a significant contribution to the advancement of science 'on a broad range of topics' (WG Report 2003: 21). It sets out the consequences for science of returning human remains (e.g. WG Report 2003: 20-1), noting that members of the scientific community, from whom it had received numerous submissions, felt deeply that collections were a 'unique and irreplaceable resource for the legitimate pursuance of scientific and other research' (WG Report 2003: 21). It also discusses at length the consequences of collecting for communities of origin (e.g. WG Report 2003: 21-3), which are best summed up here in its 'case for repatriation' (WG Report 2003: 91):

1. To many indigenous peoples the return of their ancestors to the homeland is essential to the health of the descendant community. Such a community should be allowed to decide for itself how its members are treated. Any derogation from this principle is a discriminatory subordination of indigenous peoples and a demeaning relation of them and their concerns to inferior status. It also prevents them from fulfilling a solemn obligation, the neglect of which causes acute pain. There is little question that the original taking of these remains was often morally, if not legally, wrongful, that such dispossession would not be tolerated today, and that English museums will no longer acquire indigenous remains in violation of the wishes of their parent communities. Why, then, should it make any difference that particular remains are already in the possession of the museum?
2. Until this wrong is redressed, there will be no closure in respect of past injustices and an arguable enduring violation of fundamental human rights. The physical and psychological health, and indeed the social advancement, of indigenous communities are in consequence impaired. No other class of society finds its lack of consent overridden, its autonomy subverted, and its spiritual needs unilaterally subordinated to others' interests, in this way. Equality and justice demand the return of ancestral

remains. People grieve and will continue to grieve till the spirits of their ancestors are laid to rest.

The Working Group recognised that much, if not all, of the overseas human remains in UK collections had been obtained without consent and that, 'in the majority of cases, this lack of consent persisted throughout the later acquisition of the material by the museum, and extends to its current holding and other treatment, such as research' (WG Report 2003: 23). Indeed, it saw that the relationship between researchers and indigenous peoples in the UK had been characterised by a general lack of constructive communication. This stood in stark contrast to the situation in other countries where, 'indigenous populations exist as articulate and politically active elements of society, and where the scientific community has already taken significant steps to become accountable to those communities' (WG Report 2003: 24).

Collaboration

Submissions received by the Working Group showed a wide spectrum of views within the scientific community both within the UK and overseas, from those of researchers who opposed any return of human remains, to those who would support the return of named and known individuals, to those who argued strongly in favour of working on remains only with the consent of communities. Indigenous submissions set out the reasons why human remains must be returned to communities, informed the Working Group that traditional owners must have the final decision about disposal, but also observed that decisions were for individual communities to make and that these did not necessarily preclude research. The Working Group reports that in some indigenous submissions genuine collaboration with museums was seen as desirable and beneficial (WG Report 2003: 35-7) and it gave examples of the views of those international museums who sought to do so, and why. Thus, Te Papa Tongarewa, the National Museum of New Zealand, submitted that:

> The retention of Maori and Moriori remains in UK museums and institutions can only further contribute to a lack of understanding on a cross-cultural basis. This is inconsistent with the role of museums as advocates for understanding cultures. It has been demonstrated in a number of circumstances that the repatriation of human remains can and does lead to enhanced relationships between museums and indigenous communities. It is also critical to note that repatriation of human remains has not resulted in an increase in calls for the return of all relevant cultural material. Te Papa acknowledges that ancestral remains held with the collections of museums and institutions in the UK have ongoing scientific value to the museum community. However, before museums can keep any human remains based on their research value, the museum must first be able to prove its claims of ongoing scientific value to the satisfaction of the relevant communities from which those remains originated.

9. Recent developments in the UK

These types of 'pro-collaboration' submissions persuaded the Group that consensus between indigenous claimants and museums was desirable and achievable, and that while dissension and mistrust characterised other submissions, there was evidence to suggest that, 'disagreement can be relieved by dialogue, and that dialogue can produce consensus, even in cases that seem, at first sight, intractable'. In light of this, the Working Group believes that, 'parties should work on the principle that informed consensus is the desirable outcome, and should act transparently and honestly to achieve this. Such an approach has the potential to generate otherwise unachievable benefits of continuing long term collaboration for museums, scientists, descendant communities and humanity as a whole' (WG Report 2003: 46). The circumstances of returns from Manchester Museum, the Horniman and the Royal College of Surgeons of England were presented as examples of this new collaborative approach. The Group also recognised that such collaboration could not occur without absolute transparency on the behalf of all parties, extending to:

> the nature of human remains collections, the circumstances of their acquisition, the nature of research done on them, the findings of such research, and the holding institution's position on restitution claims. Subject to appropriate consultation, and to the proper observance of standards of respect, decency and confidentiality, the collections themselves should be accessible; both to scientific inquirers and to geneaological and cultural descendants, including potential claimants. We regard it as critical that nobody with a legitimate interest should be excluded and that nothing should be hidden that can be legitimately divulged (WG Report 2003: 120).

Such a statement has considerable implications for institutions such as the Natural History Museum and the Duckworth Laboratory, neither of which have so far allowed indigenous groups access to ancestral remains.

Parallels and differential treatment

One reason why the Working Group's analysis is so different to previous museum based examinations of the repatriation issue in the UK, is its willingness to seek parallels between the treatment of human remains in museum collections and those elsewhere (whether, for example, in modern medical collections or buried in cemeteries). For example, it received information from the Home Office about requests for exhumation and location of burials within the UK and to overseas destinations, finding that these currently stood at some one thousand three hundred a year and were on the increase (WG Report 2003: 50). Also reporting a number of requests for the exhumation and repatriation of the remains of historical figures, information from the Home Office demonstrated a concern within the UK that the dead must be interred in the correct place, to the extent that relatives were requesting the exhumation and relocation of their deceased relatives to enable this to happen. The rights of people to 'treat their dead according to their own religion and culture' were safeguarded in English law – 'Beliefs and traditions are honoured to the extent that their violation may be illegal as well as socially unacceptable' (WG Report 2003: 51).

Exemplifying its position that all types of human remains require similar treatment, the Working Group conferred closely with the Retained Organs Commission (set up by the Department of Health following the Alder Hey revelations) to 'avoid potential overlap and to ensure consistency of approach'. Despite focusing on collections with different histories (The ROC concentrated on human remains acquired by institutions post-1948 and those obtained from post-mortems, surgery or biopsies, while the Working Group concentrated on museum and 'archival collections' of human remains acquired pre-1948), a close correlation is seen between the work of the two groups. In particular, the Working Group sees parallels in 'the importance of valuing diversity within society; the primacy of consent and the need to respect the wishes, rights and well-being of genealogical and cultural descendants; and the responsibility of scientific interest to show that proposed research will cause no harm to relatives and descendants' (WG Report 2003: 59). It acknowledges that there is 'strong resonance between the recent distress suffered by the relatives involved in the Alder Hey revelations and the distress of those indigenous peoples who are still mourning the loss of their ancestors taken from them decades ago' (WG Report 2003: 59). Again, such acknowledgement is a significant departure as previously few museum professionals were willing to publicly recognise that any comparison could be made in this area at all. From its analysis, the Working Group concluded that differential treatment was accorded to human remains in the UK, and that there were dangers inherent in these double standards that should be avoided:

> If we are willing to return Truganini's hair, skin, necklace and bracelet, why not her friends and compatriots? If we are willing to surrender for burial in his homeland the remains of a Brazilian who fled to England to escape persecution, why not the remains of a Maori warrior whose head was brought to England as a curio? If we are willing to release to Australia its birth certificate, why not its children? (WG Report 2003: 80).

Its analysis of contemporary law in England and Wales as it related to the 'legal status of human remains as the property of museums or other interested parties' and 'the legal restraints on the ability of museums to divest themselves of human remains' (WG Report 2003: 81) concluded that the current situation was 'seriously unsatisfactory'. The legal situation was contradictory and uncertain, and inhibited the exercise of discretion on the part of museums to relinquish remains should they wish to do so. The Group also looked at the relevance of international statutes and, in particular, independent legal advice was sought on the implications of the Human Rights Act 1998 for claims for the return of human remains.

This advice concluded that, while yet untested, it was possible that action to contest a refusal to return human remains could be taken, if stated criteria were met, under:

> Article 3 of the Convention (protection against inhuman or degrading treatment); or under Article 8 (respect for family and private life); or under Article 9 (right to freedom of thought, conscience and religion); or under Article 14 (prohibition of discrimination); or under Article 1 of Protocol 1 (protection of property). Each case would need to be considered on its merits (WG Report 2003: 86).

In light of its analysis of legal factors, the Working Group recommended, amongst other things, the removal of any statutory bar, where it existed, on the return of remains (WG Report 2003: 88-90). The Group did not support the implementation of legislation to force museums to return human remains, although it did point out that legislation might become appropriate in the light of future events such as 'the assimilation into UK law of the draft UN declaration on the rights of indigenous peoples, or a ruling that the retention of human remains offends human rights, or some legal decision that indigenous claimants have property or the right to possession over the remains of their ancestors, or other compelling circumstances' (WG Report 2003: 92). Apart from practicality, one of the main reasons put forward by the Group against mandatory legislation was that this 'could jeopardize relationships that might otherwise flourish', arguing that 'in the present climate, though we acknowledge that the spirit of trust and amity is not universal, we prefer an approach that gives such initiatives the chance to take root unhindered by adversarial and unilateral intervention' (WG Report 2003: 92). It further notes that such legislation has not always been required for the return of human remains from other countries (e.g. Canada and New Zealand), although NAGPRA is clearly the exception.

Consent

The most significant Working Group conclusion concerns the role of consent, and the recommendation that it should be adopted as a fundamental guiding principle in future decisions about the care and treatment of human remains, including their retention in museums (WG Report 2003: 95-114).

The Working Group accepts that there is little, if any, evidence to prove that human remains in museums in England and Wales were obtained with consent – 'there is virtually no positive evidence to show that items of human material which entered the possession of museums or kindred institutions before 1948 did so with the consent of the deceased individuals, or their blood relations, or their spouses, or their communities, and much positive evidence to suggest the contrary' (WG Report 2003: 107).

Nor does the Working Group believe that lack of original consent can be dismissed as mere historical fact without bearing on modern collections, as so many curators have argued. Instead, the Working Group believes that, the 'existence of the original wrong requires museums to ask themselves whether they consider it appropriate to derive a benefit from that wrong' (WG Report 2003: 108), and draws comparison with material spoliated during the Nazi Holocaust, noting that in such cases the UK Spoliation Advisory Panel must take account of the circumstances in which a museum or gallery obtained the material in question. The Working Group also disagrees with the argument that human remains can be retained because the acquisition of remains was seen as proper and correct at the time. While accepting that such acquisition may have complied with 'contemporary ethical and legal standards and with general principles of good faith' and have thus been 'immune from legal sanction and could even have conferred ownership on the museums, in so far as anyone can own human remains', nonetheless, 'such procedural regularity cannot, as a matter of logic, either constitute or take the place of consent' (WG Report 2003: 112).

These are significant findings on the side of indigenous groups who have repeatedly rejected museums' arguments that lack of original consent is immaterial in the current debate. In this, the Working Group took heed of evidence received from indigenous groups which made it plain that:

> for many people, want of original consent is not simply an academic issue. To these people, the removal of human remains without consent was a moral wrong that demands correction. In some cases, it was offensive and uncivilized (perhaps even unlawful) by the contemporary standards of the prevailing authority or society, as well as by those of indigenous communities. Where communities, beliefs and memories survive, the sense of pain and injustice could be as poignant and corrosive today as on the day of removal. Such removals are seen not only as a wrong that demands to be redressed, but as a barrier to that repose and dignity which should be extended to all human remains from the particular community. To some, moreover, the consequences of this violation and lack of consent can be understood only against a wider background of deprivation and subordination of indigenous peoples, the reversal of which is still in progress. The recovery of human remains is therefore part of a broader movement towards identity and self-worth for indigenous peoples (WG Report 2003: 108).

Given that it has such large implications for the retention of remains without the approval of appropriate indigenous authorities, it is unsurprising that it is on the issue of consent that the Group was most divided, and its conclusions are split between those of 'the minority' and those of 'the majority'. While it unanimously agreed on the principle of consent as a deciding factor in some cases, it disagreed on its use in others. In broad terms, consent was unanimously accepted as a guiding principle as it pertains to the wishes of the deceased or had been invested in close kin or relatives whose genealogical connection can be proven. This was as far as the minority would go, considering that 'outside the sphere of close family relations and direct genealogical descendants, the paramount need for consent should be supplanted by a duty of consultation' (WG Report 2003: 100) as this would offer a 'balanced all-round view which gives fair weight to social, familial and cultural associations, without allowing them to predominate in more remote cases' and would enable consideration of the scientific mission of museums, and 'the benefits that derive from its pursuit' (WG Report 2003: 101).

But the majority of the Working Group went further. It had 'serious reservations about limiting the exclusive power of consent to those who have a close and direct genealogical relationship with the deceased person, to the exclusion of others whose relationship may (in the majority's view) demand comparable respect and prominence' (WG Report 2003: 101). Instead, the majority believed that consent should be the 'paramount and universal principle' (WG Report 2003: 101), and a:

> threshold consideration in determining the legitimacy of *any* proposed treat-
> ment of human remains by museums. Once the principle is entrenched,
> attention can focus on the more important and delicate question of *who* is an
> appropriately interested person or group and *whose consent* must be given
> (WG Report 2003: 102).

It was the opinion of the majority that placing exclusive emphasis on genealogical relationships failed to accord proper recognition to cultural diversity, and attached 'predominant value to local or Western notions of kinship, and insufficient value to other belief systems'. The majority believed instead that institutions should 'look to the particular culture or belief system in identifying the proper source of consent' (WG Report 2003: 102). The minority rejoinder about practicalities and lack of available resources to undertake such recommendations was countered with an emphasis that the obligation on museums should be one of best endeavour, and that a 'central and universally accessible system' should be established to assist museums in this process which would helpfully include material evidence from claimant groups (WG Report 2003: 106).

Statement of Principles

In accordance with its brief, the Working Group suggested a Statement of Principles for the care and treatment of human remains. This statement incorporates features of principles proposed by the Chief Medical Officer in 2002 in relation to the work of the Retained Organs Commission, in the belief that there should be a substantial consistency of approach between the two areas. In brief, the Working Group's Statement of Principles includes: recognition of the unique status of human remains; that such items must always be treated with respect; that all claims to remains must be accorded full evaluation; that external reference should be sought and museums should be prepared to submit their position to external evaluation; that consensus should be the aim wherever possible (which may entail the use of an external mediator); that museums should 'manifest a cardinal concern, throughout the process of responding to requests for the return of human remains, for feelings of loss and deprivation on the part of bereaved persons and communities', and that this loss can, within some cultures, pass into each new generation. The Statement also holds that consent must be the underpinning guiding principle, that in negotiating the treatment, care or return of human remains, institutions should deal with the community of origin; and that they should:

> always use their best endeavours to show skill and sensitivity in dealing with the genealogical or cultural descendants of the deceased person. Procedures for considering claims should allow claimants adequate time and space in which to make what will sometimes be difficult decisions. Institutions should ensure that they have access to the expertise necessary to manage the complex and sensitive process involved in considering claims (WG Report 2003: 124).

The proposed Statement of Principles is another example of the Working Group's departure from previous UK professional guidelines as perhaps best exemplified by the *Restitution and Repatriation: guidelines for good practice* (Leggett 2000). By focusing on consent as a guiding principle, the Working Group's guidelines lift the decision-making process away from one that compares the scientific value of human remains with their value to indigenous groups, and instead places it solidly within the sphere of human rights.

Recommendations

Having considered all these issues, the Working Group makes a series of detailed recommendations (WG Report 2003: 148-61). These include, first, that museums should be relieved of any legal impediment to the relinquishment of remains. This issue has been addressed in Clause 49 of the Human Tissue Bill, introduced into the House of Commons on 3 December 2003, which gives nine UK bodies (the Trustees of: the Armouries, the British Museum, the Imperial War Museum, the National Maritime Museum, the National Museums and Galleries on Merseyside, the Natural History Museum, the Science Museum, and the Victoria and Albert Museum, and the Board of Governors of the Museum of London) the power to de-accession human remains:

> 49 (2) Any body to which this section applies may transfer from their collection any human remains if it appears to them to be appropriate to do so for any reason, whether or not relating to their other functions (www.parlia-

ment.the-stationery-office.co.uk/pa/cm200304/cmbills/009/04009.28-
34.html-j400).

If passed, section 49 (2) of this Bill will remove any impediment provided by the British Museum Act (1963) to the de-accessioning of human remains (see Chapter 8). Second, recommendations of the Working Group included that, for the purposes of dispute resolution, all museums should have an externally approved procedure for claims determination and that a Human Remains Advisory Panel should be established to assist in conflict resolution, although recommendations will only be advisory and not legally binding. Third, that a licensing system should be introduced with the object of 'regulating the holding, return, treatment, handling and disposal of human remains within all museums, in broad conformity with proposals currently being developed by the Department of Health for the proposed Human Tissue Bill' (WG Report 2003: 152 and see above). Fourth, that holding institutions should provide reasonable access to their collections and related information and pay 'full regard to the sacred/secret nature of human remains as recognised by particular cultures and religions and to the legitimate concerns of genealogical and cultural descendants of the deceased person' (WG Report 2003: 155). And fifth, on the issue of consent, that:

> no institution shall retain, or perform any other act in relation to, human remains where it knows or has compelling reason to believe:
>
> a. that the original removal of the remains occurred without the consent of the deceased person or that person's close family, and,
> b. that the present retention or other proposed act is without the consent of:
>   1. close family or direct genealogical descendants of the deceased person; or
>   2. where no such family or descendants are identified, those who have within the deceased person's own religion or culture a status or responsibility comparable to that of close family or direct genealogical descendants[5] (WG Report 2003: 156).

To this end, museums must be proactive and should exercise their 'best endeavours' to consult with those in a position to provide consent.

Implications

In its comprehensive analysis of factors affecting the reburial debate, the Working Group has concluded that the present situation is untenable and that the way forward for museums is to underpin decision-making with the guiding principle of consent, and to pursue resolution through communication and dialogue. The very act of seeking consent (which requires transparency in terms of collection contents, potential research, care and treatment of remains) obliges museums to open communication with indigenous groups on a new footing.

For the first time within the UK a leading body has recognised the double standards inherent in the treatment of human remains collections and judged it to be unacceptable. The very introduction of a guiding principle of consent has its roots in a desire for consistency of treatment throughout all UK collections of human remains, and implicit within this is the recognition that concerns for the appropriate treatment of human remains, whether voiced by, for example, indigenous groups or UK parents should be accorded equal respect. While it has not chosen to recommend a path of enacting legislation to force museums to relinquish human remains, by its statement on consent its position on museums' obligations to originating communities is made clear. Furthermore, the proposed licensing system requires institutions to 'subscribe publicly to a Code of Practice on the management of human remains' and that breach of this Code shall give rise to sanctions which may 'according to circumstances, include the loss or suspension of licence, or criminal penalties'. As the relevant sections of the Code reflect the Working Group's statement on consent, the provision of a licensing system does provide a means of enforcing the Group's recommendation.

Shortly after the Working Group's report was made public, Rodney Dillon, ATSIC's Commissioner for Tasmania, and Chair of its Culture, Rights and Justice Board released a Press Statement in which he congratulated the members of the Working Group but was wary of drawing positive conclusions too soon. The Australian Prime Minister welcomed the Working Group's recommendations, particularly applauding: 'the recognition ... that no institution should retain human remains without the consent of the genealogical or cultural descendants of the deceased' (*Prime Minister Media Release* 6 November 2003). The World Archaeological Congress also supported the recommendations (*WAC Media Release* 7 November 2003) while those against the report were also quick to state their views. These generally align themselves with the statement of dissent from Neil Chalmers (Director of the Natural History Museum and Working Group member) that is appended at the end of the Working Group Report. While stating his support for many of the main conclusions of the report, Chalmers dissents from 'several of the report's recommendations in their detailed formulation, and also with significant parts of the main body of the report':

> First, the report and recommendations do not provide a proper balance between the public benefits deriving from medical, scientific and other research on the one hand and the wishes of claimant communities on the other. The report is slanted heavily, both in tone and in substance, in favour of the latter. Second, some of the recommendations are disproportionately complicated and cumbersome in relation to the problems they are seeking to resolve. Third, some of the recommendations are unworkable.

9. Recent developments in the UK

It is yet too early to analyse the effects of the Working Group's findings. The Government response will be critical, as will its commitment of any monies to enable the Working Group's recommendations that will clearly require considerable funding, planning and management (see Anyon and Thornton 2002 for observations on funding requirements to facilitate NAGPRA). Whether the licensing system it proposes is cumbersome or streamlined, whether it can assist indigenous groups in the repatriation of their ancestors, and whether it will bring the treatment of all human remains in this country under a common Code of Practice has yet to be seen. It is also too early to find out which, if any, museums will voluntarily adopt the Working Group's relevant recommendations before any licensing system may oblige them to do so. The response of the wider UK Museum community is not known, and particularly those in Scotland who fall outside the Working Group's remit. The issue of fossil and sub-fossils has yet to be debated on this scale. However, despite all these unknowns, the conclusions of the Museums Association surveys on UK museums' attitudes towards repatriation, the comprehensive research of the Working Group, and the recent returns of Aboriginal human remains by institutions in Britain, demonstrate that the repatriation issue, because of the concerted efforts of indigenous groups for almost thirty years, has shifted significantly in the past decade.

10

Discussion

This book has described how indigenous human remains were widely obtained during the colonial era for scientific research conducted within a paradigm where difference was interpreted within a hierarchy of racial inferiority and superiority. It has also shown that the history of the collecting and interpretation of these remains was embedded within, and contributed to, power relations between the West and Australia's indigenous population. It has argued that the study of Aboriginal remains reified pre-existing concepts of racial hierarchy by constructing the Aboriginal body as inferior to that of the European. As Aboriginal people were perceived as the 'lowest' order of mankind and Europeans perceived as the 'highest', so the original inhabitants of the Australian continent were quintessentially the opposite of 'Us'. This positioning denigrated Aboriginal people, but at the same time elevated the scientific value of their human remains.

While it may now be apparent that racial categories were externally imposed by Western science, scholars at the time accepted these categories as fact and believed them to exist 'in nature'. The presence of numbers, statistics and equations lent authority to this science (see Gould 1978, 1981), the legacy of which is apparent today – despite scientific renunciation, it is still possible to be confronted with popular notions that the 'inferiority' of other 'races' is a 'fact' proven by science.

For two hundred years, human remains have been a source of raw material for the study of fundamental questions about human diversity and origins. The continuing value placed on skeletal remains to the study of 'us' and 'where we came from', and the importance placed on such analyses means that many holding institutions continue to assert pre-eminent rights to the remains in their collections. The reburial issue thus brings into focus the authority and status accorded to science, both today and in the past. The scientific value of human remains led to their removal from funerary sites, despite strong Western cultural traditions against desecrating the dead, laws to prevent grave-robbing, and a broad awareness that collecting was not a practice that would be supported or condoned by dispossessed communities or, indeed, necessarily by the non-indigenous population. The frequent modern claim that collecting occurred, if not in a manner considered ethical today, then in one which was considered ethical for the time (that collectors 'knew no better') does not equate with the historical evidence.

Requests by indigenous groups for the return of their ancestors' remains have been expressed at local, national and international levels for many years. Museums that continue to refuse these requests clearly consider that scientific interest in human remains establishes their right to hold such material against the wishes of originating communities. But this stance is not universal and the history of the development of the reburial debate demonstrates that many of those in the professions which study or curate human remains have increasingly recognised that ethical considerations should regulate scientific research.

Ancestors or objects

In general, indigenous human remains are perceived differently by those who contest their ownership in the reburial debate. For many scientists, remains are primarily biological data, objects that are unique sources of information about the past. For indigenous groups, human remains are primarily the dead who require appropriate treatment. The seemingly mutually exclusive nature of these meanings is a fundamental point of contention in the reburial debate. Given the apparently polarised meanings that have been attributed to remains by indigenous groups and scientists, and the fact that their status as scientific objects forms the basis of refusals to repatriate them, why is it that those in control of human remains collections do nevertheless agree to the return of some types of human remains? One answer demonstrates that, despite the great importance attributed to scientific value, and the claims to scientific objectivity, the views of those in charge of collections about what (or who) constitute 'the dead' have been highly influential in the reburial debate.

When those in control of collections agree to requests for the return of the remains of named individuals they presumably do so because they feel that such claims are understandable and justified. They thus concede that the remains of known individuals can be understandably perceived as 'the dead', whose repatriation and reburial is an appropriate and valid course of action – overruling any loss of scientific information that may result. On the other hand, when institutions refuse to return the bones of unknown individuals, it implies that these remains do not fulfil the necessary criteria to be perceived and claimed as 'the dead' (despite contrary beliefs held by claimant groups) and, consequently, cannot be justifiably repatriated. Thus, attitudes about which type of remains can or cannot be repatriated are determined more by personal notions of what type of bones can be perceived as 'the dead' than by the needs of science, explaining why it was that those categories of remains which would have been accorded respect within Western culture (recent, named and known individuals) were returned to Aboriginal communities first. Aboriginal groups drew no such distinction, considering the return of all remains to be equally important.

The fact that museum policies about which types of remains should or should not be repatriated are not uniform throughout the museum world indicates that the line which divides those remains considered to be 'the dead' and those considered to be 'objects' is a hazy one. Within the scientific community certain remains have therefore been frequently perceived very differently to others. This is also evident in the language people use to talk about remains. Talking about repatriation issues, those who request their return almost always refer to remains of whatever age or degree of provenance as if they are people – using terms such as 'he', 'she' or 'them'. Archaeologists and physical anthropologists also often use these terms (although not uniformly) but only for known individuals and rarely for ancient remains. These latter are usually described using terms such as 'it', 'material' and 'specimen', while the former are more often referred to, in the words of one senior archaeologist, as 'people' who should be 'treated with respect'. Because of the general authority accorded to science it is the way in which a scientific interest in human bones shifts their meaning from 'the dead' to 'objects' that reinforces the assumption of a scientific right to remains. For while Western culture has socially recognised and accepted 'rules' about who should rightfully care for the dead (families, relatives etc.), and where they should be placed (in cemeteries, crypts etc.), it also has recognised 'rules' about who should care for scientific objects (scientists, curators etc) and where, in turn, they should be placed (museums, research institutions etc.).

It is apparent from arguments put forward for their retention, that the great reluctance to repatriate ancient and fossil remains was based not only on the importance placed on them by science but also because they were perceived as simply too old and too anonymous to be viewed as ancestors, for whom living people could feel any connection or responsibility, and thus any legitimate claims over. The strength of this conviction is exemplified by the manner in which differing Aboriginal viewpoints have been completely rejected, usually accompanied by the accusation that any claims to these types of remains must be solely political in nature.

A recent case in which ancient European human remains were, through DNA analysis, identified as the relative of a British woman alive today, demonstrates that it may be the anonymity of ancient remains, rather than their great age, which is the deciding factor in determining whether, in the West, they are perceived as 'people' or 'objects', and consequently influences what kind of treatment of these remains is considered 'appropriate'. In this case, DNA from the frozen body of the 'Iceman' (a 5,000 year-old man discovered in the Italian Alps in 1991) identified a UK woman, Marie Moseley, as his living relative. According to Professor Bryan Sykes (Institute of Molecular Medicine, Oxford University), whose work had led to this discovery, the woman subsequently began to 'feel something for the Iceman ... to her, he was no longer the anonymous curiosity whose picture had appeared in the papers and on television. She had started to think of him as a real person and as a relative – which is exactly what he was' (Sykes 2001: 7-8).

For Moseley, her feelings of responsibility for the Iceman only came into play when scientific evidence proved that he was her ancestor. When this was provided, the fact that the Iceman was 5,000 years old, and thus separated from her by about 160 generations, seems somehow to have become irrelevant. Scientific proof had provided a bridge across the time gap. Without such proof, the Iceman would have remained an object with which she felt no connection.

In some cultures it is not only human remains which are perceived as 'people'. In some cultures material objects (which are not human remains) can have 'personhood' and are related to as ancestors, and in some cases have been returned to communities as such (see, for example, Tapsell 2000). Definitions of what constitutes a human remain or an 'ancestor' are thus not universal – nor are they necessarily static. For legislative purposes, NAGPRA has strict definitions for the items under its jurisdiction, but as Anyon and Thornton (2002: 191-2) commented in their recent analysis of what has been learned from NAGPRA, there is a need for flexibility in the interpretation of definitions. McKeown (2002: 113-14) recently explained in relation to NAGPRA:

> It should be stressed that the definitions of human remains, funerary objects, sacred objects, and objects of cultural patrimony simply define the applicability of the regulations and do not in any way attempt to restrict other concepts of 'sacredness' or 'patrimony'. Further, the four categories are not mutually exclusive.

Western perceptions of what (or who) constitute 'the dead' have therefore played a greater role than previously recognised in the development of the reburial issue and in relevant policies adopted by holding institutions.

The findings of the Working Group on Human Remains may force a shift in the way that indigenous human remains are perceived and/or managed in UK collections. Certainly, its general argument is one that recognises the social importance of human remains and places this above their role as scientific specimens. Its recognition of the legitimacy of indigenous concerns, its requirement of museums to obtain consent from appropriate authorities for the continued retention and analysis of remains, and its view that all human remains in UK institutions should be treated with a consistent approach, may mean that the frequent polarisation of 'object' vs 'ancestor' is decreased.

The return of ancestors

When returned to their community of origin, human remains are no longer primarily objects of science, but are once more perceived first and foremost as 'the dead' who must be accorded appropriate treatment. However, deciding which procedures are appropriate can confront communities with a number of complex issues, not least the question of where to bury returned remains. Many factors can influence the eventual choice of reburial site. There is a wide and strongly held belief that the dead must be interred in the deceased's place of origin, and there are dangers associated with not doing so. Where possible, remains are therefore usually reburied at or near where they were originally interred. Thus in 1988 the Kombumerri people were able to rebury remains returned by the University of Queensland Anatomy Department in an area of land less than a kilometre from their place of original excavation (Aird 2002: 305).

In most cases there is usually insufficient documentation to pinpoint the original burial site. Even when this *is* possible communities are frequently unable to reuse such areas for funerary purposes, usually because sites have been built upon and/or destroyed, or are not community owned. In such an event, preferred alternatives have included old Aboriginal burial grounds or areas associated with the tribe of the dead person. Affording protection to reburial sites is also a fundamental reason why communities have sought to acquire land for funerary purposes, few already having title to such areas. A consultation programme carried out in 1991 by FAIRA within Queensland concluded that although obtaining land for reburial was considered a high priority, 95% of the communities consulted did not have title to suitable areas (Briggs 1994: 61). Another option sometimes used has been to rebury remains in national parks, as they can provide some protection to burial sites.

Because returned remains are frequently considered to be those of traditional people most communities, regardless of the prevailing religious belief, choose to rebury in a traditional manner or with ceremony that combines both Christian and traditional elements (see Briggs 1994: 21-57). The amalgamation of Christianity and tradition that reburial ceremonies can exhibit is exemplified in the burial of Tambo on Palm Island (see Chapter 5). Tambo was not buried in the Island's Christian cemetery, but in an area (called Palm Island Side) of the settlement historically occupied by the Palm Island family, although nobody lives there at present:

> The casket was taken to Palm Island Side where a traditional burial took place followed by a Christian ceremony conducted by all of the denominations on the island. As the ceremonies finished, torrential rain began to fall as is to be expected at the funeral of an important elder (Palm Island 2002: 225).

Like others whose communities have experienced the return of remains, Palm Island talks of the effect this had on affirming community and individual identity. By according Tambo a traditional and Christian ceremony the funeral articulated respect for both Tambo's belief system and that of the Island's predominantly Christian community today. In doing so, it demonstrated the continuing relevance of the traditional past on Palm Island. The effects of Tambo's return have recently been considered by Walter Palm Island, Tambo's descendant and a senior Manbarra man (2002: 226-7):

> The great importance and significance of Tambo's return was demonstrated by his ability to bring the community together, although this could never be maintained at that level indefinitely. People talk about that sense of unity as one of their main memories of 23 February 1994. Another is the way in which the Island, so long represented in a negative way, shone positively in the media spotlight. Tambo is important for teaching other people respect for our traditions.

Tambo's return, and the inclusion of nearly all Palm Islanders in the ceremony, festivities and/or the required organisation, affirmed identity on many levels. It re-established the Manbarra as the traditional owners of Palm Island but also showed that the Bwgaman (Aboriginal and Torres Strait Islander people removed to the island in historical times), despite their origins from outside the area, all *belonged* to Palm Island:

> When I was growing up, my father's generation told their children who they were and where they came from. I knew that Palm Island was my traditional country. Other people knew where their traditional country was as well – whether they were, for example, Kalkadoon or Birri Gubba from the mainland. But in many ways this stopped happening with the passing of that generation, and the young people today do not know their real identity or are confused as to where they belong. This is significant because it contributes to the social problems that we have on Palm Island today. Participating in Tambo's return and reburial affirmed the identity of Palm Islanders as Aboriginal and as Manbarra or Bwgaman, and gave people a sense of belonging to Palm Island. Tambo has become an ancestor for all the Palm Island people, not only the Manbarra. His return reaffirmed Manbarra traditional association with the area but also confirmed that those who had arrived in historical times (the Bwgaman) belonged as well.
>
> Tambo's return strongly established the Manbarra identity, and, at the same time, it confirmed my sense of belonging to my traditional country. I feel that, because of Tambo's return, Manbarra links to our traditional country have been strongly established. Tambo's return showed that our language and our stories are important to us and that our belief system is still strong. Tambo embodies our link to a time before European contact. His return accorded a renewed respect to the Bwgaman elders and traditional forms of authority on the island (Palm Island 2002: 225).

Like choosing a suitable reburial place, determining an appropriate funerary ceremony can sometimes necessitate lengthy debate, preparation and organisation. Coupled with the necessity of acquiring suitable land for burial and, for example, raising sufficient funds to cover expenses and to facilitate community meetings, it can take some time for returned remains to be reburied. Despite the many hundreds of remains that have been reburied, such delays have attracted comment from those who oppose repatriation who have used it as evidence that communities have no real desire to have remains returned to them. US observers of the repatriation process during the decade since the enactment of NAGPRA in 1991 have isolated the need for adequate and flexible time frames as an 'essential component of repatriation legislation' enabling tribes to 'take as much time as necessary for them to make culturally appropriate decisions about repatriating certain objects and remains' (Anyon and Thornton 2002: 195). Such observations recognise that to change or develop appropriate new funerary practices may take time. There are parallels elsewhere. As noted by Hubert (1989: 134) 'the Anglican church took many decades to come up with a successful justification of cremation, which had become a widespread practice'.

As we have seen, many arguments for the retention of remains rejected indigenous requests by asserting they were solely political in nature. Both reburial campaigns and those who fight against them have used political methods and both have political implications. Repatriation issues have been debated in political forums nationally and internationally and attract political attention. However, the political nature of the campaign does not exist in a vacuum, motivated solely by its own ends, but is underpinned by cultural beliefs and obligations, evidenced not only by the testimony of numerous indigenous people today, but by the opposition to collecting that occurred historically. In his consultation with New South Wales communities when the reburial issue in Australia was at its most contentious, Webb concluded that the notion that the reburial campaign was entirely politically inspired by individuals or organisations 'opposed to "white" science' (Webb 1987a: 295) was not true, noting that such a viewpoint was 'facile and simplistic'. Nonetheless, this viewpoint is informative because it demonstrates above all a continuing lack of communication between those in charge of collections and the indigenous communities whose ancestors they curate. It is also an indication of the connection between the reburial issue and outside concepts of Aboriginal identity.

For example, the notion, still commonly held today, that Truganini was 'the last of a dying race' says much about the way in which identity is constructed by others, irrespective and dismissive of how people define themselves. Its legacy is particularly apparent in the reburial issue where requests by Tasmanian Aboriginal people for the return of their ancestors' human remains from some institutions continue to be denied on the basis that the indigenous population of Tasmania no longer exists. For example, the following statement was made in a letter by a group of UK museums to the UK Working Group on Human Remains:

A further problem has been the possible lack of mandate vested in those individuals requesting repatriation. In particular, to remove particular genotypes from the possibility of scientific investigation is akin to a form of racism if not genocide, because those genotypes would be excluded from important ways in which we may continue to investigate and define our species. Arguably, therefore, the rights of (for example) mixed blood descendants of now-extinct genotypes have not been fully taken into account, nor have their views been adequately canvassed (WG Report 2003: 37-8).

The response of Tasmanian Aboriginal authorities made the implications of the above statement clear:

> The museums' comments do not raise any new issues. The comments put a new twist on an old argument, namely that scientists and not Aborigines have the greatest call over what happens to the tissue, body parts, cell structures and so on of the Aboriginal dead. This is apparent from the language used – 'in which we [scientists] may continue to investigate' remains.
>
> Access to the human remains of Aboriginal people for genetic research is no different in nature to access for archaeological reasons. In both cases the issue is whether Aboriginal people are to have control of our heritage, culture and spiritual beliefs or whether this is all subject to the imposed desires of scientists. Our position has been made very clear on this point.
>
> Incidentally, having read the offensive language used by the museum submission we must say it is little wonder there is an increasing lack of sympathy for scientific research of us as a people. We are not animals to be described as 'pure' or 'spoiled' by inter-marriage. The use of such language reminds us of the Nazi era.
>
> We cannot resist saying that the geneticists' claim that Aborigines have no mandate to deal with the rights of our dead must be one of the best examples of pure hypocrisy we have heard for some time (WG Report 2003: 38).

Objectivity

The reburial issue has raised questions concerning the 'connections between archaeological theory, research methods and politics' (Layton 1989: 1). In particular, it has highlighted the question and status of objectivity in scientific research (Layton 1989, Zimmerman 1989a). As illustrated in discussion between, for example, Hassan (1997) and Hodder (1997), the degree of objectivity and subjectivity in archaeological research is still a matter of heated debate. It would appear that central to this debate is the ongoing issue of whether or not there is any ' "real" past somewhere "out there" which can be "discovered" and "objectively" analysed, if only we can "get at it"' (Ucko 1989: xiii). This debate, and its implications, are apparent in arguments for the retention of human remains that are predicated on the belief that skeletal remains have an enduring scientific significance, containing the answer to certain questions if only the correct techniques can be applied. According to this type of understanding, regardless of scientific practices and theories having been previously developed and discarded as incorrect, the bones themselves will *always* hold the solution to the critical questions of human origins and diversity. Indigenous groups, on the other hand, do not necessarily share this belief in archaeological science and can be suspicious of its claims to provide 'truth' about their pasts. In reference to North America, Zimmerman (2002: 97) notes Native American distrust in the discipline, tribes pointing out: 'that at one time archaeologists believed in a lost race of Moundbuilders, then the idea that Indians came over the Bering Land Bridge, then along the coasts, and now they say that others were here before Indians'.

This perception of science as somehow 'the one enterprise that draws constantly nearer to some goal set by nature in advance' (Kuhn 1962: 171) finds no place for contemporary indigenous meanings that are seen as contradicting those offered by science. Alternative meanings are considered obstructive – at worst resulting in the 'death' of the discipline. The importance and primacy accorded by science to the *permanent* scientific relevance that is claimed for human remains is highlighted by anti-reburial arguments which place this factor, and scientific objectivity, in opposition to what is viewed as the transient and emotive – and thus 'subjective' and less 'valid' – reasons put forward by indigenous groups for their return. While again open to the criticism that such views dismiss the cultural beliefs of others, they also demonstrate how difficult it has been for science to deal with the strength of genuine feeling that the reburial issue has engendered amongst claimant communities.

With the possible development of more advanced techniques in the future, the potential of future research is a common argument put forward by those against repatriating human remains, while indigenous groups have argued that museums have had their ancestors' remains for long enough, and it is now time that they were returned. Any discussion within the reburial issue about whether or not human remains are scientifically important is a diversion as it carries with it two assumptions: that scientific value imposes property rights (over and above the issue of whether there exists any property in a body) and that it legitimates research. Layton (1989: 13-14) observed that simply because human remains are considered to be of value to science, this does not mean that science consequently has rights over them:

> The assertion that 'ancient skeletons are remnants of unduplicable evolutionary events ...' is empirically testable. To continue '... which all living and future peoples have the right to know about and understand. In other words ancient human skeletons belong to everyone' (ACPAC 1986: 2) is to move to another level. There is no obvious way in which the value of an objects determines who owns it. It will determine how anxious people are to keep or acquire ownership. The analogous claim 'all peoples value good art, therefore no valuable paintings should remain in private collections' may make its political implications clearer.

In many disciplines, scientific research has proscribed limits and, as Joyce (2002) has discussed in her analysis of repatriation and academic freedom, one of the fundamental areas in which the freedom of scientific research finds almost universal limitation is in areas in which it deals with human subjects. Such research finds regulation by ethics committees in research institutions worldwide, and is often based on the ideal of free and informed prior consent. The premise that the wishes of the relevant indigenous group must be ascertained and respected after the discovery of human remains, or before analysis is undertaken, is now central to legislation and policy in countries such as the USA and Australia. The findings of the UK Working Group on Human Remains indicate that the UK may adopt a similar course.

Throughout the history of the collecting and repatriation of Aboriginal and other human remains these items have accumulated multiple layers of meaning: as ancestors, specimens, commodities, objects, artefacts, etc. Even though each group and/or individual with interests in human remains may have attributed a different significance to them, and these have sometimes been polarised, the different perceptions have been shown to be not necessarily mutually exclusive. Indeed, the boundaries between the different meanings attributed to human remains are not rigidly fixed and are frequently crossed. The flexibility of 'meaning' which exists in relation to human remains has implications for archaeology as a discipline which seeks to understand past and present societies through the interpretation of 'things'. The reburial issue demonstrates that it is difficult for science to accept that the term 'data' is also one more definition; that objects of scientific analysis can hold as many, or more, different meanings in the contemporary context as they did in the past. As various authors have discussed (see, for example, Layton 1989, Swidler *et al.* 1997), it is possible, and perhaps more instructive, to accept that different meanings can and do co-exist. Fundamentally, this requires the recognition that human remains are cultural, and not solely biological, items, and thus can have cultural significance in the present (see Layton 1989: 14-15 and Joyce 2002). The denial of the cultural status of human remains (or at the least, the according of greater value to their status as biological items), may reveal much about the realities of the practice of archaeology and anthropology, as it occurs despite the historical focus of these disciplines on documenting the cultural context of human remains through the excavation of burial sites and the analysis of funerary rituals. The reburial issue also has significance for archaeology because it provides a context for analysing its own assumptions and perceptions, and how these may govern the way in which it practices its discipline.

Arguments against repatriation have frequently framed the debate in terms of local needs versus those of humanity as a whole (e.g. Stringer 2003). In doing so, they imply that returning human remains to communities of origin is to the detriment of the wider human community. The notion that Aboriginal human remains belong to everyone has, of course, been roundly rejected by Aboriginal groups and opposed on many levels. The argument that returning remains is against the needs of wider humanity is now being supplanted amongst pro-repatriation museum professionals with a view that returning requested human remains promotes shared understanding and respect, forges mutually beneficial relationships and may help to balance the unequal relations of power that have been so central to the history of the collecting and study of human remains, and continue today. For the Director of the Manchester Museum, returning Aboriginal remains was an act that recognised 'our common humanity'. The differing opinions amongst the museum community on this aspect of repatriation also reflect the range of views about the role of museums in today's society.

Over the past thirty years indigenous campaigns have progressively established the rights of originating communities to all their ancestral remains held in Australian collections. Since the successful campaign for Truganini's skeleton and the remains contained in the Crowther Collection, scientists have largely supported Aboriginal control over the remains of named individuals, known individuals, those which were obtained in 'unethical' circumstances, and those which have demonstrable cultural or biological descendants. But, with the exception of the return of Mungo Woman, it has invariably taken government authority to enforce the return of those remains considered to be of most scientific importance. In this way, government has played a crucial role in the return of Aboriginal remains from Australian museums. With the Australian/UK Joint Prime Ministerial statement (in 2000), the DCMS Select Committee (in 2000) and now the Working Group on Human Remains (in 2003), recent developments in the UK have also seen the increasing involvement of government in the reburial debate.

It is clear that the history of the collecting of human remains is one of differential treatment. The differential treatment accorded to indigenous human remains and those of Europeans in North America provided one catalyst for the initiation of the reburial campaign in the USA. Over twenty years later, recognition of differential treatment accorded to British human remains and those of indigenous peoples in UK institutions appears also to have been fundamental to the new developments in the UK repatriation debate. Nonetheless, while there have been significant improvements, in many cases, indigenous communities still face significant obstacles in establishing their right to their ancestors' remains.

The reburial issue continues to receive widespread media attention and has tended to be a very public affair. Media coverage highlighted the controversial nature of the debate, representing it as a conflict between two polarised groups, although neither side could in reality be seen as a unified whole, and some archaeologists and indigenous people sought, and achieved, compromise. While such coverage did reflect the controversial nature of the reburial issue, it also detracted from the advances which were made to forge a working relationship between Aboriginal people and archaeologists and museums (e.g. Sim and Thorne 1990, Pardoe 1991, Aird 2002). Zimmerman (2002: 94) has observed that NAGPRA has vastly increased the amount of consultation with Native American groups, and while this may increase the complexity of archaeological practice it has nonetheless generated a wide range of new information. As perhaps the most contentious issue ever to be faced by the archaeological discipline, the reburial issue has impelled, at least in Australia, North America and New Zealand, a renegotiation of the relationship between archaeologists and indigenous people. NAGPRA has shown that repatriation legislation does not result in the emptying of museums, as initially feared by museum officials (Anyon and Thornton 2002: 191). Similarly, the recognition of indigenous ownership of human remains does not mean the permanent termination of archaeological research. For example, Schanche (2002) has written of her examination of Saami remains undertaken with community consultation and in Australia the work of Adcock *et al.* (2001), which acknowledges community support, shows that the study of ancient remains continues. Far from being the 'death' of archaeology and physical anthropology, the repatriation issue may be the process which enables these disciplines to develop a practice that by being inclusive of those whose remains they study reaches a wider audience and goes someway toward being of benefit 'to all humanity'. As demonstrated by Swidler *et al.* (1997) recognition of indigenous rights to their ancestors' remains provides the only meaningful basis upon which a new and mutually beneficial relationship can be forged between the academy and the living people whose past is the subject of enquiry.

Notes

Introduction

1. The issues raised by Alder Hey are not restricted to Britain. In New Zealand, news that Auckland Hospital had collected children's hearts for over fifty years without telling relatives caused distress to parents and caused public debate (Coddington 2002).

2. For a range of views see, for example, Bahn 1984; Duncan 1984; Doumas 1989; Hammil and Cruz 1989; Mulvaney 1989; Richardson 1989; Turner 1989; Ubelaker and Grant 1989; Zimmerman 1992; Bray and Wilson 1994; Morell 1995; Bray 1996; Weatherall 2000; Stringer 2003.

Chapter 3

1. Allport later became a major supplier of Tasmanian skeletons to Europe – providing two to the Royal College of Surgeons of England, one to the private collector Joseph Barnard Davis, one to the Anthropological Society of London, and one to the Royal Museum in Brussels (Plomley 1962).

2. This account of William Lanne's post-mortem history was first published in an extended form in *World Archaeological Bulletin* 6 (1992), 63-9.

3. See Banks 1803; Colbung 1996; Fforde 2002; Pedersen 1995.

4. Translated by F. Handley.

Chapter 4

1. For a comparison with the attitudes of nineteenth- and twentieth-century archaeologists towards the excavation of burial sites in Europe and the Middle East see Bahn (1984).

2. The body of this individual is believed to have been destroyed when the College was bombed in 1941.

Chapter 5

1. After a long campaign, which included representation by the South African Government to French authorities, an Act was recently passed in the French parliament to enable the return of Baartman's remains to South Africa (see also Gilman 1985; Wiss 1990; Fausto-Sterling 1995).

2. The remains of Pirú may have been returned by the Musée de l'Homme to Uruguay (Barbosa pers. comm.)

3. The bones of Inakayal were returned by the La Plata Museum to the Mapuche in 1994 (Endere 2002).

4. According to Poignant (1993: 49) one of the Fijians was a woman from Virginia. Cheating the public in this way may have been common practice for P.T. Barnum who, as Fausto-Sterling (1995: 30) notes, also billed an African American from Connecticut as 'Zip the What-is-it', a member of a newly discovered race who had been captured in the Gambia.

Chapter 6

1. e.g. *Federal Archaeology* Fall/Winter 1996: 35; Schanche 2002; Sellevold 2002; Podgorny and Politis 1992; *El Dia, La Plata* 18 April 1994; Endere 2002; Barbosa 2002; Koch and Sillen 1996; *Observer* 18 February 1997; Parsons and Segobye 2002; Simpson 1994: 31; Ballard 2001.

2. For more information on the NMAI Act see www.nmnh.si.edu/anthro/ repatriation/repat.htm.

Chapter 7

1. P. Brown, University of New England to B. Jones, Federal Minister for Science and Technology 29 June 1984, reproduced in Meehan 1984: 139.

2. I. Davidson, University of New England to B. Jones 20 July1984, reproduced in Meehan 1984: 142.

3. Communiqué of the 13th Meeting of the Cultural Ministers Council, Adelaide, 27 February 1998.

4. Communiqué of the 14th meeting of the Cultural Ministers Council (CMC) Sydney, 11 August 2000.

Chapter 8

1. For media reports of these events see, for example, the *Launceston Sunday Examiner* 25 February 1990; *Launceston Examiner* 27 February 1990; *Melbourne Sunday Sun* 25 February 1990; *Sunday Tasmanian* 11 March 1990; 25 March 1990; *Sydney Morning Herald* 1 February 1990, 2 February 1990, 14 February 1990, 26 February 1990.

2. The University Court is composed of: 'the rector; the principal; the lord provost of the city of Edinburgh for the time being; an assessor nominated by the Chancellor; an assessor nominated by the rector; an assessor nominated by the lord provost, magistrates and council of the City of Edinburgh; four assessors elected by the General Council; six assessors, elected from among its members by the Senatus Academicus, of whom at least two [are] readers or lecturers; such persons, not exceeding three in number of whom not more than one may hold an appointment in the University of Edinburgh, as may be co-opted by the University Court' (Universities (Scotland) Act 1966 Section 1 Part iv).

3. Subject to the review and control of the University Court, the Senatus Academicus is responsible for, amongst other things, superintending and regulating the teaching and discipline of the University and administering the University's property (Universities (Scotland) Act, 1858 Preamble 5).

Chapter 9

1. A range of witnesses gave written and oral evidence to the enquiry, including those 'concerned with or responsible for museums and museum policy, archaeology and the protection of the archaeological heritage, the legitimate trade in art and antiquities, enforcement measures against illegal trading, claims for the return of cultural property, and Government policy' (CMSSC 2000: Introduction). All Reports of the Select Committee, including published evidence, are available at www.parliament.uk/commons/selcom/cmshome.htm.

2. The UK Government noted that the terms of reference give effect to the Government's earlier undertaking to the Committee for further discussions with the relevant bodies on the need for guidance on the issue of the care of human remains (recommendation xv), on the handling of requests for their return and on the issue of access to information about holdings of human remains.

3. The report of the UK Working Group on Human Remains can be found online at www.culture.gov.uk

4. For details of the Retained Organs Commission see www.nhs.uk/retainedorgans/.

5. Part b.2 is a recommendation of the majority and not, therefore, unanimous.

Chapter 10

1. For articles written about the construction of Aboriginality see, for example, Chase 1981; Langton 1981; Cowlishaw 1987; Beckett (ed.) 1988; Lattas 1993.

Abbreviations

AAA	=	Australian Archaeological Association
AAAC	=	Australian Aboriginal Affairs Council
AAP	=	Australian Associated Press
ACPAC	=	American Committee for Preservation of Archaeological Collections
AIAS	=	Australian Institute of Aboriginal Studies, now AIATSIS
AIATSIS	=	Australian Institute of Aboriginal and Torres Strait Islander Studies
ALH	=	Allport Library, Hobart
AML	=	Ashmolean Museum Library, Oxford
ANU	=	Australian National University
AOF	=	Aborigine Office Files
ATSIC	=	Aboriginal and Torres Strait Islander Commission
CMSSC	=	Culture, Media and Sport Select Committee
DCMS	=	Department of Culture, Media and Sport
EADL	=	Edinburgh University Anatomy Department Library
ELSC	=	Edinburgh University Library Special Collections
FAIRA	=	Foundation for Aboriginal and Islander Research Action
GGAL	=	George Grey Letter Collection, Auckland Library
LAO	=	Lunatic Asylum Office
MEG	=	Museum Ethnographers Group
NAGPRA	=	The Native American Graves Protection and Repatriation Act
NHM	=	Natural History Museum, London
NL	=	National Library, Canberra, Australia
NMA	=	National Museum of Australia, Canberra
NMAI Act	=	National Museum of the American Indian Act
NSWSA	=	New South Wales State Archives
PLA	=	Parkside Lunatic Asylum
QSA	=	Queensland State Archives, Brisbane
RCSEL	=	Royal College of Surgeons of England, Library
ROC	=	Retained Organs Commission
SAM	=	South Australian Museum
SASA	=	South Australia State Archives
TAC	=	Tasmanian Aboriginal Centre
WAC	=	World Archaeological Congress
WG Report	=	Report of the Working Group on Human Remains
WI	=	Wellcome Institute, London

Bibliography

For abbreviations see the list on p. 169.

Abbie, A.A. 1967: Review. *Current Anthropology* 8 (1/2): 113-14.

Adcock, G.J., Dennis, E.S., Easteal, S., Huttley, G.A., Jermiin, L.S., Peacock, W.J., and Thorne, A. 2001: Mitochondrial DNA Sequences in Ancient Australians: implications for modern human origins. *Science* 98 (2): 537-42.

Aird, M. 2002: Development in the Repatriation of Human Remains and Other Cultural Items in Queensland. In C. Fforde *et al.* (eds) *The Dead and Their Possessions*. London: Routledge. 303-11.

Allingham, E.G. 1924: *Romance of the Rostrum*. London: Witherby.

Anderson, C. 1986: Research and Return of Objects as a Social Process. *COMA Bulletin* 19: 2-10.

Anderson, C. 1990: Repatriation, Custodianship and the Policies of the South Australian Museum. *COMA Bulletin* 24: 112-22.

Anon. 1825: On the Coincidence between the Natural Talents and Dispositions of Nations and the Development of their Brains. *Phrenological Journal* 2: 1-19.

Anyon, R. and Thornton, R. 2002: Implementing Repatriation in the United States: issues raised and lessons learned. In C. Fforde *et al.* (eds) *The Dead and Their Possessions*. London: Routledge. 190-8.

Atkinson, A.M. 1985: The Shepparton Aboriginal Keeping Place. *COMA Bulletin* 16: 9-10.

Attwood, B. 1989: *The Making of the Aborigines*. St Leonard's: Allen & Unwin.

Attwood, B. 1992: Introduction. In B. Attwood and J. Arnold (eds) 1992: *Power, Knowledge and Aborigines*. Special Edition of the *Journal of Australian Studies* 35: i-xvi.

Bahn, P. 1984: Do Not Disturb? Archaeology and the Rights of the Dead. *Oxford Journal of Archaeology* 3 (1): 127-39.

Baker, J.R. 1974: *Race*. Oxford: Oxford University Press.

Ballard, C. 2001: A.F.R. Wollaston and the 'Utakwa River Mountain Papuan Skulls. *Journal of Pacific History* 36 (1): 117-26.

Banks, J. 1803: Letter from Joseph Banks to Governor King. In *Historical Records of New South Wales* 5. Bladern, F.M. (ed.) 1897. 834-6.

Banton, M. 1977: *The Idea of Race*. London: Tavistock Publications.

Barbosa, R.M. 2002: One Hundred and Sixty years of Exile: Vaimaca Pirú and the campaign to repatriate his remains to Uruguay. In C. Fforde *et al.* (eds) *The Dead and Their Possessions*. London: Routledge. 218-21.

Barkan, E. 1988: Mobilizing Scientists against Nazi Racism 1933-1939. In G.W. Stocking (ed.) 1988: *Bones, Bodies and Behaviour*. Wisconsin: Wisconsin University Press. 180-205.

Barkan, E. 1992: *The Retreat of Scientific Racism: changing concepts of race in Britain and the United States between the World Wars*. Cambridge: Cambridge University Press.

Basedow, H. 1904: Anthropological Notes on the South Australian Government North-West Prospecting Expedition, 1903. *Transactions Royal Society of South Australia* 28: 12-51.

Basedow, H. 1935: *Knights of the Boomerang*. Sydney: The Endeavour Press.

Baudrillard, J. 1994: The System of Collecting. In J. Elsner and R. Cardinal (eds) 1994: *The Cultures of Collecting*. London: Reaktion Books. 7-24.

Beckett, J.R. (ed.) 1988: *Past and Present. The Construction of Aboriginality*. Canberra: Aboriginal Studies Press.

Beckett, J.R. 1988: The Past in the Present; the Present in the Past: constructing a national Aboriginality. In J.R. Beckett (ed.) 1988: *Past and Present. The Construction of Aboriginality*. Canberra: Aboriginal Studies Press. 191-217.

Bendyshe, T. 1865: The History of Anthropology. *Memoirs of the Anthropological Society of London* I: 335-458.

Benedict, B.M. 1990: The 'Curious Attitude' in Eighteenth-Century Britain: observing and owning. *Eighteenth Century Life* 4 (3): 59-98.

Bennett, T. 1995: *The Birth of the Museum*. London: Routledge.

Bernier, F. 1684: A New Division of the Earth, according to the Different species or Races of Men who Inhabit it. In T. Bendyshe 1865: The History of Anthropology. *Memoirs of the Anthropological Society of London* I: 360-4.

Berry, R.J.A. 1911: The Sectional Anatomy of the Head of the Australian Aboriginal: a contribution to the subject of Racial Anatomy. *Proceedings of the Royal Society of Edinburgh* 31 (v): 604-6.

Berry, R.J.A. and Robertson A.W.D. 1911: The Place in Nature of the Tasmanian Aboriginal as Deduced from a Study of his Calvarium. Part 1. *Proceedings of the Royal Society of Edinburgh* 31: 41-84.

Bieder, R.E. no date: A Brief Historical Survey of the Expropriation of Indian Remains. Unpublished manuscript.

Bischoff, C. 1931: *The Hard Road*. London: Hopkinson.

Blumenbach, J.F. 1775: *De Generis Humani Varietate Nativa*. In T. Bendyshe (ed.) 1865: *The Treatises of Johann Friedrich Blumenbach*. London: Longman, Green, Longman, Roberts & Green. 64-143.

Blumenbach, J.F. 1795: *De Generis Humani Varietate Nativa. Third Edition*. In T. Bendyshe (ed.) 1865a: *The Treatises of Johann Friedrich Blumenbach*. London: Longman, Green, Longman, Roberts & Green. 145-276.

Boas, F. 1894a: The Anthropology of the North American Indian. In G.W. Stocking (ed.) 1974: *A Franz Boas Reader: the shaping of American anthropology, 1883-1911*. New York: Basic Books. 191-201.

Boas, F. 1894b: Human Faculty as Determined by Race. *Proceedings of the American Association for the Advancement of Science* 43: 301-27.

Boas, F. 1903: Heredity of Headform. *American Anthropologist* 5: 530-8.

Boas, F. 1911: Instability of Human Types. In G.W. Stocking (ed.) 1974: *A Franz Boas Reader. The Shaping of American Anthropology, 1883-1911*. New York: Basic Books. 214-18.

Boas, F. 1940: *Race, Language and Culture*. New York: Macmillan.

Bibliography

Bowdler, S. 1992: Unquiet Slumbers. The return of the Kow Swamp burials. *Antiquity* 69: 103-6.

Bowes, J. 1914: The Australian Aboriginal. In J. Colvell and W.H. Fitchett (eds) 1914: *A Century in the Pacific 1815-1915*. London: Kelly. 151-73.

Bowler, J.M., Jones, R., Allen, H. and Thorne, A.G. 1970: Pleistocene Human Remains from Australia: a living site and human cremations from Lake Mungo, western New South Wales. *World Archaeology* 2 (1): 39-59.

Bowler, J.M., Thorne, A.G. and Polach, H.A. 1972: Pleistocene Man in Australia: age and significance of the Mungo skeleton. *Nature* 240: 48-50.

Bowler, P.J. 1992: From 'Savage' to 'Primitive': Victorian evolutionism and the interpretation of marginalised peoples. *Antiquity* 66: 721-9.

Brace, C.L. 1964: On the Race Concept. *Current Anthropology* 5 (4): 313-14, 319-20.

Bray, T.L. 1996: Repatriation, Power Relations and the Politics of the Past. *Antiquity* 70: 440-4.

Bray, T.L. and Wilson, T.W. (eds) 1994: *Reckoning with the Dead: the Larsen Bay repatriation and the Smithsonian Institution*. Washington & London: Smithsonian Institution Press.

Brennan, F.T. Consultation Document 15. Palm Island, Deed of Grant in Trust. Unpublished manuscript.

Briggs, L. 1994: The Development of the Ancestral Remains Data Base and Subsequent Queensland Community Consultation Strategy. Unpublished report.

Brocklebank, L. and Kaufman, M. 1992: An Investigation into the Identity of a Skull in the Department of Anatomy Collection, University of Edinburgh, Marked as Tasmanian XXX2, and Believed to be that of William Lanne. *World Archaeological Bulletin* 6: 70-4.

Brohier, R.L. 1933: *The Golden Age of Military Adventure in Ceylon: an account of the Uva Rebellion 1817-1818*. Colombo.

Brook, J. and Kohen, J. 1991: *The Parramatta Native Institution and the Black Town*. Sydney: New South Wales University Press.

Brown, T.A. and Brown, K.A. 1992: Ancient DNA and the Archaeologist. *Antiquity* 66 (250): 10-23.

Brues, A. 1967: Review. *Current Anthropology* 8 (1/2): 117-18.

Buchanan, A., Russell, J.G. and Torr, W.G. 1903. Report of Board of Inquiry Re: Dr. Ramsay Smith. *Proceedings of Parliamentary Papers, South Australia* 3: 1-4.

Buffon, G.L.L. 1785: *Natural History*. Translated by William Smellie. London.

Camper, P. 1794: *The Works of the Late Professor Petrus Camper on the Connexion between the Science of Anatomy and the Arts of Drawing, Painting, Statuary*. Translated by T. Cogan. London: C. Dilly.

Chase, A. 1981: Empty Vessels and Loud Noises: views about Aboriginal people today. *Social Alternatives* 2 (2): 23-7.

Chisholm, J.S. 1994: Reply. *Current Anthropology* 35 (1): 42-5.

Clark, J. 1983: Tasmanian Museum and Art Gallery. *COMA Bulletin* 12: 18-19.

Clark, J. 1990: Tasmanian Museum and Art Gallery. *Australian Archaeology* 31: 57.

Clifford, J. 1985: Objects and Selves – an Afterword. In G. Stocking (ed.) *Objects and Others, Essays on Museums and Material Culture*. Wisconsin: University of Wisconsin Press. 236-46.

Clifford, J. 1988: *The Predicament of Culture: twentieth-century ethnography, literature and art*. Harvard: Harvard University Press.

Clift, W. 1831: *Catalogue of the Contents of the Museum of the Royal College of Surgeons, London. Part III. The Human and Comparative Osteology*. London: Royal College of Surgeons.

Coddington, D. 2002: 'Heartbreak Hospital'. *North and South* June issue. 29-41.

Colbung, K. 1996: *Yagan. The Swan River 'Settlement'*. Australia Council for the Arts.

Combe, G. 1835: *The Constitution of Man Considered in Relation to External Objects*. Edinburgh: Maclachlan & Stewart.

Combe, G. 1841: *Notes on the United States of North America, During a Phrenological Visit in 1838-39-40* (3 vols). Edinburgh: Maclachlan, Stewart & Co.

Commonwealth of Australia 1997: *Bringing Them Home. Report of the National Enquiry into the Separation of Aboriginal and Torres Strait Islander Children from their Families*. Canberra: Commonwealth of Australia.

Coon, C.S. 1962: *The Origin of the Races*. New York: Knopf.

Coon, C.S. 1963: Comment. *Current Anthropology* 4 (4): 363.

Coon, C.S. 1964: Comment. *Current Anthropology* 5 (4): 314.

Coon, C.S. and Hunt, E.E. 1965: *The Living Races of Man*. New York: Alfred A. Knopf.

Coon, C.S. and Hunt, E.E. 1967: The Living Races of Man. *Current Anthropology* 8 (1/2): 112-13.

Cooter, R. 1984: *The Cultural Meaning of Popular Science*. Cambridge: Cambridge University Press.

Count, E.W. 1964: Commet. *Current Anthropology* 5 (4): 314-16.

Cove, J. 1995: *What the Bones Say: Tasmanian Aborigines, science and domination*. Ottawa: Carleton University Press.

Cowlishaw, G. 1986: Aborigines and Anthropologists. *Australian Aboriginal Studies* 1: 2-12.

Cowlishaw, G. 1987: Colour, Culture and the Aboriginalists. *MAN* n.s. 22: 221-37.

Cowlishaw, G. 1992: Studying Aborigines: changing canons in anthropology and history. In B. Attwood and J. Arnold (eds) 1992: *Power, Knowledge and Aborigines*. Special Edition of the *Journal of Australian Studies* 35: 20-31.

Creamer, H. 1988: Aboriginality in New South Wales: beyond the image of culture-less outcasts. In J.R. Beckett (ed.) 1988: *Past and Present. The Construction of Aboriginality*. Canberra: Aboriginal Studies Press. 45-62.

Cunningham, D.J. 1908: Anthropology in the Eighteenth Century. *Journal of the Royal Anthropological Institute* 38: 10-35.

Cuvier, G. 1800: Note Instructive sur les Reserches à faire relativement aux différences anatomiques des diverses races d'homme. In J. Copans and J. Jamins (eds) 1978: *Aux Origines de l'Anthropologie Française. Les Mémoires de la Société des Observateurs de l'Homme en l'An VIII*. Paris: Le Sycomore. 171-6.

Cuvier, G. 1817: Faites sur le cadavre d'une femme connue à Paris à Londres sous le nomme de Venus Hottentotte. *Mémoires du Musée Nationale d'Histoire Naturelle* 3: 259-74.

Daes, E. 1995: Protection of the Heritage of Indigenous People. *United Nations Working Group on Indigenous Populations Twelfth Session 20-29 July 1994*,

Geneva, Switzerland. The Australian Contribution 1994. Canberra: ATSIC. 125-33.

Dahl, K. 1926: *In Savage Lands: an account of a hunting and collecting expedition to Arnhem Land and Dampier Land.* London: Philip Allan & Co.

Dale, R. 1834: *Descriptive Account of the Panoramic View etc. of King George's Sound and the Adjacent Country.* London: J. Cross.

Darwin, C. 1859: *The Origin of Species.* London: Penguin.

Darwin, C. 1871: *The Descent of Man.* London: John Murray.

Davidson, I. 1991: Notes for a Code of Ethics for Australian Archaeologists Working with Aboriginal and Torres Strait Islander Heritage. *Australian Archaeology* 32: 61-4.

Davis, J.B. 1867: *Thesaurus Craniorum.* London: printed for the subscribers.

Dawson, J.W. 1880: *Fossil Men and their Modern Representatives.* London: Hodder & Stoughton.

Day, M. 1995: Humana: anatomical, pathological and curious human specimens in Sloane's museum. In A. MacGregor (ed.) 1995: *Sir Hans Sloane. Collector, Scientist, Antiquary. Founding Father of the British Museum.* London: British Museum Press. 69-71.

De Guistino, D. 1975: *Conquest of Mind: phrenology and Victorian social thought.* London: Croom Helm.

Dobzhansky, T. 1962: Comment. *Current Anthropology* 3 (3): 279-80.

Dobzhansky, T. 1963: Possibility that Homo Sapiens Evolved Independently 5 Times is Vanishingly Small. *Current Anthropology* 4 (4): 360, 364-5.

Donlon, D. and Pardoe, C. 1991: The Keppel Island and Central Queensland Coast Skeletons. A report for the Aboriginal communities of the Keppel Islands and the central coast of Queensland. Unpublished manuscript, AIATSIS ms 2980.

Donlon, D. 1992: Assessment of the Cultural Significance of Australian Aboriginal Skeletal Remains held in the National Museum of Australia. Unpublished report prepared for the National Museum of Australia, Canberra.

Donlon, D. 1993: Preliminary Examination of the Edinburgh Collection of Skeletal Remains and Methodology for Provenancing Aboriginal Skeletal Remains in Collecting Institutions. Unpublished report prepared for ATSIC.

Doumas, C. 1989: Archaeological Ethics and the Treatment of the Dead. *World Archaeological Bulletin* 4: 21-2.

Dower, A. 1923: Variations in the Inferior Nasal Region in the Skulls of Various Races. Unpublished PhD thesis. Department of Anatomy, University of Edinburgh.

Dreyfus, H.L. and Rabinow, P. 1982: *Michel Foucault: beyond structuralism and hermeneutics.* Brighton: Harvester Press.

Dubow, S. 1995: *Scientific Racism in Modern South Africa.* Cambridge: Cambridge University Press.

Duckworth, W.L.H. 1908: On the Brains of Aboriginal Natives of Australia in the Anatomy School, Cambridge University. Part 1. *Journal of Anatomy and Physiology* XLII: 69-287.

Duckworth, W.L.H. 1913: *International Agreements for the Unification (a) of Craniometric and Cephalometric Measurements, (b) of Anthropometric Measurements to be made on the Living Subject.* Cambridge: Cambridge University Press.

Duncan, T. 1984: Bones Rights now an Issue in Tasmania too. *Bulletin* 4 September 1984.

Duroux, M. 1985: Establishing a Keeping Place. *COMA Bulletin* 16: 7-8.

Edwards, C. and Read, P. (eds) 1989: *The Lost Children*. Sydney: Doubleday.

Ellis, V.R. 1981: *Trucanini. Queen or Traitor?* Canberra: Aboriginal Studies Press.

Elsner, J. and Cardinal, R. (eds) 1994: *The Cultures of Collecting*. London: Reaktion Books.

Endere, M. 2002: The Reburial Issue in Argentina: a growing conflict. In C. Fforde *et al.* (eds) *The Dead and Their Possessions*. London: Routledge. 266-83.

Erikson, P.A. 1979: Phrenology and Physical Anthropology: the George Coombe connection. *Occasional Papers in Anthropology* 6. Department of Anthropology, St. Mary's University, Halifax Nova Scotia.

Evans, R., Saunders, K. and Cronin, K. 1993: *Race Relations in Colonial Queensland*. 3rd edition. Brisbane: University of Queensland Press.

Fabian, J. 1983: *Time and the Other*. New York: Columbia University Press.

Fausto-Sterling, A. 1995: Gender, Race and Nation: the comparative anatomy of the 'Hottentot' women in Europe, 1815-1817. In J. Terry and J. Urla (eds) 1995: *Deviant Bodies: critical perspectives on difference in science and popular culture*. Bloomington & Indianapolis: Indiana University Press. 19-48.

Fforde, C. 1992a: The Royal College of Surgeons of England: a brief history of its collections and a catalogue of some current holdings. *World Archaeological Bulletin* 6: 22-31.

Fforde, C. 1992b: The Posthumous History of William Lanne. *World Archaeological Bulletin* 6: 63-9.

Fforde, C. 1992c: The 'Williamson Collection'. *World Archaeological Bulletin* 6: 20.

Fforde, C. and Ormond Parker, L. 2001: Repatriation Developments in the UK. *Indigenous Law Bulletin* 5 (6): 9-13.

Fforde, C. 2002: Yagan. In C. Fforde *et al.* (eds) *The Dead and Their Possessions*. London: Routledge.

Fforde, C. 2002: Collecting, Repatriation and Identity. In C. Fforde *et al.* (eds) *The Dead and Their Possessions*. London: Routledge. 25-46.

Fforde, C., Hubert, J. and Turnbull, P. (eds) 2002: *The Dead and Their Possessions*. London: Routledge.

Firth, R. 1938: *Human Types: an introduction to social anthropology*. London: Thomas Nelson & Sons.

Flower, W.H. 1879: *Catalogue of the Specimens Illustrating the Osteology and Dentition of Vertebrated Animals Recent and Extinct Contained in the Museum of the Royal College of Surgeons of England*. London: Printed for the College.

Flower, W.H. 1881: Presidential address to the Department of Anthropology, British Association for the Advancement of Science. In Flower, W.H. (ed.) 1898: *Essays on Museums and other Subjects Connected with Natural History*. London: Macmillan & Co. 235-50.

Flower, W.H. 1885: Classification of the Varieties of the Human Species. President's Address. *Journal of the Anthropological Institute* XIV: 378-94.

Flower, W.H. 1898: *Essays on Museums and Other Subjects Connected with Natural History*. London: Macmillan & Co.

Bibliography

Flower, W.H. 1907: *Museum of the Royal College of Surgeons of England. Catalogue of the Osteological Series. Man. Part I Vol. II.* 2nd edition. London.

Flower, W.H. and Murie, J. 1867: Account of the Dissection of a Bushwoman. *Journal of Anatomy and Physiology* 1: 189-208.

Foucault, M. 1970: *The Order of Things.* London: Tavistock.

Foucault, M. 1977: *Discipline and Punish.* Harmondsworth: Penguin.

Friedman, J.B. 1981: *The Monstrous Races in Medieval Art and Thought.* London: Harvard University Press.

Gamble, C. 1992: Archaeology, History and the Uttermost Ends of the Earth – Tasmania, Tierra del Fuego and the Cape. *Antiquity* 66: 712-20.

Gerstenblith, P. 1995: Identity and Cultural Property: the protection of cultural property in the United States. *Boston University Law Review* 75 (3): 559-687.

Gilman, S.L. 1985: Black Bodies, White Bodies: toward an iconography of female sexuality in late 19th century art, medicine and literature. *Critical Inquiry* 12: 204-42.

Goodman, A.H. and Armelagos, G.J. 1996: The Resurrection of Race: the concept of race in physical anthropology in the 1990s. In L.T. Reynolds and L. Liberman (eds) *Race and Other Misadventures: essays in honor of Ashley Montagu in his ninetieth year.* New York: General Hall Inc. 174-86.

Gould, S.J. 1978: Morton's Ranking of Races by Cranial Capacity. *Science* 200: 503-9.

Gould, S.J. 1981: *The Mismeasure of Man.* London: Penguin.

Grew, N. 1681: *Musaeum Regalis Societatis or a Catalogue of the Natural and Artificial Rarities belonging to the Royal Society and Preserved at Gresham College.* London: W. Rawlins.

Grey Turner, G. 1945: The Hunterian Museum. Yesterday and tomorrow. *The Lancet* 24 March: 359-63.

Grupe, G. and Peters, J. 2003: *Documenta Archaeologiae. Decyphering Ancient Bones: the research potential of bioarchaeological collections.* Rahden/Westf: Verlag Marie Leidorf GmbH.

Gunson, N. 1974. Australian Reminiscences and Papers of L.E. Threlkeld. Missionary to the Aborigines 1824-1859. *Australian Aboriginal Studies* 40 (2 vols). Canberra: Aboriginal Studies Press.

Haddon, A.C. 1901: *Head Hunters, Black, White and Brown.* London: Methuen & Co.

Haddon, A.C. 1924: *The Races of Man.* Cambridge: Cambridge University Press.

Haddon, A.C. and Huxley, J. 1935: *We Europeans: a survey of the 'racial' problem.* London: Jonathan Cape.

Hagelberg, E., Sykes, B. and Hedges, R. 1989: Ancient Bone DNA Amplified. *Nature* 342: 485.

Hagelberg, E. 1990: Bones, Dry Bones. *Times Higher Educational Supplement* 14 December 1990.

Hagelberg, E. 1992: DNA in Bones. *World Archaeological Bulletin* 6: 110-12.

Hall, J. 1986: President's Report. *Australian Archaeology* 22: 140-5.

Hall, R. 1983: On 'Redefining Race': concepts of race according to physical anthropologists. *Current Anthropology* 24 (4): 529.

Haller, J.S. 1971: *Outcasts from Evolution: scientific attitudes of racial inferiority, 1859-1900.* Chicago: University of Illinois Press.

Hanchant, D. 2002: Practicalities in the Return of Remains: the importance of provenance and the question of unprovenanced remains. In C. Fforde *et al.* (eds) *The Dead and Their Possessions*. London: Routledge. 312-16.

Harmer, S.F. 1912: Preface to the Second Edition. In C.T. Regan 1921: *Guide to the Specimens Illustrating the Races of Mankind (Anthropology) Exhibited in the Department of Zoology British Museum (Natural History)*. London: Printed by order of the Trustees of the British Museum. i.

Harraway, D.J. 1988: Remodelling the Human Way of Life. Sherwood Washburn and the new physical anthropology, 1950-1980. In G.W. Stocking (ed.) 1988: *Bones, Bodies and Behaviour*. Wisconsin: Wisconsin University Press. 206-59.

Hassan, F.A. 1997: Beyond the Surface: comments on Hodder's 'reflexive excavation methodology'. *Antiquity* 71: 1020-5.

Hedderley, F. 1970: *Phrenology: a study in mind*. London: L.N. Fowler & Co.

Hedges, R. 1994: Book Review. Ancient DNA: recovery and analysis of genetic material from palaeontological, archaeological, museum, medical and forensic specimens, edited by B. Herrmann and S. Hummel (1994). *Journal of Archaeological Science* 21: 861.

Hemming, S. 1985: Development of the Issue. *COMA Bulletin* 16: 22-31.

Hermann, B. and Hummel, S. (eds) 1994: *Ancient DNA: recovery and analysis of genetic material from palaeontological, archaeological, museum, medical and forensic specimens*. Berlin: Springer-Verlag.

Hodder, I. 1997: 'Always momentary, fluid and flexible': towards a reflexive excavation methodology. *Antiquity* 71: 691-700.

Hollander, B. 1920: *In Search of the Soul and the Mechanism of Thought, Emotion and Conduct*. New York: E.P. Dutton & Co.

Hollinsworth, D. 1992: Discourses on Aboriginality and the politics of identity in urban Australia. *Oceania* 63 (2): 137-55.

Hooper-Greenhill, E. 1992: *Museums and the Shaping of Knowledge*. London: Routledge.

Houzé, E. and Jacques, V. 1884: Les Australiens du Musée du Nord. *Bulletin de la Société d'Anthropologie de Bruxelles* III-IV: 53-153.

Hoyme, L. 1953: Physical Anthropology and its Instruments. *Southwestern Journal of Anthropology* 9: 408-30.

Hubert, J. 1989: A Proper Place for the Dead: a critical review of the 'reburial issue'. In R. Layton (ed.) 1989: *Conflict in the Archaeology of Living Traditions*. London: Routledge. 131-66.

Hubert, J. 1992: Dry Bones or Living Ancestors? Conflicting Perceptions of Life, Death and the Universe. *International Journal of Cultural Property* 1: 105-27.

Hull, J. 1960: Catalogue of Crania. Unpublished manuscript.

Hunt, J. 1866: On the Application of the Principle of Natural Selection to Anthropology. *Anthropological Review* IV: 320-40.

Hunt, J. 1867: On the Doctrine of Continuity applied to Anthropology. *Anthropological Review* V: 110-20.

Hunt, J. 1870: On the Acclimatisation of Europeans in the United States of America. *Anthropological Review* VIII: 109-37.

Hunter, J., Roberts, C. and Martine, A. 1996: *Studies in Crime: an introduction to forensic archaeology*. London: Batsford.

Bibliography

Isaac, B. 2002: Implementation of NAGPRA: The Peabody Museum of Archaeology and Ethnology, Harvard. In C. Fforde *et al.* (eds) *The Dead and Their Possessions*. London: Routledge. 160-70.

Jacobs, J.M. 1988: The Construction of Identity. In J. Beckett (ed.) 1988: *Past and Present. The Construction of Aboriginality*. Canberra: Aboriginal Studies Press. 31-43.

Janke, T. 1998 *Our Culture Our Future. Report on Australian Indigenous Cultural and Intellectual Property Rights*. Prepared for the Australian Institute of Aboriginal and Torres Strait Islander Studies and the Aboriginal and Torres Strait Islander Commission.

Johnston, W.R. 1988: *A Documentary History of Queensland*. Brisbane: Queensland University Press.

Jones, P.G. 1985: Museums and Sacred Material: the South Australian Museum's experience. *COMA Bulletin* 16: 16-21.

Jones, P.G. 1987: South Australian Anthropological Research: the board for Anthropological research and its early expeditions. *Records of the South Australian Museum* 20: 71-92.

Jones, S. 1994: Crossing Boundaries. *Museums Journal* July: 29.

Joyce, R. 2002: Academic freedom, stewardship, and cultural heritage: weighing the interests of stakeholders in crafting repatriation approaches In C. Fforde *et al.* (eds) *The Dead and Their Possessions*. London: Routledge. 99-107.

Jukes, J.B. 1847: *Narrative of the Surveying Voyage of HMS Fly Commanded by Capt. F.P. Blackwood, R.N. in Torres Strait, New Guinea, and other islands of the Eastern Archipelago during the years 1842-1846. Together with an excursion into the interior of the Eastern part of Java*. London: T. & W. Boone.

Kames, H. 1778: Preliminary Discourse, Concerning the Origin of Men and of Languages (second edition). In H.F. Augstein (ed.) 1996: *Race: the origins of an idea 1760-1850*. Bristol: Thoemmes Press. 10-23.

Keefe, K. 1988: Aboriginality: resistance and persistence. *Australian Aboriginal Studies* 1: 67-81.

Keith, A. 1931: *Ethnos, or the Problem of Race Considered from a New Point of View*. London: Kegan Paul & Co.

Keith, A. 1950. *An Autobiography*. London: Watts.

Kelso, A.J. 1967: Review. *Current Anthropology* 8 (1/2): 120.

Kennedy, M. 1985: *Born a Half-Caste*. Canberra: Aboriginal Studies Press.

Klaatsch, H. 1907a: Schlussbericht über meine Reise nach Australien in den Jahren 1904-1907. Translated by B. Stehlik 1986: Hermann Klaatsch and the Tiwi, 1906. *Aboriginal History* 10: 65-76.

Klaatsch, H. 1907b: Some Notes on Scientific Travels Amongst the Black Population of Tropical Australia in 1904, 1905, 1906. *Proceedings of the Australian and New Zealand Association for the Advancement of Science* 11: 577-92.

Klaatsch, H. 1923: *The Evolution and Progress of Mankind*. London: T. Fisher Unwin Ltd.

Krings, M., Stone, A., Schmitz, R.W., Krainitzki, H., Stoneking, M. and Paabo, S. 1997: Neanderthal DNA Sequences and the Origin of Modern Humans. *Cell* 90: 1930.

Koch, E. and Sillen, A. 1996: Rites of Passage. *New Scientist* June: 30-3.

Kuhn, T.S. 1962: *The Structure of Scientific Revolutions*. 3rd edition (1996). Chicago and London: University of Chicago Press.

Kuklick, H 1991: *The Savage Within: the social history of British anthropology*. Cambridge: Cambridge University Press.

L.P. 1695: The Second Part of the First Essay Concerning the Peopling and Planting of the New World, and Other Remote Areas. In T. Bendyshe 1865b: The History of Anthropology. *Memoirs of the Anthropological Society of London* I: 365-71.

Lahn, J. 1996: Finders Keepers, Losers Weepers: a 'social history' of the Kow Swamp remains. *Ngulaig* 15.

Lampert, R. 1983: Aboriginal Remains and the Australian Museum. *COMA Bulletin* 12: 19-20.

Langford, R. 1980: Our Heritage – Your Playground. *Australian Archaeology* 16: 1-6.

Langton, M. 1981: Urbanising Aborigines: the social scientists' great deception. *Social Alternatives* 2 (2): 16-22.

Lattas, A. 1993: Essentialism, Memory and Resistance: Aboriginality and the politics of authenticity. *Oceania* 63 (3): 240-67.

Lawrence, W. 1819: *Lectures on Physiology, Zoology and the Natural History of Man, delivered at the Royal College of Surgeons*. London.

Lawrence, W. 1822: *Lectures on Physiology, Zoology and the Natural History of Man, delivered at the Royal College of Surgeons*. London.

Lawrence, W. 1823: *Lectures on Physiology, Zoology, and the Natural History of Man*. 3rd edition. In Augstein, H.F. (ed.) 1996: *Race: the origins of an idea 1760-1850*. Bristol: Thoemmes Press. 90-126.

Lawrence, W. 1844: *Lectures on Comparative Anatomy, Physiology, Zoology and the Natural History of Man*. 9th edition. London: John Taylor.

Layton, R. 1989: Introduction: conflict in the archaeology of living traditions. In R. Layton (ed.) 1989: *Conflict in the Archaeology of Living Traditions*. London: Routledge. 1-21.

Leggett, J. 2000 *Restitution and Repatriation: guidelines for good practice*. London: Museums and Galleries Commission.

Lewin, R. 1984: Extinction Threatens Australian Anthropology. *Science* 225: 393-4.

Littlefield, A., Lieberman, L. and Reynolds, L.T. 1982: Redefining Race: the potential demise of a concept in physical anthropology. *Current Anthropology* 23 (6): 641-7, 652-3.

Livingstone, F.B. 1962: On the Non-existence of Human Races. *Current Anthropology* 3 (3): 279.

Lloyd, G.E.R. (ed.) 1978: *Hippocratic Writings*. London: Penguin.

Lovelace, A. 1994: A Special Case. *Museums Journal* July: 30.

Lunsingh Scheurleer, T.H. 1985: Early Dutch Cabinets of Curiosities. In O. Impey and A. MacGregor (eds) 1985: *The Origin of Museums: the cabinets of curiosities in sixteenth and seventeenth century Europe*. Oxford: Clarendon Press. 115-20.

Lumholtz, C. 1889: *Among Cannibals: account of four years travels in Australian and of camp life with the Aborigines of Queensland*. London: John Murray.

Bibliography

Macalister, A. 1892: Report of the Department of Human Anatomy. *Cambridge University Reporter* June, 936-7.

Macalister, A. 1893: Report of the Department of Human Anatomy. *Cambridge Reporter* June 8 1893: 959-60.

Macalister, A. 1897: Human Anatomy, Report of the Professor. *Cambridge Reporter* June 4 1897: 1036-7.

MacGillivray, J. 1852. *Narrative of the Voyage of HMS Rattlesnake*. London.

McGuire, R.H. 1989: The Sanctity of the Grave: white concepts and American Indian burials. In R. Layton (ed.) 1989: *Conflict in the Archaeology of Living Traditions*. London: Routledge. 167-84.

McGuire, R.H. 1992: Archaeology and the First Americans. *American Anthropologist* 94 (4): 816-36.

Mackay, D. 1985: *In the Wake of Cook: exploration, science and empire, 1780-1801*. Victoria: Victoria University Press.

Mackenzie, G.R. 1820: *Illustrations of Phrenology*. Edinburgh: A. Constable & Co.

MacKenzie, J.M. (ed.) 1990: *Imperialism and the Natural World*. Manchester: Manchester University Press.

McKeown, C.T. 2002: Implementing a 'True Compromise': the Native American Graves Protection and Repatriation Act. In C. Fforde *et al.* (eds) *The Dead and Their Possessions*. London: Routledge. 108-32.

MacLeod, R. 1982: On Visiting the Moving Metropolis: reflections on the architecture of imperial science. *Historical Records of Australian Science* 5: 1-16.

MacLeod, R. (ed.) 1988: *The Commonwealth of Science: ANZAAS and the scientific enterprise in Australasia 1888-1988*. Oxford: Oxford University Press.

MacLeod, R. and Rehbock, P.F. (eds) 1988: *Nature in its Greatest Extent: Western science in the Pacific*. Honolulu: University of Hawaii Press.

Macquarie, L. Unpublished Diary. NSWSA CY Reel 301.

Macquarie, L. (8 June 1816) Despatches. NSWSA: CY Reel 896

Mansell, M. 1990: The Case for Bringing Shiney Home. *Australian Financial Review* 28 June 1990.

Markus, A. 1988: Australian Governments and the Concept of Race. In M. de Lepervanche and G. Bottomley 1988: *The Cultural Construction of Race*. Sydney Studies in Society and Culture 4. Sydney: University of Sydney. 46-59.

Marx, K.F.H. 1865: Life of Blumenbach. In T. Bendyshe (ed.) 1865a: *The Anthropological Treatises of Johann Friedrich Blumenbach*. London: Longman, Green, Longman, Roberts & Green. 3-45.

Maury, A., Pulszky, F. and Meigs, J.A. 1857: *Indigenous Races of the Earth*. Philadelphia: J.B. Lippincott & Co.

Mavalwala, J. 1967: Review. *Current Anthropology* 8 (1/2): 122.

Meehan, B. 1971: The Form, Distribution and Antiquity of Aboriginal Australian Mortuary Practices. Unpublished MA thesis, University of Sydney.

Meehan, B. 1984: Aboriginal Skeletal Remains. *Australian Archaeology* 19: 122-47.

Meigs, J.A. 1858: *Hints to Craniographers*. Philadelphia: Merrihew & Thompson.

Milicerowa, H. 1955: *Crania Australica*. Polska Akademia Nauk Zakland Antropologii. Materialy I Prace Anthropologizne no. 6.

Molleson, T. 2003: Body of Evidence: museum collections, why they were brought together, their value today and public future. In G. Grupe and J. Peters (eds)

Documenta Archaeologiae. Decyphering Ancient Bones: the research potential of bioarchaeological collections. Rahden/Westf: Verlag Marie Leidorf GmbH. 17-28.

Monro, A. 1813: *Outlines of the Anatomy of the Human Body.* Edinburgh: Archibald Constable & Co.

Monro, A. 1825: *Elements of the Anatomy of the Human Body in its Sound State.* Edinburgh: John Carfrae & Son.

Monroe, D.L. and Echohawk W. 1991: Deft Deliberations. *Museum News* 70 (4): 55-88.

Montagu, A. 1963a: What is Remarkable About Varieties of Man is Likenesses, not Differences. *Current Anthropology* 4 (4): 361-3.

Montagu, A. 1963b: Reply. *Current Anthropology* 4 (4): 363-4.

Montagu, A. 1964a: Comment. *Current Anthropology* 5 (4): 317.

Montagu, A. 1964b: On Coon's 'The Origin of the Races'. In Montagu (ed.) 1964: *The Concept of Race.* 228-41.

Montagu, A. 1974: *Man's Most Dangerous Myth.* Oxford: Oxford University Press.

Morrell, V. 1995: Who Owns the Past? *Science* 268: 1424-6

Morris, A.G. 1996: Trophy Skulls, Museums and the San. In P. Skotnes (ed.) 1996: *Miscast: negotiating the presence of the Bushmen.* Cape Town: University of Cape Town. 67-79.

Morton, S.G. 1839: *Crania Americana.* Philadelphia: J. Dobson.

Moyal, A. 1993: *A Bright and Savage Land.* 2nd edition. London: Penguin.

Mulvaney, J. 1989: Bones of Contention. *The Bulletin* 9 October.

Mulvaney, J. 1991: Past Regained, Future Lost: the Kow Swamp Pleistocene burials. *Antiquity* 65: 12-21.

Myers, F. 1994: Culture-Making: performing Aboriginality at the Asia Society Gallery. *American Ethnologist* 21 (4): 679-99.

Nott, J.C. 1844: *Two Lectures on the Natural History of the Caucasian and Negro Races.* Mobile: Dade & Thompson.

Nott, J.C. and Gliddon G.R. 1854: *Types of Mankind.* London: Trubner & Co.

Novotny, V., Iscan, M.Y. and Loth, S.R. 1993: Morphologic and Osteometric Assessment of Age, Sex and Race from the Skull. In M.Y. Iscan and R.P. Helmer (eds) *Forensic Analysis of the Skull.* New York: Wiley-Liss. 71-88.

O'Connor, D. and Quirke, S. 2003: Introduction: mapping the unknown in Ancient Egypt. In D. O'Connor and S. Quirke (eds) *Encounters with Ancient Egypt: Mysterious Lands.* London: UCL Press. 1-21.

Ogilvie, G. and Ogilvie, L. 1874: Inventory of the Phrenological Museum. Edinburgh. Unpublished manuscript.

O'Keefe, P.J. 1992: Maoris Claim Head. *International Journal of Cultural Property* 2 (1): 393-4.

Ormond Parker, L. 1997a: Ancestral Remains Project Brief European Archival Research (February-August 1997). Available at www.faira.org.au/issues.html.

Ormond Parker, L. 1997b: A Commonwealth Repatriation Odyssey. *Aboriginal Law Bulletin* 3 (90): 9-12.

Ormond Parker, L. (forthcoming): Indigenous Peoples' Rights to their Cultural Heritage. *Public Archaeology.*

Palm Island, W. 1996: *Walter Palm Island Speaks on Palm Island.* Central Queensland Land Council Aboriginal Corporation 2 (2).

Palm Island, W. 2002: Tambo. In C. Fforde *et al.* (eds) *The Dead and Their Possessions*. London: Routledge. 222-8.

Pardoe, C. 1991: Eye of the Storm. *Journal of Indigenous Studies* 2 (1): 16-23.

Pardoe, C. 1992. Arches of Radii, Corridors of Power: reflections on current archaeological practice. In B. Attwood and J. Arnold (eds) 1992: *Power, Knowledge and Aborigines*. Special Edition of the *Journal of Australian Studies* 35. 45-62.

Pardoe, C., and Donlon, D. 1991: The Roth Collection and Other Aboriginal Skeletal Remains from the Keppel Islands and Central Coast of Queensland: description and analysis. Unpublished report for the Australian Museum. AIATSIS ms 2980.

Parsons, N. and Segobye, A. 2002: Missing Persons and Stolen Bodies: the repatriation of 'El Negro' to Botswana. In C. Fforde *et al.* (eds) *The Dead and Their Possessions*. London: Routledge. 245-55.

Patterson, H. 1854: Memoir of S.G. Morton. In J.C. Nott and G.R. Gliddon 1854: *Types of Mankind*. London: Trubner & Co. xvii-lvii.

Pearce, S.M. (ed.) 1992: *Museums, Objects and Collections: a cultural study*. Leicester: Leicester University Press.

Pearce, S.M. (ed.) 1994a *Interpreting Objects and Collections*. London: Routledge.

Pearce, S.M. 1994b: Introduction. In S.M. Pearce (ed.) 1994: *Interpreting Objects and Collections*. London: Routledge. 1-6.

Péron, F. 1807-1816: *Voyage de Découvertes aux Terres Australes. Exécuté par ordre de Sa Majesté l'Empereur et Roi, sur les corvettes le Géographe. Le Naturaliste, et la Goelette le Casuarina, pendant les Années 1800, 1801, 1802, 1803 et 1804. Tome Premier.* Paris: De l'Imprimerie Impériale.

Plomley, N.J.B. 1962: A List of Tasmanian Aboriginal Material in Collections in Europe. *Records of the Queen Victoria Museum, Launceston* n.s. 15: 1-16.

Podgorny, I. and Politis G. 1992: Que Sucedio en la Historia? Los Esqueletos Araucanos del Museo de La Plata y la Conquista del Desierto. *Arqueologia Contemporanea* 3: 73-9.

Poignant, R. 1992: The Grid on Contested Ground: at Pickford's Freight Store. *The Olive Pink Journal* 4 (1): 17-22.

Poignant, R. 1993: Captive Aboriginal Lives: Billy, Jenny, Little Toby and their companions. *Working Papers in Australian Studies* 87. Sir Robert Menzies Centre for Australian Studies, Institute of Commonwealth Studies, London.

Pomian, K. 1990: *Collectors and Curiosities*. Oxford: Polity.

Powledge, T.M. and Rose, M. 1996: The Great DNA Hunt. *Archaeology* 49 (5): 36-44.

Prentis, M.D. 1991: The Life and Death of Johnny Campbell. *Aboriginal History* 15 (1-2): 138-51.

Prichard, J.C. 1813: *Researches into the Physical History of Mankind*. London.

Prichard, J.C. 1843: *The Natural History of Man*. London: H. Balliere.

Proctor, R. 1988: From *Anthropologie* to *Rassenkunde* in the German Anthropological Tradition. In G.W. Stocking (ed.) 1988: *Bones, Bodies and Behaviour*. Wisconsin: Wisconsin University Press. 138-79.

Queensland Museum Pamphlet, no date: Some information for Aboriginal people concerning Human Remains held in the Queensland Museum. AIATSIS Library p. 15211.

Rabinow, P. (ed.) 1984: *The Foucault Reader*. London: Penguin.

Rahtz, P. 1985: *Invitation to Archaeology*. Oxford: Blackwell.

Raines, J.C.B. 1992: One is Missing: Native American Graves Protection and Repatriation Act: an overview and analysis. *American Indian Law Review* 17 (2): 639-64.

Ramsay Smith, W. 1907a: The Place of the Australian Aboriginal in Recent Anthropological Research. *Report of the Eleventh Meeting of the Australian Association for the Advancement of Science*: 558-76.

Ramsay Smith, W. 1907b: The Inca Bone: its homology and nomenclature. *Proceedings of the Royal Society of Edinburgh* XXVIII (VII): 588-94.

Ramsay Smith, W. 1908: The Evolution of Man's Teeth Founded upon a Study of the Development of the Australian Aboriginal. *Journal of Anatomy and Physiology* 42: 126-31.

Ramsay Smith, W. 1913: Australian Conditions and Problems from the Standpoint of Present Anthropological Knowledge. *Presidential Address to the Section of Anthropology of the Australian Association for the Advancement of Science*. Melbourne: Government Printer.

Ramsay Smith, W. 1924: *In Southern Seas: wanderings of a naturalist*. London: John Murray.

Regan, C.T. 1921: *Guide to the Specimens Illustrating the Races of Mankind (Anthropology) Exhibited in the Department of Zoology British Museum (Natural History)*. London: Printed by Order of the Trustees of the British Museum.

Relethford, J.H. 2001: Absence of Regional Affinities of Neandertal DNA with Living Humans does not Reject Multiregional Evolution. *American Journal of Physical Anthropology* 115: 95-8.

Reynolds, H. 1981: *The Other Side of the Frontier*. Harmondsworth: Penguin.

Reynolds, H. 1989: *Dispossession: Black Australians and white invaders*. St. Leonards: Allen and Unwin.

Reynolds, H. 1990: *With the White People: the crucial role of Aborigines in the exploration and development of Australia*. Harmondsworth: Penguin.

Richards, M.B., Sykes, B.C. and Hedges, R.E.M. 1995: Authenticating DNA Extracted from Ancient Skeletal Remains. *Journal of Archaeological Science* 22: 291-9.

Richardson, R. 1988: *Death, Dissection and the Destitute*. London: Pelican.

Richardson, L. 1989: The Acquisition, Storage and Handling of Aboriginal Skeletal Remains in Museums: an indigenous perspective. In R. Layton (ed.) 1989: *Conflict in the Archaeology of Living Traditions*. London: Routledge. 185-8.

Robertson, J.H. 1979: More on Skeletal Analysis and the Race Concept. *Current Anthropology* 20 (3): 617-19.

Robertson, J.H. and Bradley, R.J. 1979: On Skeletal Analysis and the Race Concept. *Current Anthropology* 20 (2): 414-15.

Rolleston, H.D. 1888: Description of the Cerebral Hemisphere of an Adult Australian Male. *Journal of the Anthropological Institute* XVII: 32-42.

Rushton, J.P. 1994a: Cranial Capacity Related to Sex, Rank, and Race in a Stratified Random Sample of 6,325 U.S. Military Personnel. *Intelligence* 16: 401-13.

Rushton, J.P. 1994b: Comment. *Current Anthropology* 35 (1): 41-2.

Ryan, L. 1974: Report to the Australian Institute of Aboriginal Studies on Truganini. Unpublished manuscript. AIATSIS pMs 1436.

Ryan, L. 1981: *The Aboriginal Tasmanians*. St Lucia: University of Queensland Press.

Rydell, R.W. 1984: *All the World's a Fair: visions of empire at American international expositions, 1876-1916*. Chicago: University of Chicago Press.

Said, E. 1978: *Orientalism: Western conceptions of the Orient*. London: Penguin.

Said, E. 1994: *Culture and Imperialism*. London: Vintage.

Sampson, C. 1988: Aboriginal Keeping Places. *COMA Bulletin* 20: 20-3.

Sauer, N. 1992: Forensic Anthropology and the Concept of Race: if races don't exist, why are forensic anthropologists so good at identifying them? *Social Science in Medicine* 34 (2): 107-11.

Sawday, J. 1995: *The Body Emblazoned*. London: Routledge.

Schanche, A. 2002: Saami Skulls, Anthropological Race Research and the Repatriation Question in Norway. In C. Fforde *et al.* (eds) *The Dead and Their Possessions*. London: Routledge. 47-58.

Schupbach, W. 1985: Some Cabinets of Curiosities in European Academic Institutions. In O. Impey and A. MacGregor (eds) 1985: *The Origin of Museums: the cabinets of curiosities in sixteenth and seventeenth century Europe*. Oxford: Clarendon Press. 169-78.

Sellevold, B. 2002: Skeletal Remains of the Norwegian Saami. In C. Fforde *et al.* (eds) *The Dead and Their Possessions*. London: Routledge. 59-62.

Semon, R. 1899: *In the Australian Bush and on the Coast of the Coral Sea*. London: Macmillan & Co.

Severn, J. M. no date: *Phrenology: the language of the mental faculties. Definitions, combinations etc.* Published by the Author, printed by the Westbourne Press, Hove.

Shanklin, E. 1994: *Anthropology and Race*. Belmont: Wadsworth.

Sheets-Pyenson, S. 1988: *Cathedrals of Science: the development of colonial natural history museums during the late nineteenth century*. Kingston and Montreal: McGill-Queen's University Press.

Sim, R. and Thorne, A. 1990: Pleistocene Human Remains from King Island, Southeastern Australia. *Australian Archaeology* 31: 44-51.

Simpson, M. 1994: Burying the Past. *Museums Journal* July: 28-32.

Simpson, M. 1997: *Museums and Repatriation: an account of contested items in museum collections in the UK, with comparative material from other countries*. London: Museums Association.

Simpson, M. 2002: The Plundered Past: Britain's challenge for the future. In C. Fforde *et al.* (eds) *The Dead and Their Possessions*. London: Routledge. 199-217.

Skotnes, P. (ed.) 1996: *Miscast: negotiating the presence of the Bushmen*. Cape Town: University of Cape Town Press.

Slee, J. 1991. 'Few Qualms About Taking Heads'. Letter to the Editor, *The Bulletin* 1991, 3 December. 7.

Soemmering 1784: On the Physical Difference Between the Ape and the Negro. Mainz.

Sollas, W.J. 1911: *Ancient Hunters and their Modern Representatives*. London: Macmillan & Co.

Southworth, E. 1994: A Special Concern. *Museums Journal* July: 23-5.

Specht, J. and MacLuchlich C. 1996: Changes and Challenges: The Australian Museum and indigenous communities. In P.M. McManus (ed.) 1996: *Archaeological Displays and the Public: museology and interpretation*. London: Institute of Archaeology, University College London. 27-49.

Stallybrass, P. and White, A. 1986: *The Politics and Poetics of Transgression*. London: Methuen.

Stanton, W. 1960: *The Leopard's Spot: scientific attitudes toward race in America 1815-59*. Chicago: University of Chicago Press.

Stehlik, B. 1986: Hermann Klaatsch and the Tiwi, 1906. *Aboriginal History* 10 (1-2): 59-76.

Stepan, N. 1982: *The Idea of Race in Science*. Oxford: Macmillan Press.

Stepan, N. 1985: Biology: races and proper places. In J.E. Chamberlain and S.L. Gilman (eds) 1985: *Degeneration: the dark side of progress*. New York: Columbia University Press. 25-120.

Stern, M. 1971: *Heads and Headliners: the phrenological Fowlers*. Norman: University of Oklahoma Press.

Stewart, S. 1984: *On Longing: narratives of the miniature, the gigantic, the souvenir, the collection*. Baltimore and London: Johns Hopkins University Press.

Stocking, G.W. 1968: *Race, Culture and Evolution*. 2nd edition (1982). Chicago: University of Chicago Press.

Stocking, G.W. 1974: The Basic Assumptions of Boasian Anthropology. In G.W. Stocking (ed.) 1974: *A Franz Boas Reader: the shaping of American anthropology, 1883-1911*. New York: Basic Books. 1-20.

Stocking, G.W. 1985: Essays on Museums and Material Culture. In G.W. Stocking (ed.) 1985: *Objects and Others: essays on museums and material culture*.Wisconsin: Wisconsin University Press. 3-14.

Stocking, G.W. 1988: Bones, Bodies and Behaviour. In Stocking (ed.) 1988: *Bones, Bodies and Behaviour*. Wisconsin: Wisconsin University Press. 3-17.

Stokes, J.L. 1846: *Discoveries in Australia*. London: T. & W. Boone.

Stringer, C. Bones of Contention. *Telegraph* 12 November 2003.

Stringer, C. and McKie, R. 1996: *African Exodus: the origins of modern humanity*. New York: Holt.

Sumner, R. 1980: The German Image of Australian Aborigines. *Australia 1888* 5: 116-30.

Sumner, R. 1993: Amalie Dietrich and the Aborigines: her contribution to Australian anthropology and ethnography. *Australian Aboriginal Studies* 2: 2-19.

Sutton, P. 1986: Anthropological History and the South Australian Museum. *Australian Aboriginal Studies* 1: 45-51.

Swidler, N., Dongoske, K.E., Anyon, R., and Downer, A.S. (eds) 1997: *Native Americans and Archaeologists: stepping stones to common ground*. London: AltaMira Press.

Sykes, B. 2001: *The Seven Daughters of Eve: the science that reveals our genetic ancestry*. W.W. Norton and Co.

Symons, J. 2003: 'How Not to Move a Library'. Friends of the Wellcome Library and Centre for the History of Medicine: Newsletter. Issue no: 31: 1-2.

Tapsell, P. 2000: *Pukaki: a comet returns*. Auckland: Reed.

Bibliography

Tasmanian Aboriginal Centre 2000: Memorandum Submitted to the House of Commons Committee: Culture Media and Sport Inquiry into *Cultural Property: Return and Illicit Trade*.

Tasmanian Aboriginal Centre 2001: Submission to the Department for Culture, Media and Sport. Working Group on Human Remains. Available at www.culture.gov.uk/cultural_property/wg_human_remains/Submissions_Section_5.htm

Taylor, T. 1946: Opening Statement of the Prosecution December 9, 1946. In G.J. Annas and M.A. Grodin (eds) 1992: *The Nazi Doctors and the Nuremberg Code: human rights in human experimentation*. Oxford: Oxford University Press. 67-93.

Thomas, N. 1991: *Entangled Objects: exchange, material culture and colonialism in the Pacific*. London: Harvard University Press.

Thomas, N. 1994: *Colonialism's Culture: anthropology, travel and government*. Oxford: Polity Press.

Thorne, A.G. 1971: Mungo and Kow Swamp: morphological variation in Pleistocene Australians. *Mankind* 8: 85-9.

Thorne, A.G. and P.G. Macumber 1972: Discoveries of Late Pleistocene man at Kow Swamp, Australia. *Nature* 238: 316-19.

Thornton, R. 2002: Repatriation as Healing the Wounds of the Trauma of History: cases of Native Americans in the United States of America. In C. Fforde *et al.* (eds) *The Dead and Their Possessions*. London: Routledge. 17-24.

Tickner, R. 1994: Statement on Behalf of the Australian Government. *United Nations Working Group on Indigenous Populations Tenth Session 20-31 July 1992 Geneva, Switzerland. The Australian Contribution*. Canberra: ATSIC. 90-1

Topinard, P. 1885: Presentation de trois Australiens vivants. *Bulletin de la Société d'Anthropologie, Paris* 3: 683-98.

Topinard, P. 1890: *Anthropology*. London: Chapman & Hill.

Tucker, W.H. 1994: *The Science and Politics of Racial Research*. Chicago/Urbana: University of Illinois Press.

Turnbull, P. 1991. Ramsay's Regime: The Australian Museum and the procurement of Aboriginal bodies, c. 1874-1900. *Aboriginal History* 15 (2), 108-21.

Turnbull, P. 1993: Ancestors not Specimens: reflections on the controversy over the remains of Aboriginal people in European scientific collections. *Contemporary Issues in Aboriginal and Torres Strait Islander Studies* 4: 10-35.

Turnbull, P. 1994: To What Strange Uses: the procurement and use of Aboriginal peoples' bodies in early colonial Australia. *Voices* 4 (3): 5-20.

Turnbull, P. no date: The Uses and Meanings Made of the Ancestral Remains of Aboriginal People by British Anatomists, c. 1788-1830. Unpublished working paper.

Turnbull, P. 1999: Indigenous Bodies and Enlightenment Anthropology. In A. Calder, J. Lamb and B. Orr (eds) *Voyages and Beaches: Pacific encounters, 1769-1840*. Honolulu: University of Hawaii Press.

Turnbull, P. 2002: Indigenous Australian People, Their Defence of the Dead, and Native Title. In C. Fforde *et al.* (eds) *The Dead and Their Possessions*. London: Routledge. 63-86.

Turner, A.L. 1919: *Sir William Turner: a chapter in medical history*. Edinburgh: Blackwood & Sons.

Turner, E. 1989: The Souls of My Dead Brothers. In R. Layton (ed.) 1989: *Conflict in the Archaeology of Living Traditions*. London: Routledge. 188-94.

Turner, W. no date: MS Notebook. Held at Edinburgh University Library: Special Collections Anatomy Box 21; 922 (25).

Turner, W. 1878: Notes on the Dissection of a Negro. *Journal of Anatomy and Physiology* XIII: 382-6.

Turner, W. 1879: Notes on the Dissection of a Second Negro. *Journal of Anatomy and Physiology* XIV: 244-8.

Turner, W. 1886: *The Comparative Osteology of Races of Men (comprising parts XXIX and XLVII of the zoological series of reports on the scientific results of the voyage of H.M.S. Challenger)*. Edinburgh.

Turner, W. 1891: Double Right Parietal Bone in an Australian Skull. *Journal of Anatomy and Physiology* XXV: 473-4.

Turner, W. 1897: Notes on the Dissection of a Third Negro. *Journal of Anatomy and Physiology* XXXI: 624-6.

Turner, W. 1900: An Australian Skull with Three Supernumerary Upper Molar Teeth. *Journal of Anatomy and Physiology* XXXIV: 273-4.

Turner, W. 1901: Address on Public Museums in Edinburgh to the Museum Association, Edinburgh Conference. *Museums Journal* 1: 7-23.

Turner, W. 1908: The Craniology, Racial Affinities, and Descent of the Aborigines of Tasmania. *Transactions of the Royal Society of Edinburgh* XLVI (II): 365-404.

Turner, W. 1909: The Aborigines of Tasmania. Part II. The Skeleton. *Transactions of the Royal Society of Edinburgh* XLVII (III): 411-54.

Tylor, E.B. 1889: Anthropology. In D.W. Freshfield and W.J.L. Wharton (eds) 1889: *Hints to Travellers, Scientific and General*. London: Royal Geographic Society. 373-4.

Tylor, E.B. 1894: On the Tasmanians as Representatives of Palaeolithic Man. *Journal of the Anthropological Institute* XXIII: 141-52.

Tyler, W. 1993: Postmodernity and the Aboriginal Condition: the cultural dilemmas of contemporary policy. *Australian and New Zealand Journal of Sociology* 29 (3): 322-42.

Ubelaker, D.H. 1989: *Human Skeletal Remains: excavation, analysis, interpretation*. Washington: Taraxacum.

Ubelaker, D.H. and Grant, L.G. 1989: Human Skeletal Remains: preservation or reburial? *Yearbook of Physical Anthropology* 32: 249-87.

Ucko, P.J. 1975: Review of AIAS Activities, 1974. *Australian Institute of Aboriginal Studies Newsletter* 3: 6-17.

Ucko, P.J. 1989: Foreword. In R. Layton (ed.) 1989: *Conflict in the Archaeology of Living Traditions*. London: Routledge. ix-xvii.

Ucko, P.J. 1992: Introduction. *World Archaeological Bulletin* 6: 1-3.

Ucko, P.J. 1992b: Non-Darwinian Reasons for the Collection of Human Skeletal Remains: an example from Russia. *World Archaeological Bulletin* 6: 5-8.

Uren, M. 1948: *Land Looking West: the story of Governor James Stirling in Western Australia*. Oxford: Oxford University Press.

Urla, J. and Terry, J. 1995: Introduction. Mapping Embodied Deviance. In J. Terry and J. Urla (eds) 1995: *Deviant Bodies: critical perspectives on difference in science and popular culture*. Bloomington & Indianapolis: Indiana University Press. 1-18.

Bibliography

Visser, R.P.W. 1985: *Zoological Works of Petrus Camper (1722-1789)*. Amsterdam: Rodopi.

Vogt, C. 1864: *Lectures on Man: his place in creation, and in the history of the earth*. London: Longman, Green, Longman, Roberts and Green.

Wagner, R. 1856: The Anthropological Collection of the Physiological Institute of Göttingen. In T. Bendyshe (ed.) 1865: *The Anthropological Treatises of J.F. Blumenbach*. London: Longman, Green, Longman, Roberts & Green. 347-55.

Walker, R.B.N. 1866: On the Alleged Sterility of the Union between Women of Savage Races with Native Males, after having had Children by a White Man; with a few remarks on the Mpongwe tribe of Negroes. *Memoirs Read Before the Anthropological Society* II: 283-7.

Wallace, A.R. 1864: The Origin of Human Races and the Antiquity of Man Deduced from the Theory of 'Natural Selection'. *Journal of the Anthropological Society* II: clviii-clxxxvii.

Wallace, C. 1984: *The Lost Australia of François Péron*. Nottingham: Nottingham Court Press.

Waring, H. 1933: Royal College of Surgeons of England, Annual Report to the Council 1933. London.

Watson, H.C. 1836: *Statistics of Phrenology: being a sketch of the progress and present state of that science in the British Isles*. London.

Weatherall, R. 2000: 1989: Aborigines, Archaeologists and the Rights of the Dead. Paper presented at 1989 WAC Inter-Congress, Vermillion, South Dakota. Available at www.faira.org.au/lrq/archives/200102/stories/dead_rights.html.

Weaver, S. 1984: Struggles of the Nation-State to Define Aboriginal ethnicity: Canada and Australia. In G.L. Gold (ed.) 1984: *Minorities and Mother Country Imagery*. Social and Economic Papers 13, Institute of Social and Economic Research, Newfoundland. 182-211.

Webb, S. 1987a: Reburying Australian Skeletons. *Antiquity* 61: 292-6.

Webb, S. 1987b: The Aboriginal Community Liaison Program Carried out in the Murray Valley and Tasmania. Unpublished report.

West, I. 1987: *Pride and Prejudice: reminiscences of a Tasmanian Aborigine*. Canberra: Aboriginal Studies Press.

Wettenhall, G. 1989: The Murray Black Collection Goes Home. *Australian Society* December 1988/ January 1989 issue. 17-19.

White, C. 1799: *An Account of the Regular Gradation in Man and in Different Animals and Vegetables*. London: C. Dilly.

Williamson, G. 1857: *Observations on the Human Crania in the Museum of the Army Medical Department, Fort Pitt, Chatham*. Dublin: McGlashan & Gill.

Wishart, E. 1990: Queen Victoria Museum and Art Gallery. *Australian Archaeology* 31: 55.

Wiss, R. 1990: Lipreading: speaking for/as the other. Feminism, postmodernism and difference. Unpublished honours thesis. Department of Anthropology, Australian National University.

Wolfe, P. 1999: White Man's Flour. In P. Pels and O. Salemink (eds) *Essays on the Practical History of Anthropology*. Ann Arbor: University of Michigan Press. 196-240.

Wolpoff, M. and Caspari, R. 1997: *Race and Human Evolution: a fatal attraction*. New York: Simon and Schuster.

Wood Jones, F. 1928: Claims of the Australian Aborigine. *Report of the 18th Meeting of the Australian Association for the Advancement of Science (Australia and New Zealand) Western Australian Meeting Perth August 1926*. Perth: F.W. Simpson.

Zimmerman, L. 1987: Webb on Reburial: a North American perspective. *Antiquity* 61: 462-3.

Zimmerman, L. 1989a: Made Radical by my Own: an archaeologist learns to accept reburial. In R. Layton (ed.) 1989: *Conflict in the Archaeology of Living Traditions*. London: Routledge. 60-7.

Zimmerman, L. 1989b: An Opinion about Some of the Challenges and Opportunities for Archaeology and the Osteological Sciences offered at the WAC Inter-Congress. *World Archaeological Bulletin* 4: 23-8.

Zimmerman, L. 1989c: Human Bones as Symbols of Power: aboriginal American belief systems towards bones and 'grave-robbing' archaeologists. In R. Layton (ed.) 1989: *Conflict in the Archaeology of Living Traditions*. London: Routledge. 211-16.

Zimmerman, L. 1992: Archaeology, Reburial, and the Tactics of a Discipline's Self-Delusion. *American Indian Culture and Research Journal* 16 (2): 37-56.

Zimmerman, L. 2002: A Decade After the Vermillion Accord: what has changed and what has not. In C. Fforde *et al.* (eds) *The Dead and Their Possessions*. London: Routledge. 91-8.

Index

29; hybridity 18, 19; natural selection 27, 28, 29; slavery, its support of 19-20; species, definition of 18-19
Port Lihou (Muralug) 61
Prichard, John Cowles 11, 18
Pryor, Monty 122, 124
public: dissection, outcry over 66; theft of Aboriginal bodies, attitudes to 46, 47-8, 49, 50, 66; grave robbing, attitudes to 46, 47, 64-5, 66, 75
punitive raids 53-4

Queen Victoria Museum 102
Queensland: grave robbing 55; racism 79, 80; supply of ancestral remains from 57
Queensland Museum 97
Queensland University 111-12, 115-16, 157

race: ancient Greek explanation of 7-8; anthropological debates on 37-8, 39-40; biblical tradition 8-9; classification 13-14; cultural causation of racial differences 8, 14-15; definition of 35, 36, 37-8; environmental causation of racial differences of 7, 11, 14, 17-18, 27; extinction 28-9, 79; metric studies of 10, 11, 33-4, 35, 37, 40-1, 78-9, 153; Plinian tradition 8, 9; racial hierarchies 9, 11, 12, 14, 16, 19, 20, 21, 22, 24, 28-9, 32, 33-4, 79, 80, 153; racial 'types' 35; skulls, use of to define racial characteristics 10-11, 14, 18, 20-1, 24, 30-1; tenacity of 39-41
racism 10, 79, 80, 160; Nazi race ideology 37, 38; scientific 39, 40
Ramsay, E.P. 74
reburial 2-3, 94-103; Aboriginal attitudes to 110, 111; archaeological opposition to 107, 108; ceremonies of 109, 111-12, 121, 123, 156, 157, 158, 159; of fossil remains 112, 113, 114, and identity 159; international significance of 90, 105, 154; Keeping Places 105, 114, 115; origins of 2-3, 50, 89, 96-7, 100-1, 105, 119, 120; polarisation of 108-9, 163-4; and politics 108, 111, 159; spiritual significance of 94, 95, 96, 110, 111,

141-2, 154; *see also* Aborigines, repatriation
repatriation 2, 94-7, 116-17; Aborigines' role in 123, 125, 133, 135, 137, 138, 139; archaeological opposition 90-1, 99, 102-3, 106-8, 112-13; archaeological support 101, 102, 154; funding of 126, 151; and indigenous rights 110, 111, 160, 162; museum opposition to 138, 159-60; museum policies 117-18, 126-30, 132-3, 137, 154-5; NAGPRA 3, 92-4, 156, 159, 164; from overseas institutions 119-23, 125-6, 127, 133, 138-40, 143; polarisation of 108-9, 138, 159, 163-4; and politics 108, 111, 120-1, 159; scientific opposition to 90-1, 138, 142; spiritual significance of 94, 95, 96, 110, 141-2, 154; Working Group on Human Remains 3, 4, 95, 127, 128, 137-8, 140-51, 156, 159-60, 163; *see also* Aborigines, reburial
Retained Organs Committee 144
Retzius, Anders 33
Robinson, Arthur 43, 73
Robinson, George Augustus 56
Rockhampton 115
Rolleston, George 57, 58, 74
Rolleston, H.D. 31-2
Rolleston, William 57, 58
Roth, W.E. 56
Royal Anthropological Institute 37
Royal College of Surgeons of England 13, 25, 45, 57, 58, 59, 63, 69, 70, 74, 89; Odontological Museum 126; organisation of 78; repatriation of Aboriginal ancestral remains 63, 137, 138, 139-40, 143
Royal College of Surgeons, Dublin 122
Royal Geographical Society 61
Royal Society of Tasmania 45, 46, 47, 71, 98; *see also* Truganini

Saami 3, 164
science: absence of indigenous understandings in 160, 161; and objectivity 160-1; racism 39, 40; repatriation, opposition to 90-1, 138, 142; scientific capital, acquisition of 72-3, 74, 75
Semon, Richard 54

www.ingramcontent.com/pod-product-compliance
Lightning Source LLC
Chambersburg PA
CBHW062025270326